Rhetoric Made Plain

Second Edition

Anthony C. Winkler

Jo Ray McCuen

Glendale College

 HARCOURT BRACE JOVANOVICH, INC.

New York / San Diego / Chicago / San Francisco / Atlanta

ISBN: 0-15-577075-6

Library of Congress Catalog Card Number: 78-53130

Printed in the United States of America

Page 368, listing copyrights and acknowledgments,
constitutes a continuation of the copyright page.

PREFACE

The second edition of *Rhetoric Made Plain* is a logical extension of the first. Rhetorical principles are still laid down lucidly and simply; concepts are as heavily exampled and as carefully explained as before; theory is still held to the minimum necessary for practical instruction. Nevertheless, we have not been content merely to parrot ourselves in this new edition. Rather, we have made some specific changes, many suggested by users of the first edition, all intended to make the book more usable and practical.

Our general discussion of rhetoric has been entirely rewritten, and the chapter on voice and style has been substantially revised. In the progression from outline to paragraph to essay we now explore the journalistic paragraph and narration as a method of expanding the thesis. We have increased the number of examples of denotation and connotation, and, in response to users' requests, we have included an extensive discussion of deductive and inductive reasoning. New exercises and examples have also been added throughout the book.

To guide students more successfully through the painstaking process of revision, we now use an actual student paper as illustration. Toward the same end, we follow one student through the entire process of a research paper. This method enables us to catalog the minor and major obstacles students will meet, and to counsel them on how to deal with these difficulties. Moreover, the research paper and all elements of the second edition conform to the latest recommendations and suggestions of the Modern Language Association as put forth in their *MLA Handbook* (1977).

Our approach to this second edition echoes the philosophy of the first edition: "Throughout the book we have tried to practice what we preach: Write plainly."

Anthony C. Winkler and Jo Ray McCuen

CONTENTS

1

PREWRITING

1

What do you mean by rhetoric?

DEFINITIONS OF RHETORIC
AUDIENCE AND WRITING
PURPOSE AND WRITING
FORM AND CONTENT
EXERCISES

The suspicion that rhetoric involves emptiness or guile in the use of words is both ancient and durable. "You call a man a thief," wrote Persius, complaining in 45 A.D. about rhetoric, "and he answers you with figures of speech." A character from the work of contemporary Italian author Alberto Moravia declares: "And I am, in fact, inclined to rhetoric—that is, to the substitution of words for deeds." In *The Final Days,* an oral exchange between Richard Nixon and Gerald Ford is described, with the word "rhetoric" being used to denote inflated yet meaningless talk:

> Ford had always been a loyal party man, and his relationship with Nixon had never been more personal than that. Both men had been in politics for decades, and both were accustomed to the formality that smooths ups and downs, political shifts, changes of fortune. Both were used to falling back, in moments of potential embarrassment, on rhetoric.

Swayed by such cynical impressions of rhetoric, students are sometimes startled to discover that rhetoric is brazenly taught in freshman composition. Moreover, a glance through the speech books in a bookstore reveals a staggering number of texts with the word "rhetoric" wriggling on their covers, adding to the suspicion that the English and speech departments are fighting one another for the right to instill premeditated glibness in the minds and hearts of innocents. What does "rhetoric" mean in these contexts? A useful point to begin this text is to clarify the meaning of the word "rhetoric" as it is generally understood by teachers of English.

DEFINITIONS OF RHETORIC

Rhetoric has been defined in many ways over the centuries. To Isocrates in 350 B.C., rhetoric was "the science of persuasion"; twenty years later, Aristotle defined rhetoric as "the faculty of discerning in every case the available means of persuasion." A nineteenth-century British logician, Richard Whately, saw rhetoric as "the art of argumentative composition." Common to all of these definitions is the suggestion that rhetoric involves the strategies used by a speaker or writer in attempting to communicate with an audience.

Rhetoric, in fact, exists because of the richness and variety of language. If a statement could be communicated in only one way, rhetoric would never have appeared on the earth. For rhetoric is chiefly the art of effective linguistic choice; and the indisputable basis for choice is the existence of alternatives. This paragraph, for instance, could have been written in a thousand different ways that said essentially the same thing. Its final form was shaped by the rhetorical sense of the writer. Faced with nearly endless alternatives, the writer—guided by his sense of the audience as well as the purpose of the text—has written the paragraph as it appears. The choice was dictated not only by grammar, but also by rhetoric. *Grammar prescribes the correct use of words to form grammatical sentences; rhetoric suggests the most effective use of the most effective words to form the most effective message, effectiveness in every case being measured by the impact of the message on the audience.*

Consider, for instance, the rhetorical impact of a one-word message exchanged during the Second World War. The besieged town of Bastogne, Belgium, was defended by tattered bands of American troops and encircled by a superior force of German units. The German commander sent the following message offering terms of surrender:

> To the U.S.A. Commander of the encircled town of Bastogne.
>
> The fortune of war is changing. This time the U.S.A. forces in and near Bastogne have been encircled by strong German armored units . . .
>
> There is only one possibility to save the encircled U.S.A. troops from total annihilation: that is the honorable surrender of the encircled town.
>
> If this proposal should be rejected, one German Artillery Corps and six heavy A.A. Battalions are ready to annihilate the U.S.A. troops in and near Bastogne . . .
>
> All the serious civilian losses caused by this artillery fire would not correspond with the well-known American humanity.
>
> The German Commander

The American brigadier general commanding the town's defenses sent the following reply:

> To the German Commander:
> —Nuts!
> The American Commander

Grammatically, "nuts" may leave something to be desired. But as a rhetorical device, it is a stinging rebuff and ideally suited to the purpose of the message—to express defiance and contempt for surrender.

Compared to rhetoric, grammar is rigid and unforgiving. Just as "one plus one equals three" is always arithmetically incorrect, "The went store to I" is always ungrammatical. The rules of grammar are based on customary language usage, and English-speaking people do not customarily say "The went store to I." On the other hand, the strategies of rhetoric vary with audience and purpose—variables that can never be completely anticipated. What is rhetorically effective for one audience and purpose may be grossly inappropriate in another context. That a writer must adapt diction, detail, emphasis, content, tone, and style to suit both the audience and purpose of the writing is a rule both of common sense and of rhetoric.

Some of this adapting to audience and purpose is simply unteachable—being a matter of sensitivity, common sense, and talent. An English instructor in a freshman composition class cannot anticipate every conceivable purpose a student may have for writing, nor every imaginable audience to whom that writing may someday be directed. Neither, we might add, can any textbook. But it does not follow that writing cannot be taught. The American author Ambrose Bierce put the case for teaching writing this way:

> There is a good deal of popular ignorance about writing; it is commonly thought that good writing comes of a natural gift and that without the gift the trick cannot be turned. This is true of great writing, but not of good. Anyone with good natural intelligence and a fair education can be taught to write well, as he can be taught to draw well, or to play billiards well, or shoot a rifle well, and so forth; but to do any of these things greatly is another matter.
> —Ambrose Bierce, "To Train a Writer"

The authors of this text essentially agree with Bierce's view. No amount of schooling in rhetoric will make the ungifted writer great. But betterment can be expected in the writing of students who conscientiously apply themselves to the study of rhetoric.

AUDIENCE AND WRITING

Most of us automatically and unconsciously adapt our written and spoken words to suit the intended audience. A student will not address a professor in the same language he would a close friend; will not write his great grandmother a letter using the same style and vocabulary as he would with a lover; and will not answer an essay question with the words he might scribble on a bathroom wall. These modifications, drastic and slight, are made because people desire to write not merely grammatically, but effectively. Our rhetorical sense tells us that the professor will probably not appreciate being addressed as a close friend; that the great grandmother has different interests and presumptions than a young lover; and that bathroom graffiti will not win points on an essay examination. Other than babies, who will determinedly babble ''goo-goo'' whether addressing a grandmother, a cat, or the President of the United States, human beings, in their desire to express themselves effectively, make rhetorical concessions of one kind or another to their audiences.

Nowhere is the rhetorical concession to audience more evident than in magazine publishing. Magazines unashamedly cater to the life-styles, educational levels, and tastes of their audiences. Here, for example, is how a well-known pulp magazine, *True Romance,* characterizes its audience and editorial needs in *Writer's Market 1977,* a publication listing markets open to the work of free-lance writers.

> High-school educated, blue collar wives make up the vast majority of our audience. Most of them have young children. All are family and love oriented. . . . We are looking for timely, exciting, emotional first person stories on the problems that face today's young women. The narrators should be sympathetic, and the situations they find themselves in should be intriguing, yet realistic. Every story should have a strong romantic interest, and every plot should reach an exciting climax. All stories should be written in the first person, and the subject matter should be approached with sincerity. Emphasis should be placed on the love interest, and the stories should have a strong moral tone.

Here are some typical story titles from the January 1977 issue of *True Romance:*

> I Put My Wife Up For Sale!
> It's the only way I could keep her.
>
> ''Daddy's a Dirty Old Man!''
> Can my teenager's accusation be true?
>
> Honeymoon for Four
> What a way to start our marriage!

The opening paragraph of ''Daddy's a Dirty Old Man'' gives an example of the simple diction and trite images used throughout the story—made necessary by the presumed limitations in the reading skills and vocabulary of the magazine's audience.

> My heart sank when I saw Norma come into the kitchen for breakfast late that Saturday morning. She looked as if she'd been through hell on earth.
> Her eyes had the puffiness of somebody who has had a sleepless night. But it wasn't the bags under her usually bright eyes that tore my heart—it was the anguish in them.

The characters in the story are tailored to reflect the interests, enthusiasms, habits, and preoccupations of the magazine's devotees. The main character, a philandering father, drinks beer, worries about inflation, and patronizes a place called Mabel's Tavern.

Mademoiselle magazine, also listed in *Writer's Market 1977,* caters to an entirely different audience from that of *True Romance,* but pampers its readers no less energetically:

> Directed to college educated women between the ages of 18 and 25. . . . Particular concentration on articles of interest to the intelligent young woman that concern the arts, education, careers, European travel, current sociological and political problems. Articles should be well researched and of good quality. . . . We are not interested in formula stories and our subject matter need not be confined to a specific age or theme.

Pitched at a more affluent, better educated, and younger audience, *Mademoiselle* regales the reader with a feast of articles about travel idylls, current fads, beauty secrets, psychological horrors, and success formulas. Taken from the January 1977 issue, here are some typical article titles:

Sex: The New Definition of Normal
Depression: How to Kick It
The Good Life on Maui
The Truth About Cellulite, Binge-eating, Sweating, and Other Beauty Bores.

A short story in the January 1977 issue, entitled "Mrs. Crocker," also reflects the presumed life-style and education level of the magazine's audience. The opening paragraph of the story gives the flavor of its language.

> Leona Crocker was a stern looking woman who wore thick-rimmed glasses and her hair close to her head. A wary woman, she always blinked twice, slowly, before answering any direct questions and never went anywhere without a large canvas bag full of coffee cake and a camera and her latest address book. Mrs. Crocker hated hotels.

Most of the primary characters in the story are professional people, presumably because college-educated women aspire to a profession. Mrs. Crocker's husband is a doctor; a friend teaches at the university. The characters in the story dine at expensive, modish restaurants, ordering entrees like "scampi a la Marsala" from menus written in a foreign language, reminisce about vacations spent abroad, listen to opera music, and have books like *The Diary of Anne Frank* and *Wuthering Heights* (typical college-level reading) casually lying around. The story is written in language that is studiously stylish and pretty; the vocabulary is more complicated, and the descriptive detail more plentiful than in the *True Romance* story.

PURPOSE AND WRITING

Common to *True Romance, Mademoiselle,* or any other magazine, the principle of adapting content and language to the tastes of specific readers illustrates the effect an audience exerts on commercial writing. Numerous examples can also be cited to demonstrate a similar rhetorical adaptation of writing and speaking to varying purposes. Here, for instance, is an excerpt taped from a popular radio show, illustrating how language is used for the purpose of entertaining:

> That's Patty Baby and that's the girl with the dancing feet and that's Freddy Cannon there on the David Mickie show in the night time ooohbah scubadoo how are you booboo. Next we'll be Swinging on a Star and sssshhhhwwwooooo and sliding on a moonbeam. Waaaaaaa about that . . . one of the goodest guys with you . . . this is lovable kissable D.M. in the p.m. at 22 minutes past nine o'clock there. . . .

Contrast this chitter with the formal language used by John F. Kennedy at his Inaugural Address for the purpose of enunciating the goals, aims, and ambitions of the incoming administration.

> Now the trumpet summons us again—not as a call to bear arms, though arms we need—not as a call to battle, though embattled we are—but a call to bear the burden of a long twilight struggle year in and year out, "rejoicing in hope, patient in tribulation"—a struggle against the common enemies of man: tyranny, poverty, disease and war itself.
>
> Can we forge against these enemies a grand and global alliance, north and south, east and west, that can assure a more fruitful life for all mankind? Will you join in that historic effort?

Both examples demonstrate the changeable character of language, and its capacity for adapting to the different purposes of human communication.

If professional writers are required to adapt their language to different audiences and purposes, for the sake of realism it follows that a similar adaptability ought to be demanded from the prose of student writers. Students do not write in a vacuum. The purpose for their writing—admittedly not the most glamorous—is to pass a course. In effect, a course in writing aims at standardizing the student's style to bring it in line with contemporary usage. The instructor's knowledge of the accepted and current modes of writing, as well as of the accepted and current techniques involved in assembling a paper, makes him or her an ideal, representative audience.

To overlook these simple facts of audience and purpose would be extraordinary, yet it is remarkable how often students do, as attested to by their complaints about the phoniness of classroom writing assignments. It is no more artificial to write an essay defining freedom for the purpose of passing a course than to write a field report for the purpose of informing a sales manager about the annual sales in a certain territory. Both assignments involve an audience and a purpose to which the writer must adapt. To help students adapt their prose accordingly, we offer the following commentary on the teacher as audience, along with a few tips on what English teachers most appreciate and most abhor about student writing.

1. Aim for originality in your writing.

Whenever a classwork assignment is given, the teacher is treated not merely to one paper on the assigned topic, but to innumerable versions of the same paper by different students. Boredom, fatigue, and madness threaten the instructor who goes home on a weekend with a hundred student papers on "The Meaning of Freedom." Chances are, fifty students will parrot simplisms about freedom that they picked up in high-school civics classes. The other fifty will try to clout the teacher senseless with fine-spun, reworked clichés lifted straight out of the Constitution. Almost everyone will begin the paper with a flat and insipid opening line like "Freedom is the ability to do as one pleases"; or, "Freedom means that the individual has the right to choose his own destiny"; or, "What is freedom? Many have pondered this question since the beginning of civilization."

Rhetorical tip: Try for originality. Tell a story that you think exemplifies the meaning of freedom. Don't quote the Constitution, the Bill of Rights, or Patrick Henry; quote the *I Ching,* or Abigail Van Buren. The point is not to be eccentric, outlandish, or cute, but to anticipate and avoid the endless plague of platitudes that most of your classmates will use. Even if your essay is not that good, by its very originality will the teacher be startled, revived, and refreshed.

2. Write in plain, ungarbled English.

Most teachers are looking for and are prepared to admire unpretentious, down-to-earth prose. They are not especially fond of nor do they encourage the use of extravagant metaphors and serpentine analogies in student writing. Here, for example, is a student paragraph choked with gibberish figures of speech:

> The poetry of Keats possesses an ethereal quality removed from reality yet still containing questions as to the validity of reality. Keats uses poetry as a vehicle to convey himself away from the pain of his existence, to promote the ideal qualities of life seen in mythology and legend. This fanciful chariot of imagery removes him from reality and allows him to question his values without undermining his ideals.
>
> *Translation:* Keats wrote escapist, mythological poetry.

One possible reason for this calamitous passage is the student's misapprehension of the kind of writing English instructors admire. This passage is not it; indeed, the passage is more representative of writing that English teachers typically dread.

3. Be generous in the use of specific detail.

A widespread failing of student writing is its lack of specific detail. The passage below, intended to be a description of spring, is a typical rendering of this fault in its utmost glory:

> Spring is the season following winter and before summer. The temperature is usually very mild and the weather quite nice. Flowers are in bloom and whatever snow or ice on the ground starts to melt. Most people welcome spring because it brings relief from the severity of winter. Spring is my favorite time of the year.

This passage, supposedly descriptive, contains little specific concrete detail. All kinds of writing are utterly dependent for force and strength on the use of detail, but descriptive writing especially so. Much student writing is characterized not by an overabundance of detail but by a universal lack of it. In contrast to the student's attempt at describing spring, consider this passage taken from *Anna Karenina*, by Leo Tolstoy, which describes a Russian spring:

> In the morning the bright sun rose and quickly devoured the thin ice covering the water, and the warm air all around vibrated with the exhalation of the reviving earth. The old grass turned green again and the young grass thrust out its needle-sharp blades, the buds swelled on the guelder-rose, the currant bushes, and the sticky, resinous birch trees; and in the gold-besprinkled willows the honey bee, which had only just emerged from its hive, flew about humming. Invisible larks broke into song over the velvet of the young, sprouting corn and the ice-covered stubble; peewits began to cry over the marshes and the low reaches of the rivers and streams, still overflowing with brownish water, and cranes and wild geese flew high across the sky, uttering their loud, spring cries. The cattle, their winter coats only partly shed and bald in patches, began to low in the pastures; bandy-legged lambs frisked round their bleating mothers, who were losing their fleece; swift-footed children ran about the quickly drying paths marked with imprints of bare feet; the merry voices of peasant women rose over the pond; and the axes of the peasants repairing their ploughs and harrows rang in the yard. Real spring had come.

The contrast in the use of detail is so obvious that it is unnecessary to belabor the point.

The English language has a vast supply of insipid, meaningless adjectives. Some of these are: cute, beautiful, bad, good, pretty, nice, sweet, interesting, ugly. These words are not bad in themselves but when joined in grim succession to various nouns, they portray reality in a drab shade of gray. The antidote is simply to use as much specific, concrete detail in your writing as humanly possible.

We have not exhausted the characteristics that you should either strive for or avoid in your writing, but merely highlighted some of them. Further chapters of this book will deal with these and other characteristics in much greater detail. For now, you may view lack of plain language, lack of originality, and lack of specific detail as the three deadliest sins of writing that you should do your utmost to avoid.

FORM AND CONTENT

The written word is theoretically divisible into two components: form and content. Content refers to *what* is said; form, to *how* it is said. Since these two terms will repeatedly come up in later discussions, we will briefly elaborate on this distinction here.

Language is variable both in form and content. It is possible to say the same thing in different ways—varying the form but not the content—and to say different things in the same way—changing the content but not the form. Here, for instance, are some examples of the same thing said in different ways.

1. I bought my sister a present for her birthday.
2. I purchased a present for my sister to commemorate her birthday.
3. I acquired a gift for Sis, which I gave her on her birthday.
4. On the birthday of my sister, I handed her a gift.

To say that these sentences differ significantly in content would be to quibble. Essentially, they say the same thing, differing either in the arrangement of words or in the actual words themselves. The changes are variations not of content but of form.

Content is an easier concept to understand than form and requires less illustration.

1. I ate my breakfast.
2. I ate my canary.

These sentences differ because the underlying acts they describe are irreconcilably different. No amount of sameness in the language of these sentences can disguise the differences in their content.

In college writing classes, essays are judged on the basis of both form and content. It is possible for a student to submit written work that is acceptable in form but objectionable in content. Here, for instance, is a paragraph taken from a student's essay on poetry that the instructor faulted for poor content.

> I have just finished reading Wordsworth's "Prelude," hundreds of lines of humorless, dull, pompous poetry. The Romantic poets apparently allowed nature to turn them into weirdos. They couldn't see the sun piercing the clouds without having some wild mystical fit, and they couldn't look at flowers, lakes, or trees without popping a sermon. Give me Emily Dickinson any day. At least when she sees a mushroom, she writes about it as a mushroom.

The instructor objected to the student's content as presumptuous and illogical. William Wordsworth is considered by critics to be one of the greatest English poets and for the student to simply dismiss him as a ''weirdo'' is as unpardonable as characterizing Abraham Lincoln as a ''creep.'' This does not mean, of course, that an individual is not entitled to a personal opinion both of Wordsworth and of Lincoln. It simply means that the formality of the classroom environment requires that likes and dislikes be couched and expressed in reasonably logical and restrained terms. Here, taken from another student's essay, is a similar objection against Wordsworth, but made less offensively:

> Wordsworth's "Prelude" is too long and philosophical for me to enjoy. While I can appreciate the lyrical descriptions of lovely landscapes, the bitter attacks against city life, and the detailed accounts of personal incidents, still the language of the poem seems excessively lofty and the philosophic musings too abstract for my taste. I prefer short, direct poems, such as those of Emily Dickinson.

For an illustration of a passage that suffers from bad form, consider the following:

> Another trend that some suggest has weakened the instrumental structure of the family is the decline of family ascribed relations and status and the increase in achieved relations and status. Status was once gained mainly through family affiliation. Today status is gained through the cultivation of relationships external to the primary family unit. The danger seen by some in the advent of such varied external relations is that they have a tendency to make the individual decide that the family as a lifelong relationship is too restrictive for personal gratification. Thus he will choose to function independent of interrelations.

Contrast the above with the paragraph below, which expresses more or less the same idea in a more effective form.

A striking difference between today's family and the family of fifty years ago is the fact that fifty years ago family members were satisfied to get their sense of importance from their family. If, for example, the parents were farmers, then farming was accepted as the social status of the family. But today, most people refuse to be confined by their families' social tags. They prefer to identify with the achievements of work associates or friends. Many sociologists see this shift in identity as weakening the family as a force in our society.

These illustrations point out what we have said earlier: the purpose of a course in rhetoric is to criticize both the *form* and *content* of your writing. Intermingled throughout the chapters of this book are suggestions for avoiding errors both in *form* and *content* along with instructions on how to remedy deficiencies in each area.

EXERCISES

1. Study the following paragraphs; then comment on audience and purpose.

   a. At first our Greg was a model child. Healthy, happy, unfailingly sweet-tempered, he was a total joy as a baby. When he was one year old, he thought that everything mother and father wanted him to do was wonderful. His second birthday passed, and he remained cooperative and adorable. Aha, I thought, the "terrible twos" that everyone complains about must result from inadequate attention and discipline.

   Then Greg turned 2¾ years old. Suddenly we had an obnoxious monster in the house. His favorite word was "No!" and he used it constantly. At the simplest request he would stamp his feet and cry. It took a battle to get him to put on clothing he had previously worn happily. Favorite foods were thrown on the floor. It became almost impossible to take him shopping because he would lie down in the store and refuse to move. There was constant tension in the house, and my husband and I became irritable, too. We felt as if we were living on the slopes of a volcano, and we found ourselves giving in to Greg too much in order to avoid the threatened eruptions.

   b. Others will debate the controversial issues, national and international, which divide men's minds. But serene, calm, aloof, you stand as the nation's war guardians, as its lifeguards from the raging tides of international conflict, as its gladiators in the arena of battle. For a century-and-a-half you have defended, guarded, and protected its hallowed traditions of liberty and freedom, of right and justice.

Let civilian voices argue the merits or demerits of our processes of government: whether our strength is being sapped by deficit financing indulged in too long; by federal paternalism grown too mighty; by power groups grown too arrogant; by politics grown too corrupt; by crime grown too rampant; by morals grown too low; by taxes grown too high; by extremists grown too violent; whether our personal liberties are as firm and complete as they should be.

These great national problems are not for your professional participation or military solution. Your guidepost stands out like a tenfold beacon in the night: duty, honor, country.

c. To give Eleanor her due, any suspicion as to the slightest inclination on her part towards Mr. Slope was a wrong to her. She had no more idea of marrying Mr. Slope than she had of marrying the bishop, and the idea that Mr. Slope would present himself as a suitor had never occurred to her. Indeed, to give her her due again, she had never thought about suitors since her husband's death. But nevertheless it was true that she had overcome all that repugnance to the man which was so strongly felt for him by the rest of the Grantly faction. She had forgiven him his sermon. She had forgiven him his low church tendencies, his Sabbath schools, and puritanical observances. She had forgiven his pharisaical arrogance, and even his greasy face and oily vulgar manners. Having agreed to overlook such offences as these, why should she not in time be taught to regard Mr. Slope as a suitor?

d. Earthquakes are often accompanied by a roaring noise that comes from the bowels of the earth. This phenomenon was known to early geographers. Pliny wrote that earthquakes are "preceded or accompanied by a terrible sound." Vaults supporting the ground give way and it seems as though the earth heaves deep sighs. The sound was attributed to the gods and called theophany.

The eruptions of volcanoes are also accompanied by loud noises. The sound produced by Krakatoa in the East Indies, during the eruption of 1883, was so loud that it was heard as far as Japan, 3,000 miles away, the farthest distance travelled by sound recorded in modern annals.

e. I beg you to excuse a father who dares to approach you in the interests of his son.

I wish to mention first that my son is 22 years old, has studied for four years at the Zurich Polytechnic and last summer brilliantly passed his diploma examinations in mathematics and physics. Since then he has tried unsuccessfully to find a position as assistant, which would enable him to continue his education in theoretical and experimental physics. Everybody who is able to judge praises his talent, and in any case I can assure you that he is exceedingly assiduous and industrious and is attached to his science with a great love.

2. Write different paragraphs giving advice on how to drive safely in the rain. Address one to an audience of business people who drive Cadillacs. Address the other to an audience of Hell's Angels who drive motorcycles.

3. Which of the following suffers from bad form? Why?

   a. I returned and saw under the sun, that the race is not to the swift, nor the battle to the strong, neither yet bread to the wise, nor yet riches to men of understanding, nor yet favour to men of skill; but time and chance happeneth to them all.

   b. Objective consideration of contemporary phenomena compels the conclusion that success or failure in competitive activities exhibits no tendency to be commensurate with innate capacity, but that a considerable element of the unpredictable must invariably be taken into account.

4. Which of the following suffers from bad content?

   a. The debate over whether or not a writer should split an infinitive rages on, mainly in the classroom. In the real world, infinitives are ceaselessly split by the great, the near great, and the good among the literary populace. Infinitives have been admirably cleaved by Hemingway, Fitzgerald, Salinger, and Fowler. Such writers would never dream of saying, "Safeguards should be provided to prevent *effectually* financiers from manipulating these reserves." Or, "Both the U.S. and Russia have done ill in not combining to forbid *flatly* hostilities." Only the very timid who live in mortal dread of the grammarian's scolding would dare give life to such tortured, wooden sentences.

   b. Idiots and schoolmarms who have nothing better to do than grind their mandibles over the preservation of obsolete grammatical rules are the only people who still cling to the belief that infinitives should not be split. Sentences must be twisted, words wrenched, and euphony abandoned, all for the sake of keeping the "to" trotting meekly and uninterruptedly behind the verb like a microscopic cart pulled by a gargantuan donkey. These fools would do anything to preserve a rule that not even Shakespeare himself attended to. Well, I say if bananas and decisions can be split, so can infinitives.

2
*What should
I sound like?*

Voice—the unique mannerisms of language that distinguish one writer's work from another—is lamentably absent from the essays of most students. Instructors are annually amazed at how students, distinctively recognizable in person, can end up sounding like well-meaning robots on paper. The peculiar wit, the special gaiety, the unique sensitivity of the individual, disappear under an onslaught of humdrum phrasing. The cause is clearly psychological. Afraid of seeming stupid, silly, or presumptuous, most students would rather mumble in their essays and be safe, than roar and be found out. The result is an endless succession of dreary essays that sound anonymous and alike.

The world of learning, we grant, is a trying place. Students, blundering about in this world, are often keenly aware that they have none of the learning and expertise of the specialists who teach them. They are daily lectured by professors and perplexed by textbooks. Each student painfully accumulates evidence of personal inadequacy—real or imagined. The history professor laughs at their ideas; the chemistry professor looks astonished at their denseness; the literature teacher expresses amazement at their clumsy interpretations of poems. On top of all this misery, the composition instructor expects these same bewildered students to write fluent and distinguished essays.

Many students react to these pressures by grinding out papers that sound as if the writer has been recently anesthetized. Original opinion is scantily expressed; much bowing and scraping is made to authority; personal notions are apologized for with a barrage of "I believe," "I think," and "It-is-my-humble-opinion." An obsession to conform takes hold of students, leading them to snuff out all personal flair. Only the honorably insipid words of the lexicon, "nice," "beautiful," "interesting"—as inoffensive as curds of cottage cheese—are found in paragraph after paragraph of safe, colorless sentences.

A similar snuffing-out of originality occurs in young children when they first begin school. Imagination and natural curiosity are lost as the children are crammed into prearranged patterns of learning. We grant that the rigors of society demand that certain conventions be followed and that it would be chaotic to live in an environment where every individual behaved outland-ishly and unpredictably. Nevertheless, we are all endowed with personal trademarks and there is no reason why our uniqueness should not be re-vealed on paper. Great writers invariably project their indefinable selves into their style of writing. Hemingway is recognizably Hemingway on whatever parchment you find him. To help you to project your own indefinable self in your writing, we offer the following suggestions.

SOUND LIKE YOURSELF

When you write, you should sound like yourself. How does a writer do this? The answer is, by not sounding like someone else. If you do not strain for special effects in your writing, it will come out sounding like your own.

The way to project this natural sound on paper is to stick with the vocab-ulary you already know and with the sentence types you use in your daily speech. There is nothing deficient about your everyday vocabulary. One es-timate says that the average freshman in college has a vocabulary of 100,000 words. The same freshman can generate several different sentence types in a half-hour conversation. In short, if you are at all average, you have enough linguistic lumber in your head to build a book. This is not to say that you should never use a new word or try out a new sentence pattern. But what you already know should be the basis for your writing: use the old as the es-sential structure, and use the new to add a dash of interest or variation.

You may object that an instructor can never know the vocabulary or the speech sentence patterns of each student and therefore cannot know when a student is deviating from the familiar in his writing. It is true that a teacher cannot be familiar with every student's usual vocabulary and usual way of speaking. But when a student plunges into the exotic in his writing, a cramped and forced manner creeps into the style because the student is no longer writing through his own voice. If you do not use your own voice, you cannot tell whether what you say sounds phony because your whole style is now a massive put-on. Professional writers regularly assume other voices in their writing, but this is a skill that comes with practice and is not easily achieved by the beginning writer.

So, to begin with, you should write with your own voice. Most of your skill with the language up to now has been acquired through speaking it. Linguists used to believe that grammar was something that had to be learned apart from the language; now they recognize it as a set of rules built into the language skills of every native speaker. You select words and frame them into a grammatical context almost instinctively. Even if you speak a dialect or so-called broken English, you still have a built-in, consistent usage pat-tern that guides the way you phrase a sentence or use a word. *Grammatical* is not synonymous with *proper;* more accurately it means *consistent.* Grammar is a body of rules of consistency. All speakers use these rules so that other speakers can understand them. "I ain't here" is therefore grammatical, although some might not consider it proper. "I here ain't" is ungrammatical, because it is inconsistent with customary usage. If all the speakers of the language agreed that "ain't" should always be placed after an adverb, then "I ain't here" would become the ungrammatical form, while "I here ain't" would be accepted by linguists as the grammatical usage. As a native speaker of the language you have already acquired a built-in consistency pattern that is almost instinctive and always grammatical. If you use your speech as a model for your writing, you take advantage of innate skills that come from a lifetime of speaking English.

Read your writing aloud to yourself!

Reading your writing aloud will give you a chance to compare the way you write with the way you talk. If you come across any word or sentence in your writing that sounds artificial or pretentious you should change it so that it sounds like something you would say. It does not necessarily follow that in sticking to your normal speech style you are going to sound like everybody else. This seems to be a prominent fear that goads students into using big words and constructing boa-constrictor sentences. At college age you have already accumulated enough distinctive mannerisms in the way you speak to give your speech an individual style. By projecting your talking voice into your writing you will sound naturally and uniquely like yourself, just as you do in your speech.

Although sounding natural is of basic importance, sounding *un*natural is not the only thing that can go wrong with your writing. Writing is prone to other failings. You could sound natural and be a poor speller; you could sound natural and argue in circles; you could sound natural and still be boring. In these cases your writing would still not be effective, and you would probably get a low grade in freshman English, even if your instructor thought you were naturally boring. But in this chapter we address ourselves to the matters of natural word and sentence choice; other problems will be discussed later.

SAY WHAT YOU REALLY BELIEVE

The following paragraph was written by a student in response to the question: "Why do some teenagers like to hang around the streets in gangs?"

Some parents have problems keeping their teenagers off the streets. The teenager is hyper or restless and wants to release his energy. So, after studies are finished, he goes out and cruises the streets with little or nothing else to do. Left to their own devices, teenagers often get into trouble. In some cases parents work late or work at night and are thus not around to see their children leave the house, so they don't know where their children are. This is potentially a dangerous situation. Greater efforts should be made by our society to reduce street gangs.

A safe, dull, and mediocre paragraph. It reads as if the student had thought: "If I say something harmless and noncontroversial I won't get into trouble." The instructor replied with a yawn and a mediocre grade. Ironically, the writer's true attitude toward the question was neither dull nor neutral; it was vehement. She had spent a summer working with inner-city youths and had come away outraged at the wretched home life that drove them into the streets to seek companionship. She blamed the problem partly on the self-righteous neglect of the indifferent middle class and wanted to say so, but she thought the instructor might be a conservative who would take offense. She therefore decided to suppress her feelings and play classroom politics in the essay. But honest people lie as badly in writing as they do in talking; before she knew what had happened, she had written a vacuous, boring essay. With some encouragement, this student was persuaded to rewrite the essay and express the way she really felt. Here is a paragraph from the rewritten version.

Teenagers seek the streets because they are desperately lonely and because any place seems more attractive to them than the dump they call "home"—where Father lies on the broken-down couch, drunk, and Mother denies the ugliness of her tattered existence by listening to grating tape recordings of Reverend Ike promising her pie in the sky. The walls of the apartment are grease-stained and the curtains look like cheesecloth chewed up by rats. The voices of quarreling neighbors fill the air with oaths, and the hallways perenially smell like canned oyster soup. Is it any wonder that a lusty teenager escapes such a trap? It fills me with anger to realize how often we self-righteously heap blame on such youngsters. But, safely tucked away in our nice, clean, middle-class lives, what are we doing to make the inner city a place where a youngster can have a decent home?

The difference between the first and second version is mainly a matter of gumption and honesty. The student simply forgot about appeasing the instructor and expressed the way she really felt on the issue. A vast majority of instructors not only welcome this sort of honesty in essays written by their students but desperately crave it. Most English instructors, in fact, would rather read a vigorously written student paper that contradicts and blasts their own views than have to plough through a colorless, toadying essay. Differences of opinion, after all, can be settled by logic and evidence.

There is another wrinkle to being honest that we ought to mention: namely, that you may express what you believe is genuinely your own opinion only to find that the instructor nevertheless labels it as trite or stale. This sort of deficiency cannot be blamed on language or style, but on shopworn thinking. Obviously, if you are content to parrot popular, shallow opinions then you are settling for mass-minded mediocrity and deserve to be rebuffed. Research and honest inquiry into an issue will quickly lead you to formulate your own opinion that differs in content, substance, and detail from the views of the herd. Expressed in your essay, this opinion will carry conviction since it is truly your own.

DEVELOP A CLEAR VOICE

Human beings have a virtually limitless capacity for misunderstanding each other in both speech and print. The burden, therefore, is on the writer to express ideas with unmistakable clarity. Among student populations, a prime cause of fuzzy expression is word clutter. The cure for clutter is rewriting and pruning. But behind the creation of word clutter is usually the age-old student strategy to fuzz one's meaning a little so that if an opinion is wrong, it will only be mildly so. Politicians fuzz for a similar reason. Consider the following scenario. A bridge has been proposed across a river running through a certain town. It is opposed by some and favored by others. The politician representing this town is meeting with his constituents to discuss, among other matters, the bridge. One crusty old gentleman gets up and growls: "How do you feel about the bridge?" Our politician is uncertain to which camp the old gentleman belongs. He therefore replied in the following style:

> Engineering and construction techniques, as everybody in this room realizes, have taken giant steps and accomplished many miracles in making the edifices look attractive and at the same time be functional. My feeling about this bridge is that if it can be located at a site agreeable to all and if all parties concerned can arrive at a meaningful compromise about its utility and practicability and desirability, then we certainly should consider its feasibility with reference to the needs of the community.
>
> *Translation:* I'll tell you how I feel about the bridge when you tell me how you feel about the bridge.

Similarly, a student is asked to write an essay saying how she feels about female police officers. Decidedly in favor of them, she nevertheless chooses to hedge a little:

> In general, female police officers are denigrated in our society because people are of the mistaken persuasion that certain anatomical differences in women severely limit their capabilities to deal with the demanding problems with which they are beset.

What she really wanted to say was:

> The idea that female police officers are too fragile and dainty to do the job required of them is rubbish. As a matter of fact, my neighbor, who is a police sergeant, tells me that for assignments, such as taming drunks, caring for lost children, and even breaking up domestic quarrels, women are more skilled than men.

The difficult lot of the English instructor is to convince the student that the second opinion is better expressed than the first because it is clearer, more forceful, and more direct. But that, indeed, is plainly the case. Directness and forcefulness in student prose are devoutly wished for by many bewildered English instructors who, year after year, have been vainly trying to get a grip on the slippery phrasing of the insecure, cautious student.

Here are some more examples of cluttered, slippery phrasing taken from an essay interpreting "Flowering Judas," a short story by Katherine Anne Porter.

> *Cluttered:* In "Flowering Judas" we have the story of a tale about a young woman called Laura, considered at great length until we catch a glimpse of her total self, of which I see the subconscious character of her tortured by guilt.
>
> *Better:* "Flowering Judas" is the story of Laura, a young woman subconsciously tortured by guilt.
>
> *Cluttered:* Laura would not necessarily agree with this analysis if she were asked, but that has little bearing on the facts since Laura does not understand her own motives, and at one point in the story, which goes on for five pages, this is made clear when we are told that Laura instinctively crosses streets cautiously and that she feels a slow inexplicable chill whenever she has the bad fortune of being in her boss Braggioni's presence.
>
> *Better:* That Laura does not understand her own motives is clear when we are told that instinctively she crosses streets

> cautiously and that she feels a slow, inexplicable chill in the presence of her boss, Braggioni.

The cure for clutter is pruning, honesty, and the willingness to risk one's grade on the clear expression of heartfelt opinions.

BEWARE OF BIG WORDS

Behind every big word there is a little word. A case in point is *lachrymose*. *Webster's New World Dictionary* defines it:

> lachrymose: 1. inclined to shed many tears; tearful 2. causing tears; sad.

The lacrimal gland is the tear gland in the eye, so *lachrymose*, which is derived from *lacrimal*, comes to mean *tearful*. But in a choice between *lachrymose* and *tearful*, you should settle for *tearful*. It is a word most people can understand, and you want to be understood. And since every big word is propped up by a little word, to understand *lachrymose* your reader needs to know the meaning of *tearful*. Let us assume that you are dealing with a special kind of reader who knows 99,999 words, but he does not know the meaning of either *tears*, *lachrymose*, or *sad*. He reads the definition of *lachrymose*, and is still lost because he does not know what *tearful* means. He looks up the word *tears* since he deduces that the *-ful* is a suffix to the word *tears*. He finds the following definition:

> tear: 1. a drop of the salty fluid secreted by the lacrimal gland, which serves normally to lubricate the eyeball and in weeping flows from the eye 2. anything resembling this, as a drop of transparent gum; tearlike mass . . .

Notice that while the definition of *lachrymose* shuttled the reader back to the little word *tear*, the definition of *tear* gives a direct description of what a tear is. This stacking effect of big words over little words is common in English. The big word is stacked over the little word and draws its meaning from it; the little word, in contrast, points directly to the idea or object it stands for. Ordinarily a big word is twice removed from its meaning while a little word sits directly on top of its meaning.

The temptation to use a big word instead of a little one is strong, and most people at some point in their lives have to resist it or risk being hooked on big words forever. This temptation is most irrestible during the student years. One of the authors of this book was once hooked on the big word and wrote the following in a student newspaper:

Advocates of *anthropocentric, geocentric* and *ethnocentric* attitudes are cordially invited to attend the astronomy lab class taught by Mr. John E. Bowen. The class meets for 3 hours each week (one session) during which time actual experiments and measurements are conducted by students. If education is primarily of an *iconoclastic* nature, then this class must be the *slaughterhouse* of *egocentric idealism.*

This author now repents for having used the italicized words. The author also noticed that during his addiction to the big word, he also became addicted to making pompous phrases out of them, usually by joining two big words with an *of* as in "the slaughterhouse of egocentric idealism." Now, years later, and reeling with the excruciation of his embarrassment over this past foible, he mainly abstains from it, except for an occasional relapse.

Never use a word just because it is big!

If you are trying to communicate an idea in writing, you should choose words for their precision rather than for their size. Sometimes the bigger word, particularly if it has a technical meaning, will be more precise. But usually the little word is more precise and has more of an edge to it. Moreover, by sticking with the vocabulary you regularly use (which has its share of both big and little words), your writing will sound like your own.

A final note of warning on words: if you unearth a word you especially like and are determined to use, wait until you have seen it used in the context of several sentences before using it in your own writing. The dictionary definition of a word, no matter how up-to-date, usually lags behind its usage definition. To get the full flavor of a word, you need to know how various writers are currently using it. In Chapter 7 we will discuss additional aspects of the meaning of words, how words work, and how you choose the right word.

KEEP YOUR POINT OF VIEW CONSISTENT

Your point of view is determined by the pronoun you use to refer to yourself in your writing. There is a finite number of such pronouns. You may call yourself *I*, which introduces a personal relationship between yourself and your reader.

> I have always depended on myself.

You may call yourself *we*. More formal than *I*, this form is sometimes referred to as the royal *we* because it is used by kings in referring to themselves. The use of *we* introduces distance between the writer and the material.

> We have always depended on ourselves.

You may call yourself *one,* which is excessively formal and not recommended. The use of *one* gives an air of universality to whatever it is you are trying to say.

> One has always to depend on oneself.

Finally, you may leave out any reference to yourself.

> People should always depend on themselves.

Ordinarily, *I* is the preferred form, depending on your assignment and on your instructor. If you have any doubt about which pronoun you should use in referring to yourself, ask your instructor. More often than not, if you are writing an essay about a nonpersonal subject, you can avoid ever having to refer to yourself at all. Instead of saying,

> In this paper, I will describe the folkways of the Trobriand Islanders as they were cataloged by Malinowski.

you can say,

> This paper will describe the folkways of the Trobriand Islanders as they were cataloged by Malinowski.

The *I* is invisible, but assumed. However, if your instructor asks you to write an essay describing a personal experience, *I* is the pronoun you should use.

Choose your pronoun with care, because once you select a pronoun for yourself, you are obliged to use it throughout the entire essay. If you begin by referring to yourself as *I,* you must not switch to *we* in the middle.

USE SUBORDINATION TO JOIN CHOPPY SENTENCES

Fashions change in the lengths of hemlines and also in the lengths of sentences. We are less charitable today to the long, serpentine sentence than people were, say, in the days of Benjamin Franklin when brocaded writing was regarded as a mark of literary skill. Students, however, rarely write long sentences; rather, they commit the opposite sin of piling up a succession of short, childish sentences. The cure for this defect is subordination—the combining of related sentences through the use of relative pronouns, parenthetical expressions, modifiers, or appositives. Here is an example of choppy student writing:

> Abraham Lincoln was President during the Civil War. He was born in a log cabin. He freed the slaves.

Here are various subordinated versions:

> Abraham Lincoln, who was President during the Civil War and who freed the slaves, was born in a log cabin.
>
> Abraham Lincoln, who freed the slaves, was born in a log cabin and was President during the Civil War.
>
> Born in a log cabin, Abraham Lincoln—President during the Civil War—freed the slaves.

Here are some more examples of choppy sentences joined through subordination into longer, more effective sentences.

> *Choppy:* In life we must learn two things. We have to control ourselves. We must live in peace with our neighbors. If not, we shall not even be in a position to regret it.
>
> *Subordinated:* Unless we learn to control ourselves and to live in peace with our neighbors, we shall not even be in a position to regret it.
>
> *Choppy:* A week passed. Then the divers descended into the murky water. They poked around the seaweed and kelp. Then they found the cable. It was solid copper.
>
> *Subordinated:* When a week passed, the divers descended into the murky water, where they poked around the seaweed and kelp until they found the solid copper cable.
>
> *Choppy:* First he selected a lancet and sterilized it. Then he gave his patient a local anesthetic. Then he lanced the infected finger.

> *Subordinated:* After selecting a lancet and sterilizing it, he gave his patient a local anesthetic and lanced the infected finger.

Notice, by the way, that short, choppy sentences joined by conjunctions still sound childish:

> Abraham Lincoln was President during the Civil War and was born in a log cabin and freed the slaves.

It is best to use a variety of sentence types in essays. Short, medium, and long sentences will work together to keep your reader's interest.

EXERCISES

1. The following sentences do not catch the flavor of today's speech. Rewrite them using more current language.

   a. No man who knows aught would deny the existence of God.
   b. I shall ever esteem my acquaintance with you as a felicitous circumstance.
   c. The insatiable swilling of wine doth weaken the senses.
   d. He is a great nomenclator of authors, but he does not read books.
   e. He was somewhat revived at this testimony of her good disposition toward him.
   f. We learned to eat after the manner of their country.
   g. He is not in a humor to harken to an epistle steeped in dullness.
   h. Prithee, accept my sincerest approbation.
   i. We could entreat her to fetch us some medicine from the apothecary.
   j. Betwixt me and them me thought I saw a wall that did compass about a huge mountain.

2. The following sentences contain stilted or pedantic language. Rewrite them to project a "talking voice."

   a. An individual with whom I am moderately well acquainted invited me to accompany him to New York to examine works of artistic merit.
   b. Overmobility while dancing connotes lack of talent as regards bodily coordination.
   c. For a long period of time the men gazed at that circuitous water-filled channel running between rocky elevations.
   d. His speech was delivered with exceeding perspicacity.
   e. Come with me, my love, to gaze at all the arboreal growths.

     f. Many university professors exhibit a tendency toward loquaciousness.

     g. Three conditions today militate against optimum marital harmony.

     h. All the while the university is systematically desiccating the integrated community of Morningside Heights.

3. Pretend that your best friend has asked you for some written advice on how to make adjustment to college as smooth as possible. Answer the request in a brief letter. (Remember to be yourself; after all, you are writing to your best friend.)

4. Which of the following sentences would be acceptable in a written assignment?

     a. Your plan bugs me.

     b. There are bugs in your plan.

     c. He plans to buy a bug.

     d. He told the salesman to bug-off.

     e. There is a bug on the windowpane.

     f. He is a bug about windowpanes.

     g. They drove him to the bug-house.

     h. The telephone is bugged.

5. In the following passage, Sherlock Holmes, the English detective, outlines a theory to his colleague, Dr. Watson:

The facts, as I read them, are something like this: This woman was married in America. Her husband developed some hateful qualities, or shall we say he contracted some loathesome disease and became a leper or an imbecile? She flies from him at last, returns to England, changes her name, and starts her life, as she thinks, afresh. She has been married three years and believes that her position is quite secure, having shown her husband the death certificate of some man whose name she has assumed, when suddenly her whereabouts is discovered by her first husband, or, we may suppose, by some unscrupulous woman who has attached herself to the invalid. They write to the wife and threaten to come and expose her.

     a. Underline all words in the above that you no longer use in the same way in your own speech.

     b. Circle all the words you do not know, look up their meanings, and write the word you would use in place of it in your own speech.

     c. Rewrite the passage until it sounds the way you would say it.

6. This passage is taken from court testimony. Rewrite it so that the judge, who understands no slang at all, can read it.

Well, the dude arrives at around 8, and man he's stoned. I ain't never seen such a stoned dude. So she says to him, "Man, you're stoned." Next thing I know, he wants to fight. He don't like nobody telling him he's stoned. So I said, "Cool it, baby, this here ain't no fighting issue." Then he wants to fight me. So I back off, since the dude's stoned, you know, and when a dude's stoned, he's stoned. I looked at my watch then; it was 8:15. So I thought to myself, "This is not my pad. I was just cruising when the chick tells me to come in, so why should I stay and hassle this scene, man?" I said to myself, "You better split." So I split. Just as I was splitting, I looked at my watch. It was 8:20, on the nose.

7. Use subordination to join the following sentences.

    a. The time passed. They grew tired. I became very sleepy.

    b. John Bold died. She earnestly implored her father, Mr. Harding, to come and live with her. But Mr. Harding declined. He remained with her for some weeks as a visitor.

    c. He had said very nice things about her books. He had had the tact to say things that did not make her feel embarrassed. Many people could make her feel embarrassed almost without trying.

8. Rewrite the following sentences, eliminating unnecessary word clutter.

    a. It is the best of all not to fertilize your lawn and grass in any year that is exceedingly dry from lack of rain or snow.

    b. One of the best of all recommended ways to improve and enhance the quality of your spelling is to keep a meticulous and painstaking record of the words that you have tended to misspell.

    c. An experienced driver, one who has driven for quite a time on the road, does not generally fear heavy traffic.

    d. Never in a million years will citizens of America be able to comprehend and understand the Asian mind.

    e. It was a curious, odd, little, and miniscule company that had assembled and gathered to do honor to this old, aged, kindly bachelor.

    f. The reason why I did not go to school yesterday is because of the fact that I was sick.

    g. Last week, I made my way into town to shop for and buy a quantity of groceries.

    h. The immensities and endless expanses of the universe are invisible and cannot be seen even with the most powerful telescope.

3

What's a thesis?

When you set out on a trip, you ought to be able to answer two questions: Where am I going? How do I plan to get there? It is pointless to start out the door in your nightshirt, without any destination in mind. As a rule, fruitful trips need to be planned.

The same is true about writing. Except for the once-in-a-blue-moon genius who, without formal planning, can spin out verbal clusters that make your spine tingle, people write better when they spend a little effort in prewriting, that is, thinking about their project and plotting it. While all of us are aware that some people naturally write better than others, this is no reason why everyone cannot at least write clearly, logically, and even persuasively. It is simply a matter of practice in following the rules. The more you write, the better you get. If you are a poor writer, your best guarantee for improvement is constant writing. Keep a diary; write letters to friends; take notes on instructors' lectures. You learn to write by writing, not by reading *about* writing—just as a pianist learns to play the piano by playing, not by reading manuals on how to play.

Because writing is a mental art, not a mechanical skill, no one can supply you with an exact recipe for the perfect final product. Nevertheless, certain guidelines are useful, and we will begin with some suggestions on subject selection.

Do not belittle your writing skill.

You have received a writing assignment. First, you must get your thoughts under control. The trouble with your thinking is not (as you often claim) that you have no thoughts on a subject, but that too many thoughts come tumbling in too fast for you to notice any direction among them. You may reflect, mull, daydream, meditate, ponder, consider, muse, and fantasize—all in a brief period about one subject. These flights of thought are a good sign. All you need to do is select one thought that will generate other thoughts that can be used as appropriate development.

The subjects of your essays may sometimes be determined for you by the wording of the assignment. Your instructor may ask you to attack or defend a certain quotation, to contrast views on a given subject, to state three effects resulting from one cause. But when you have a free choice, try to avoid endless indecision and total blanks by taking the following steps.

Free-associate in order to create ideas.

First, learn to free-associate about the general area in which you intend to write. Say your topic is student life. Simply spend five minutes jotting down whatever comes to your mind when you think of student life. Avoid telling yourself that your thoughts are stupid or trivial or trite. Do not stop writing. When no thought intrudes, write, ''I can't think of anything.'' Your paper may look something like this:

1. I forget everything I learn.
2. Our campus needs faculty reform.
3. Some teachers are boring.
4. I can't think of anything.
5. Why do I have to know grammar?
6. Sometimes the best-looking students have no personality.
7. Computerized classrooms are showing up everywhere.
8. I like classes where the teacher allows us to rap.
9. Speaking up in front of the class still scares me.
10. Miss Grundy is a drag.
11. Do students who have money get a better education than students who don't?
12. I can't always write what I think.
13. I still don't know what to major in.
14. I can't think of anything.
15. Are required courses really a help to education?
16. If I flunked, my parents would kill me.
17. College makes you more independent.
18. A pass-fail system would relax academic pressure.
19. Plato said that education makes good men—bull!
20. What makes a really good instructor?
21. Organized student groups don't turn me on.

Zoom in on the best random thought.

Next, after you have allowed your thoughts to explore a topic in this random way, you will be confronted with the need to focus, since you have only a limited time in which to write a 500-word essay. So you look over your list and choose number 20, "What makes a really good instructor?" Of all ideas listed, this one appeals to you most. Now you must no longer free-associate, but rather you must *zoom in* by consciously asking questions that probe the area. Try to formulate questions that you could answer effectively with a general statement, which could then be developed in detail. Six such questions could be:

1. Are the most popular instructors necessarily the best?
2. Are programed textbooks always effective?
3. Who was my best instructor?
4. How can instructors make education relevant?
5. What are the three most important characteristics of a good instructor?
6. Are instructors the main reason for student apathy on today's campus?

Write a thesis that predicts, controls, and obligates.

Now you have reached the crucial part of your prewriting because any answer to one of the above questions, when carefully stated, can serve as a *thesis* for your essay. Here are possible answers for all six questions:

1. The most popular instructors are not always the best because often they place showmanship above learning.
2. Two disadvantages of programed textbooks are that they are boring because they restrict learning to tiny increments and that the reader tends to forget what he has learned as the mind feels cluttered with intellectual debris.
3. Mr. Higginbottom was my best instructor.
4. An instructor makes education relevant by bringing the real world into the classroom.
5. The three most important characteristics of a good instructor are: competence, imagination, and fairness.
6. Instructors who are incompetent, overly involved in research, or too concerned with politics directly contribute to student apathy on the college campus.

Do not be afraid that your thesis narrows your general topic too much. Composition students rarely fail in that direction; in fact, most of the time they write blanket theses laden with such imprecise and general words as *interesting, great, fine,* and so on. You will always be safe if your thesis restricts you to a specific area that you can handle within the limits of the time and the length allotted.

From the above six answers, you can see that the *thesis* of your essay is a statement in which the *key words* of your essay are nested. Your thesis summarizes your whole essay in one sentence. Sometimes a thesis contains only one key word; sometimes it contains more. The following theses contain one key word, which is italicized.

> 1. My first day on campus was a *frightening* experience.
> 2. I am a *jealous* person.
> 3. Investing in the stock market is *risky*.

Most of the time, however, a thesis will contain several key words, as in the following:

> 1. Soviet children are *members of collectives*—nurseries, schools, camps, youth programs—that emphasize *obedience, self-discipline,* and *subordination* of the self to the group.
> 2. I have nothing but *anxiety* followed by *disappointment* when I have accepted a blind date.
> 3. Good English is *clear, appropriate,* and *vivid.*
> 4. Riding a bicycle to work has *several advantages* over driving a car.

Occasionally, almost every word in a thesis will be a key word, as in the following:

> 1. *When "crimes" are committed in which there are no victims,* as in homosexuality, abortion, and prostitution, *these cannot be called criminal acts.*
> 2. *If the United States is to survive, it will have to conserve its natural resources more carefully* than it has in the past.
> 3. Good science fiction writers *do not invent the situations in their stories;* rather they *predict* them *from what they observe to be possible.*

The precision with which you formulate your thesis helps to determine the quality of your entire essay. A good thesis *predicts, controls,* and *obligates.*

THE THESIS PREDICTS

If you were to state as your thesis *America has had a feminist bias since the beginning of its history,* your reader would guess that your essay will probably deal with such factors as woman's role in the colonies and in the settlement of the frontiers. Your reader would not expect you to deal exclusively with Betty Friedan's book *The Feminine Mystique,* which is about today's woman. And if your thesis is *Yesterday's young revolutionaries have affected three institutions: the courts, the family, and the church,* your reader would predict that you will describe some specific changes that occurred in courts, in family relations, and in religious worship as a result of the youth revolution. A reader would be very confused if instead you analyzed the diction in one of Stokely Carmichael's speeches. When carefully planned, your thesis will predict the general direction in which your essay will move, and it will dictate what sort of explanation or evidence you must provide. This is why it is important that you avoid dead-end theses, such as the following:

1. Speeding on freeways is dangerous.
2. A relationship exists between eating and gaining weight.
3. Before the Civil War, American slaves were oppressed.
4. In America, movie stars are often admired.

Such statements are so self-evident that they require no further argument; in other words, they lead nowhere.

THE THESIS CONTROLS

Consider the following thesis: *Today, religion is no longer the uncontested center and ruler of human life because Protestantism, science, and capitalism have brought about a secularized world.* In this example, the structure on the essay is inherent in the thesis. The advantage of such a thesis is that in committing the writer during the prewriting stage, it controls him during the writing. The essay will quite naturally fall into four sections:

1. A description of medieval society when religion was the center of human existence.
2. An explanation of how Protestantism secularized human beings.
3. An explanation of how science secularized human beings.
4. An explanation of how capitalism secularized human beings.

This thesis functions as a skeletal outline giving the writer direction and organization for his essay. He will not scratch his head and bite his nails in anxiety over where to start and what to include. The thesis has laid the groundwork. It functions as a rough sketch, which he can fill with details, much like the artist painting a portrait from his sketch.[1]

---

[1] For information on how the thesis controls various types of paragraph development, turn to Chapter 6.

THE THESIS OBLIGATES

Confused, vague, unfocused writing is often the result of a writer's refusal to stick to his thesis. If your thesis is *Police officers spend more time controlling traffic and providing information than enforcing the law,* then you are obligated to prove that this is so without flying off into a rhapsody about the heroism of police officers in pursuit of bank robbers. Free-association techniques must be dropped once you begin developing your essay. Again, if your thesis is *California college students are sexually more liberated than their New York counterparts,* then that is the point you are committed to discuss. You must not digress on the intellectual superiority of New York colleges or weave in a few facts about vegetarianism in California unless these subjects are somehow related to the sexual behavior of students in California and New York. Good writing maintains strict unity by sticking to the key words of the thesis. In turn, the thesis must be worded so that it obligates the writer to deal with only one dominant idea. Consider this thesis: *Obscenity is a class concept, and the courts have made decisions on censorship that indicate that they are legally confused.* Here the first part of the thesis calls for an extended definition of obscenity. The reader wants to know what the author means by ''class concept.'' But the second part calls for an analysis of the confusion apparent in court decisions. To be really helpful, a thesis must commit the writer to deal with one dominant idea only. Any essay that starts out with a double purpose will most likely fall into two parts that have no connection with each other. If, however, you believe that two separate ideas are related, then you should show that relationship in the thesis. Looking back at the thesis about obscenity, it could be reworded to show a connection between the two ideas: *Because obscenity is a class concept that changes as society progresses, the courts have made some contradictory decisions on censorship.* When a thesis does not obligate you to one dominant idea, it allows you to ramble on about a subject without restriction and to fill your paragraphs with irrelevancies, digressions, or clutter, so that your finished essay may be like an abandoned thrift shop, where everything lies about in profuse disorder.

THE STATEMENT OF PURPOSE

Some essays may be purposeful without really developing a main idea. Research papers often fall into this category. For instance, if you want to list the steps involved in decorating a Christmas tree, or to demonstrate how to ski parallel, or to trace the conflict leading to open antagonism between East Pakistan and India, your paper will not have a controlling idea, but it will have a clear purpose. It would be pointless to try to force a thesis on such a paper. Yet, writing down a statement of purpose is helpful in order to announce to your reader what you plan to do. Public speakers often do this when they announce what they plan to talk about. The following statements of purpose give the reader a clear idea of what the writer intends:

1. The purpose of this essay is to list some of the aspects of prison life that brutalize rather than reform inmates.
2. In this paper I intend to list five characteristics of the typical "now" movie.
3. This essay will identify and evaluate the present leaders of the feminist movement.
4. My report deals with the major demands of the Chicano rebellion—what they are and which ones have been partly met.
5. By tracing the etymology of *nice, brave, enthrall, idiot, villain,* and *acid,* I intend to illustrate how some words in the English language have undergone amelioration and others pejoration.

SEVEN ERRORS TO AVOID WHEN COMPOSING A THESIS

1. A thesis cannot be a fragment; it must be expressed in a sentence.

   Poor: How life is in a racial ghetto.

   Better: Residents of a racial ghetto tend to have higher death rates, higher disease rates, and higher psychosis rates than do any other residents of American cities.

2. A thesis must not be in the form of a question. (Usually the answer to that question could be the thesis.)

   Poor: Should eighteen-year-olds have the right to vote?

   Better: Anyone who is old enough to fight a war is old enough to vote.

3. A thesis must not contain such phrases as *I think.* (They merely weaken the statement.)

   Poor: In my opinion most men wear beards because they are trying to find themselves.

   Better: The current beard fad may be an attempt on the part of men to emphasize their male identity.

4. A thesis must not contain elements that are not clearly related.

   Poor: All novelists seek the truth; therefore some novelists are good psychologists.

   Better: In their attempt to probe human nature, many novelists appear to be good psychologists.

5. A thesis must not be expressed in vague language.

Poor: Bad things have resulted from religion being taught in the classroom.

Better: Religion as part of the school curriculum should be avoided because it is a highly personal and individual commitment.

6. A thesis must not be expressed in muddled or incoherent language.

Poor: Homosexuality is a status offense because the participants are willing so that the relationship is voluntary in character rather than the type described in a victim-perpetrator model.

Better: When participants in a homosexual act are consenting adults, then homosexuality should be considered a status rather than a criminal offense.

7. A thesis should not be written in figurative language.

Poor: Religion is the phoenix bird of civilization.

Better: As long as humans can conceive the idea of a god, religion will rise to give us a spiritual reason for existence.

One final word of advice: be astute in your approach to writing. Figure out who your readers are and what appeals to them. Remember that composition instructors are forever flooded with repetitive papers—"Five Arguments against Capital Punishment," "Football Is Becoming Too Commerical," "The Grading System as an Outdated Mode," "The Legalization of Marijuana," and so forth, *ad nauseam.* Anything you write that is different will come to your teacher as a welcome spark of excitement during a tedious labor. If you have a choice of writing about capital punishment, prison reform, or the Chinese origin of goldfish, by all means write about the goldfish. The subject itself may cause your instructor to stir from the catatonia caused by reading the fifteenth paper dealing with smog in Los Angeles, each one stating inexorably, with little variety, that smog in Los Angeles is bad and something should be done about it. We state this point about originality not primarily to make the job of instructors more cheery, but to encourage students to release the freshness and inventiveness too often kept locked up inside them.

When you have compiled a free-association list of thoughts on a topic do not choose the most obvious idea or question simply because supportive details can be easily supplied. Whatever is obvious to you will probably be so to everyone else, too. Choose the off-beat comment, the eccentric question, or the unusual idea. If, however, you really want to write about such a common topic as your car, then at least treat the subject in a different manner. Describe the old jalopy as if it were an old man with a crackly voice, suspenders broken, body sagging, and spirit half-dead. If you insist on writing about capital punishment, then at least be for or against it for your own reasons, and not for everybody else's. Taking a close look at your readers in order to make your subject interesting to them is a good investment.

EXERCISES

1. Free-associate for five minutes about the word *adolescence* writing down your ideas as they come to your mind. Do not stop writing. If nothing comes to you, write, "I can't think of anything." Do the same for the words *war, poverty,* and *girl.* Choose one list and narrow it down to a thesis by following the steps outlined on pages 38–39.
2. Find a picture that expresses some aspect of today's society, such as violence, youthful idealism, promiscuity, or religious piety; then write down a thesis that could serve as an appropriate caption.
3. Look back to page 39 and underline the key words in the six theses presented.
4. Which of the following three theses is the best? Support your judgment with reasons.

   a. Forest fires are enormously destructive because they ravage the land, create problems for flood control, and destroy useful lumber.
   b. Installment buying is of great benefit to the economy, having in mind the consumer to use a product while she pays for it and being like forced savings.
   c. Television is a handicap.

5. The following are poorly worded theses. Analyze their weaknesses in terms of the previous discussion and rewrite each to make it clear and effective.

   a. In my opinion, birth control is the most urgent need in today's world.
   b. Just how far should the law go in its tolerance of pornography?
   c. How missionaries are sent to primitive areas in order to introduce Western civilization.
   d. The study of psychology is fascinating.
   e. Education should train all young people for jobs, and blacks are impatient with conditions today.
   f. Slang is the speech of him who robs the literary garbage carts on their way to the dumps.
   g. Our trip to the island of Kauai was great.
   h. Three factors may be singled out as being especially militating against the optimum adjustment that partners in the marriage relationship should experience, as money, culture, and education.

i. The problem with sound pollution is, How much longer can our ears bear the noise?

j. The noteworthy relaxation of language taboos both in conversation and in print today.

k. My feeling is that educationists are just as infatuated with jargon as sociologists.

4

How do I organize?

METHODS OF ORGANIZING

The mental survey
Brainstorming on paper
The card sketch
The formal outline

THE OUTLINE CONVENTION

Creating the outline
Choosing between a topic and a sentence outline
The advantages of organizing by the outline method
The outline and the paragraph

EXERCISES

Before we discuss how to organize, we should discuss what organization is, why it is important, and who should organize.

What is organizing? Organizing is planning your essay before writing it. The plan will show what topics you intend to take up, in what sequence, and with what degree of emphasis.

Why organize? It is easier to write from a plan than to create at random. The organized essay is mapped out in advance. This allows you to conceptualize it from beginning to end—in a sense, to see it in miniature. Lapses of inspiration and unforeseen difficulties are not entirely eliminated by organizing. But even if you stall in mid-essay, at least you will know where you have to go.

Who should organize? Almost everyone who has not had much experience at writing should organize. Later, after you have had more practice with writing essays, you may wish to venture out on the sea of spontaneity without a map. However, in the beginning your writing will probably benefit from organizing.

METHODS OF ORGANIZING

Before you do anything else, write your thesis at the top of a sheet of paper in order to keep it firmly in mind. Every word in your essay must lead the reader back to your thesis, so it is best to have it in front of you as a constant reminder. The next step can be accomplished in a number of ways, depending on your subject and on the deftness of your memory.

The Mental Survey

One way to organize is simply to sit back and write the essay in your mind. Close your eyes, ponder your thesis, and then decide what information you plan to include and in what order. You mentally work through a subject. You analyze and debate. You extract thoughts from the briny deep of your mind, review them, and consider alternatives. You treat your ideas as if they were watermelons that need to be smelled, turned over, and thumped before you buy them. Quite frankly, this approach demands a compulsive mind capable of great order and logic. Few writers are able to remember a plan fixed only in their minds.

Brainstorming on paper

An easier, surer method is to write down everything that comes to your mind about the thesis. Write down your ideas in full sentences as they occur. Of course, this method requires time because it will demand that you rewrite carefully in order to end up with a polished product. But if your teacher has encouraged you to prepare your essay ahead of in-class writing, this is one method you may find useful. It will help you over that dreadful ''I'm-a-complete-blank'' hump. The fact that you can write down ideas uncensored makes you less panicky about what you will sound like. After you have written down all your ideas, group them together into a common-sense sequence. In order to save time, limit yourself to key ideas and avoid irrelevant details.

The card sketch

A favorite method among writers is to think of three to five subtopics that would make good lead sentences for each individual paragraph in the essay. Write each subtopic as a sentence on a separate card; then, when you have written down as many topic sentences as you will need (three to five for a 500-word essay), arrange them so they appear in the proper logical sequence. Now you can jot down details on the cards to go along with the topic sentences. The advantage of this system is that you can keep rearranging (and adding or rejecting) the cards until they appear in the order in which you want to develop your subject. This informal card sketch will give you a framework for your ideas and will help you pinpoint what you want your reader to get from your paper. Like the brainstorming method, it reduces the paralyzing frustration of not knowing where to start. A card sketch of the thesis *Blind dates are not worth the time and trouble they cause you* might look something like the cards on pages 51–52.

The formal outline

The formal outline is a schematic summary of your essay. It reflects, in compact form, the gist of what you plan to write. Some teachers require an outline with the research paper, so you may end up preparing one no matter which method of organizing you use. Even if you used, say, the card sketch method, you would still have to recast your notes into conventional outline form.

1.

Anticipating a blind date is nerve-racking.
   You imagine her to be threateningly
   glamorous, or
   You imagine her to be hideously ugly.

2.

The moment of meeting is inevitably awkward.
   Some of the stupid things you say:
      "Gee, what a happy surprise!"
      "Sure was cool of Bill to fix me
      up with you."
   "Hi, so you're Petula. I hope you
      like me."

> *3.*
>
> My experience with blind dates so far has been disappointing.
>
> My first one was so timid that we spent most of the evening staring silently.
>
> My second one spent my money as if I had an endless supply.
>
> My most recent one kept putting me down because I wasn't living with a woman.

Outlining, as a method of organizing, has one decided advantage: its end-product is a complete and systematic map of the entire essay. None of the other methods of organizing—the mental survey, brainstorming, or the card sketch—yields as complete or as finished a plan as the outline.

THE OUTLINE CONVENTION

A convention has evolved for the formal outline. Main ideas are designated by Roman numerals I, II, III, IV, V, and so on. Subideas branching off the main ideas are designated by capital letters A, B, C, and so on. Examples of these subideas are marked by Arabic numerals 1, 2, 3, 4, and so on, while details that support the examples are indicated by lower case letters a, b, c, and so on. The lineup looks like this:

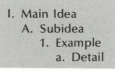

```
I. Main Idea
  A. Subidea
    1. Example
      a. Detail
```

The outline convention dictates that main ideas start at the left of the page, and that subideas are indented. As you move from left to right, you move from the more important to the less important.

Every workable outline is the natural outcome of questions you ask yourself when you first think about putting your ideas on paper. You ask your-self, Which pieces of information should go first? Which parts of my notes should get major attention, which minor, and which should be brought in as incidental but necessary details? As you answer these questions, you natu-rally begin to outline, that is, to create a shorthand version of your paper.

Creating the outline

To create an outline, begin with the thesis or the statement of purpose of the essay and divide it into smaller ideas. These main ideas are then aligned in the order in which they will be discussed in the essay.

Here, for instance, is a thesis: *Extremes in temperature can have danger-ous effects on mountain climbers.* To make this thesis arguable, you must break it down into smaller ideas. In this case, the thesis itself suggests a two-part division.

> I. The dangerous effects of excessive heat
> II. The dangerous effects of excessive cold

The thesis is now divided into two main ideas, each indicated by a Roman numeral.

It is impossible to divide anything into less than two parts. In this case, we have divided the thesis into two parts. In any outline, if you have a Roman numeral I, you must have at least a Roman numeral II.

Note that we are proceeding from the general to the specific. We began with a general idea—the thesis—and divided it into two smaller and there-fore more specific parts. When anything is divided, an idea, a number, or an apple, its parts must be smaller than the whole.

The two parts are still too large to be manageable in an essay, and must be divided again. A knowledge of mountain climbing during extreme weather conditions suggests the next breakdown:

> I. The dangerous effects of excessive heat
>   A. Heat exhaustion
>   B. Heat stroke
>   C. Heat cramps
>
> II. The dangerous effects of excessive cold
>   A. Surface frostbite
>   B. Bodily numbness
>   C. Final drowsiness

As you can see, a structure to the essay has begun to evolve. You now know what you are going to discuss, and in what order.

The preceding example is called a two-level outline, and is based on the division of the thesis into two main ideas (first level), each of which is divided into three subideas (second level). All you need to do now is to research and supply specific examples and supporting detail under each subidea. You need examples of heat exhaustion, heat stroke, heat cramps, and so on.

When both example and detail are included in the outline, it is called a four-level outline. (A three-level outline is one that includes examples but no details.) Here is a sample four-level outline:

TYPES OF COMEDY

Thesis: Comedy can be divided into two kinds, each with a different purpose: comedy to reform the foolish and comedy to entertain the bored.

I. Comedy to reform the foolish
  A. Satire
    1. Ridiculing systems
      a. Swift's "Modest Proposal"
      b. Voltaire's *Candide*
    2. Ridiculing persons
      a. Dryden's "MacFlecknoe"
      b. Newspaper cartoons of political figures
  B. Burlesque
    1. Putting down the sacred
      a. Shaw's *Arms and the Man*
      b. Musical *Hair*
    2. Elevating the lowly
      a. "Ode to a Wart"
      b. Pope's "Rape of the Lock"

II. Comedy to entertain the bored
  A. Comedy of manners
    1. Verbal wit
      a. Wilde's *The Importance of Being Earnest*
      b. Coward's *Private Lives*
    2. Situation comedy
      a. Fielding's *Tom Jones*
      b. "I Love Lucy" television show
  B. Farce
    1. Exaggerated movements
      a. Charlie Chaplin
      b. "Laugh-in" television show
    2. Exaggerated costuming
      a. Circus clowns
      b. Flip Wilson's "Geraldine"

Choosing between a topic and a sentence outline

Some outlines are topic outlines; others are sentence outlines. A topic outline is one in which the entries are not complete sentences, but fragments that state the topic; a sentence outline is one in which entries are complete sentences.

Your decision as to whether to use a topic or a sentence outline depends on how complete a breakdown you need. If your subject is simple and all you need are key words or ideas to serve as guideposts so that you will not get sidetracked, or if you wish merely to set down some major trends, categories, and stages, then a topic outline will be more convenient than a sentence outline (see, for example, the topic outline earlier in this chapter on page 54). But if your subject is dense or in an area new to you, then a topic outline may waste your time and serve no purpose. Consider the following *topic* outline:

Thesis: *An assessment of the future of our cities reveals two emerging trends.*

I. The megalopolis
   A. Definition
      1. Cluster
      2. System
   B. Two major organizational problems
      1. Transcendence
      2. Coordination

II. Shift in decision-making
   A. Local decisions
      1. Facts not known
      2. Outside agencies
   B. Federal government
      1. Increase of power
      2. Local restrictions

This topic outline is of no value to a person not thoroughly initiated into the problems of city governance. A student writing a paper based on such a flimsy outline is bound to sweat out the results and will probably end up scratching the outline and starting all over again. Now look at the following *sentence* outline on the same subject:

Thesis: *An assessment of the future of our cities reveals two emerging trends.*

I. The megalopolis is replacing the city.
   A. Megalopolis can be defined in two ways.

1. A megalopolis is a cluster of cities.
2. A megalopolis is a system of interwoven urban and suburban areas.
   B. Two major organizational problems of the megalopolis will need to be solved.
1. One problem is how to handle questions that transcend individual metropolitan areas.
2. Another problem is how to coordinate the numerous activities in the megalopolis.

II. Decision-making is shifting from local control to higher echelons of public and private authority.
   A. The growing scale of the urban world often makes local decisions irrelevant.
1. Local agencies may not know all of the facts.
2. National policies may supersede local decisions.
   B. The federal government moves into the picture.
1. The extent of federal involvement increases as the city grows.
   a. Federal long-range improvement plans are used.
   b. Grant-in-aid programs become necessary.
2. Assistance from the federal government imposes local restrictions.
   a. Federal policies make sure that no discrimination takes place in the areas of housing, employment, and education.
   b. Federal representatives check on local installations to make sure that they are up to federal standards.

The advantage of a good sentence outline is that it supplies all the basic information you need in order to write your essay; you will not waste time drumming up inept examples as you race the clock for time, your mind in a dither and your pen tapping the desk aimlessly. In fact, by merely adding a few transitional phrases to effect coherence, and by rounding out the bare ideas with some details, you can shape your essay into final form with content as well as direction.

Use a topic outline when stressing basic organization only. Use a sentence outline when stressing details as well as organization.

The advantages of organizing by the outline method

Organizing by the outline method has one significant advantage: an outline allows you to see the entire essay in miniature and to examine its structure as a whole. When you are immersed in the essay, it is easy to become fascinated with individual phrases and sentences while losing sight of the structure. But in an outline structural defects stand out clearly. Here are some examples:

> *Poor:* Thesis: *The police have two different roles, the criminal and the noncriminal.*
>
>   I. The criminal role
>
>   II. The noncriminal role
>   A. Traffic control
>   B. Personal counseling
>   C. Providing information

If this outline were followed, a lopsided essay would result. The thesis claims that there are two roles for the police. The outline ignores the first role, while developing the second. Such lopsidedness is glaringly visible in an outline, but less so in an essay.

> *Rewrite:* Thesis: *The police have two different roles, the criminal and the noncriminal.*
>
>   I. The criminal role
>   A. Prosecution of lawbreakers
>   B. Enforcement of court decisions
>   C. Crime prevention
>
>   II. The noncriminal role
>   A. Traffic control
>   B. Personal counseling
>   C. Providing information

> *Poor:* Thesis: *Four reasons dominate why college students drink.*
>
>   I. Rebelling against parents
>   II. Escaping problems or conflicts
>   III. Certain schools are labeled as party schools
>   IV. Giving in to social pressure

Idea number III is not a reason why college students drink; it is merely a statement about some colleges. If a section of the essay were developed around this area, it would seem an intrusion into the logic.

> *Rewrite:* Thesis: *Three reasons dominate why college students drink.*
>
>   I. Rebelling against parents
>   II. Escaping problems or conflicts
>   III. Giving in to social pressure

These and other defects of structure, emphasis, or order are easier to spot in an outline than in an essay.

The outline and the paragraph

Depending on how long your essay is and how involved your treatment is of its subideas, you may want to structure your outline so that each main idea consumes a separate paragraph in the essay. However, there are no hard-and-fast rules for converting an outline into an essay. The general rule of thumb is one of reasonable equivalence: that is, if you have a main idea that is divided into three subideas in the outline, then each subidea should be more or less equally treated in the essay. You should not, in other words, devote four paragraphs to one of the three subideas, while cramming the other two into a single paragraph. An idea should receive approximately the same emphasis in the essay that it gets in the outline.

Use an outline to fix approximate limits to your essay and to set up a sequence of topics and ideas that will be followed, more or less, in the essay. Bear in mind always that the outline is simply a means to an end, and not the end itself. If, in the act of writing, you fall under the spell of inspiration and hit on a fantastic new idea or way of treating your subject, do not be inhibited by the thought of deviating from your outline. The point is to write a good essay; the outline is simply a means of doing that.

> **Organize your essay by one of four methods:**
> **Mental survey**
> **Brainstorming on paper**
> **Card sketch**
> **Formal outline**

EXERCISES

1. Choose one of the following theses and formulate a card sketch. Number the cards in the order in which you wish them to appear.

   a. Getting a driver's license from the Department of Motor Vehicles is a harrowing experience.
   b. The feminist movement is heading in the wrong direction.
   c. Sadism in today's movies is excessive.
   d. Most of the world's environmental problems could be solved by population control.
   e. Fad diets do not work in weight control.
   f. Popular music today has a different purpose from that of ten years ago.

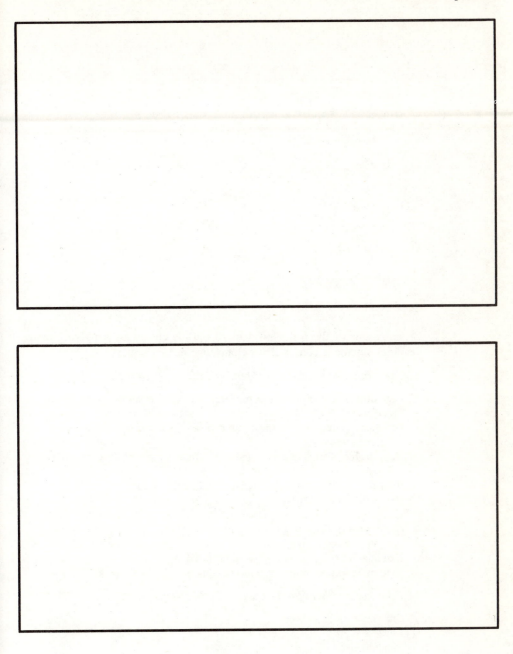

2. Organize one of the following lists of outline entries by supplying main headings for those entries that belong together.

a. *The Catherine Phillips Murder Case*

Tape of threatening phone call to victim's accountant a short while before accident

Defendant's pregnancy by husband at time of accident pointed to as evidence of love

High degree of barbiturates found in the bloodstream of dead husband's body

Evidence of affair between defendant and family friend

Extreme hatred of husband

Claim that she loved husband and needed him as father of child

Secret plan of defendant to marry lover

An empty gasoline can in the back seat of car after accident

Extramarital affair passed off as mild flirtation

Lure of $100,000 insurance policy of husband

b. *Information Sheet for Track and Field Events*

Showers

Lockers

Sophomores

Tartan for long jump, pole vault, high jump

Printed results mailed

Juniors

Three awards for each division

Seniors
Awards for first, second, third place
Dressing rooms
Cement for shotput, hammer, and discus rings
Freshmen
Results announced and posted at meet
Crushed brick for track
Duplicate awards for ties
Towels
Award presentation immediately following finals

3. Develop a two-level sentence outline from one of the following theses and main ideas:

   a. *Thesis: Food manufacturers package their products in order to sell them.*

      I. Bright colors catch the consumer's attention.
      II. Catchy slogans convince the consumer to buy.

   b. *Thesis: Photography fills some basic human needs.*

      I. It makes a person pause in the rush through life.
      II. It helps a person to focus on some enriching aspect of surroundings.
      III. It serves to sharpen a person's memory.

   c. *Thesis: A hit record in the pop field must follow three rules in order to appeal to the "now" generation.*

      I. It must have a snappy melody.
      II. It must have socially aware lyrics.
      III. It must be dressed up in a razzle-dazzle instrumental sound.

4. Mark those entries in which the logical progression of thought breaks down in the following outlines. (Stick to one organizational principle.)

   a. *Thesis: Rummage sales can be a waste of time and money.*

      I. I feel inferior buying someone's castoffs.
      II. Often the items I buy turn out to have flaws.
      III. The Rose Bowl rummage sale attracts people from all over.
      IV. One of the hottest rummage sale items is blue jeans.
      V. I am tempted to buy just because the price is cheap.
      VI. The customers at rummage sales are pushy.

   b. *Thesis: Accidents while skiing on snow can be avoided by following some simple rules.*

      I. Avoid skiing during heavy snowfalls.
      II. Slow down on crowded slopes.
      III. Austria's slopes are dangerously steep.
      IV. Rest when you are tired.
      V. Wet spots often turn into ice patches.

    VI. Do not use faulty equipment.

    VII. Stay away from areas beyond your ability.

  c. *Thesis: American political assassins have acted on nonpolitical impulses.*

      I. They are pathetic loners.

     II. A fantasy world is their reality.

    III. The victim is usually a surrogate parent image.

    IV. European assassinations, unlike ours, have been the results of elaborate plots.

     V. The assassin is seeking the same "fame" that the victim has.

5. Scrutinize the following sentence outline for errors in form and in content. Write an improved version.

Thesis: Acupuncture as a cure for illness and a painkiller has attracted serious attention in the United States.

    I. A definition of acupuncture may be useful.
      a. Inserting needles at selected points in the human body
        1. To cure illness
        2. To stop pain

    II. Despite its effectiveness, acupuncture remains a scientific mystery.
      A. Not even the Chinese, who discovered the art, know how it works.
      B. Various theories have been suggested.
        1) Variations in the skin's electrical resistance
        2) Changes in the skin's density
        3) Blocking of nerve sensations
        4) No theory has been scientifically confirmed.

    III. The needles are usually silver.

    IV. Thorough studies of the use of acupuncture are needed before it can be used widely in the United States.
      1. The Chinese have used acupuncture for 2½ millenniums.
        a. They spend years learning the method.
      2. Some harm could occur.
      3. Major blood vessels or nerve passageways could be damaged.
      4. Acupuncture's anesthetic effects are not the same for all people.

II
WRITING

5

How do I get from outline to paragraphs?

An essay is made up of two components: the sentence and the paragraph. The sentence is the basic unit of grammar, the paragraph the basic unit of organization. For the sake of overall clarity, therefore, the paragraph conventions need to be observed as scrupulously as the conventions of grammar.

Many college students who can drum up readable sentences often find it impossible to assemble these into a comprehensible paragraph—a failure due usually to one of two errors: 1. the paragraph is not limited to a main idea; 2. the paragraph does not decisively make a point.

THE TOPIC SENTENCE IN THE PARAGRAPH

Basically, the paragraph convention specifies that every new idea be treated in a separate paragraph. A shift to a new paragraph alerts the reader to the entrance of a new idea or to a major new development in an old idea. The paragraph format is simply a convenient layout for the ideas in an essay. Separate ideas are blocked off and indented in separate squares of print; the ideas are therefore less jumbled, more emphatic, and easier to follow.

Each paragraph consists of one general idea, called the *topic sentence,* supported by a group of specific ideas. In other words, each paragraph is dominated by one big idea serving as an umbrella for a number of smaller ideas. The smaller ideas have a single purpose—to stress and clarify the big idea. To illustrate this point, let us suppose that you have just completed the following outline for an essay entitled "My Grandmother":

MY GRANDMOTHER

Thesis: My Grandmother Corley was a terrifying woman.
I. My Grandmother Corley taught me religion by fear.
   A. She made hell seem like a torture chamber.

B. She threatened that my guardian angel would leave me if I offended him.

C. She reminded me daily that God kept a record of all my deeds and thoughts.

D. She made me memorize hymns about the despair caused by sin.

II. My Grandmother Corley tyrannized our household.

A. All her requests were commands shouted in a high, piercing voice.

B. She had temper tantrums if anyone dirtied her carpet.

C. Once she threw a vase at my grandfather when he came home tipsy.

D. Even when she was eighty years old, my aunts and uncles tiptoed meekly about the house whenever they knew that her arthritis had put her in a bad mood.

The best way to begin your essay is with an introductory paragraph that contains your general thesis. This paragraph is an attention-getter and therefore flexible in nature. Your job here is simply to begin the essay and introduce its thesis. (See pages 80–82 for good introductory paragraphs.)

The essay about your grandmother could open in this way:

"What was your grandmother like?" a friend asked me some time back. I have been thinking about an answer ever since. From the time of her death ten years ago, this unusual woman has remained in my memory as an unbridled phenomenon of nature. She was part mountain, part tiger, and part God. In short, *my Grandmother Corley was a terrifying woman.*

As you can see, this beginning paragraph consists of a question, some analogies, and finally the thesis. Note that the thesis is the final sentence of the first paragraph. It is not there by law, but by custom and convenience. The thesis could just as easily be the first sentence of the first paragraph, but stating the thesis in the last sentence of the first paragraph allows for some introductory preamble, which makes it seem less abrupt.

Now we come to the first paragraph in the body of the essay. Again, here is the paragraph in outline form:

I. My Grandmother Corley taught me religion by fear.

A. She made hell seem like a torture chamber.

B. She threatened that my guardian angel would leave me if I offended him.

> C. She reminded me daily that God kept a record of all my deeds and thoughts.
> D. She made me memorize hymns about the despair caused by sin.

Notice that the biggest idea in the above outline is the sentence: "My Grandmother Corley taught me religion by fear." It is the topic sentence, which will notify the reader of the main point of the upcoming paragraph and make the argument easier to follow. Notice also that statements A, B, C, and D contain smaller and more specific ideas that serve to stress and clarify the bigger idea in the topic sentence. That is the way most paragraphs progress—from a big idea to smaller ideas. With a little exaggeration we can actually give the paragraph a visual shape:

Big

> My Grandmother Corley taught me religion by fear.
> She made hell seem like a torture chamber.
> She threatened that my guardian angel would leave me if I offended him.

Smaller

> She reminded me daily that God kept a record of all my deeds and thoughts.
> She made me memorize hymns about the despair caused by sin.

Sometimes it is wise to end a paragraph by referring back to the topic sentence, in which case the shape of the paragraph would be like this:

Topic Sentence

> My Grandmother Corley taught me religion by fear.
>
> She made hell seem like a torture chamber.
> She threatened that my guardian angel would leave me if I offended him.

Smaller ideas

> She reminded me daily that God kept a record of all my deeds and thoughts.
> She made me memorize hymns about the despair caused by sin.

Back to topic sentence

> Very early in life religion for me became a source of deep anxiety.

In a paragraph, the big idea stated in the topic sentence should trigger off the smaller ideas that support it. The best way to accomplish this is to think in concrete or specific images. Here is a suggested paragraph:

My Grandmother Corley taught me religion by fear. In her Calvinistic way she did her best to scare me into heaven. For instance, she made hell seem like a torture chamber where sinners would spend "millions of billions of years" (I used to try to count that high) chained to big rocks, screaming for mercy and deliverance from the yellow sulphurous flames that Satan fanned daily. Another tactic was to shake her finger at me and say, "Young Lamb, your guardian angel will fold his wings and depart if you hurt his feelings by doing wrong. Then you will have no protection from dangers, and you could fall over a cliff, or get kicked by a horse, or get ptomaine poisoning." Furthermore, I was reminded every day by her mournful voice that God kept a record of all my deeds and thoughts. "Oh my child," she would wail, shaking her white head, "He hears every little word you speak, sees every secret deed you perform—be the room ever so dark and be you ever so alone. He writes it all in His book, posted for the Day of Judgment!" How I used to writhe in agony and embarrassment thinking about all the things I had said and done when I was all by myself. But Grandmother's favorite pastime was preaching against sin. She portrayed it as an ugly monster, summarizing her whole attitude in the words "Sin is an abomination unto the Lord." She made me memorize countless hymns about the despair caused by sin. Most of them I have forgotten, but I still remember one particular lament that began, "I was sinking deep in sin, far from the peaceful shore. . . ." Yes, very early in life religion for me became a source of deep anxiety.

Every paragraph must be dominated by a big idea, called the topic sentence, which is supported by smaller ideas and specific details.

Topic sentences that serve more than one paragraph

A single topic sentence will sometimes serve as an umbrella for two or more paragraphs, each supporting the topic sentence by adding a new idea, a different angle, or another perspective. Here is an example:

This entire exercise in restraint would teach us the most valuable lesson of all: that the quality of our lives will be enriched if we make fewer demands on our resources. "Less is more" is a paramount tenet of environmental reform, and it is time for us to recognize its specific benefits.

> Less horsepower, smaller cars, and fewer autos mean more safety, healthier urban environments, more constraints on suburban sprawl, more efficient use of fuel. Less oil consumption for fuel means more oil to share with our children and theirs, more energy self-sufficiency, more oil for use in basic industrial processes. Less investment in highways means more money for efficient public transportation, more open space, more investment in cheap, fast intercity trains.
>
> The bonuses of "less is more" are vast. The choice facing the American people is not between growth and stagnation, but between short-term growth and long-term disaster. We can continue to pursue the growth policies of the past and let urban decay, exorbitant prices, and risks to our national security dictate stringent remedial policies a few years from now. Or we can exercise restraint and learn to live comfortably, within our means.
>
> —Stewart Udall, "The Last Traffic Jam"

The topic sentence states that "our lives will be enriched if we make fewer demands on our resources"—a contention on which both subsequent paragraphs shed additional light. The second paragraph gives examples of what is meant by "less is more" while the final paragraph challenges the reader to put into practice the "less is more" philosophy by exercising restraint in the use of natural resources. However, to avoid writing either fragmented or undeveloped paragraphs, beginning writers will find it safer to use a separate topic sentence for each paragraph.

LEVELS OF GENERALITY IN A PARAGRAPH

The sentences in paragraphs vary widely in levels of generality. Some are highly general; others are minutely specific. To illustrate these levels of generality, sentences in the following paragraph are numbered on a scale of 1 to 4, 1 being the most general and 4 the most specific.

> 1 A bright splash of color has brightened New York recently.
>
> 2 The pedestrian bridge connecting Manhattan with Ward's Island has been painted in bright primary hues.
>
> 3 The span was painted yellow.
>
> 4 It's a vivid signal yellow that would make taxicabs envious.
>
> 3 The towers were painted blue.
>
> 4 You could say that the blue towers represent the gravity line that connects sky and water.

> 3 The control booths were painted red.
>
> 4 The red was needed to complete the scheme of principal colors.
>
> 2 New Yorkers are falling in love with this vibrant *objet d'art*.
>
> 3 Drivers blink and smile.
>
> 3 Children fish under the bridge as if it were their private clubhouse.
>
> 1 As a matter of fact, painting the Ward's Island Bridge is like placing a permanent rainbow over a drab part of New York.

Here is this same paragraph assembled in uninterrupted form:

> A bright splash of color has brightened New York recently. The pedestrian bridge connecting Manhattan with Ward's Island has been painted in bright primary hues. The span was painted yellow. It's a vivid signal yellow that would make taxicabs envious. The towers were painted blue. You could say that the blue towers represent the gravity line that connects sky and water. The control booths were painted red. The red was needed to complete the scheme of principal colors. New Yorkers are falling in love with this vibrant *objet d'art*. Drivers blink and smile. Children fish under the bridge as if it were their private clubhouse. As a matter of fact, painting the Ward's Island Bridge is like placing a permanent rainbow over a drab part of New York.

The point we wish to stress is that sentences in a paragraph can vary in levels of generality. The topic sentence in this paragraph is marked as 1 and is directly supported by all sentences numbered 2. Sentences numbered 3 directly support a 2 while sentences numbered 4 directly support a 3. The number of levels of generality in a paragraph depends on the topic sentence being developed. The topic of the following paragraph is simple enough to require only two levels of generality:

> 1 Christmas, as we all know, is a great big birthday party for the world, and everybody overdoes.
>
> 2 There can't be too much plum pudding, wassail, tree ornaments, street-corner Santas, garish department-store displays, or expensive gifts.

72

> 2 Everyone suddenly subscribes to the economics of "Buy now; pay later."
>
> 2 And all of us insist that we must have a smashingly good time.

1 Christmas is the world's moment of crass excess.

A paragraph is built up by various levels of generality.

CHARACTERISTICS OF THE WELL-DESIGNED PARAGRAPH

A well-designed paragraph has characteristics of 1. unity, 2. coherence, and 3. completeness.

Unity

A paragraph must have unity: its sentences must stick to the dominant idea or topic of the paragraph. A weakness apparent in many student papers is lack of unity, which means that somewhere in its development the paragraph strays away from the topic sentence; that is to say, the writer is somehow sidetracked from his purpose. Here is an example:

> 1. A fairy tale is a serious story with a human hero and a happy ending. 2. The hero in a fairy tale is different from the hero in a tragedy in that his progression is from bad to good fortune, rather than the reverse. 3. *In the Greek tragedy "Oedipus Rex," for example, the hero goes from highest fortune to lowest misery, but in the end he recognizes his error in judgment and maintains a noble posture despite profound suffering. 4. The audience watching him is purged of pity and fear through what Aristotle labeled a "catharsis."* 5. The hero in a fairy tale usually has a miserable beginning. 6. He is either socially obscure or despised as being stupid and lacking in heroic virtues. 7. But in the end, he has surprised everyone by demonstrating his courage, consequently winning fame, riches, and love. 8. We clearly see this bad-to-good-fortune progress in stories like "Cinderella," "Sleeping Beauty," and "The Frog Prince."

The topic sentence of this paragraph promises to give a definition of the fairy tale. Unfortunately, part of the paragraph drifts away from the definition. The writer is tricked into trouble by sentence 2, which is still acceptable because it helps define the fairy tale by saying what it is not—it is not a tragedy. But this allusion to tragedy then lures the writer into two additional sentences that describe a Greek tragedy and explain Aristotle's idea of catharsis. These two sentences add nothing to the definition of a fairy tale; they should therefore be left out. Sentences 5, 6, 7, and 8 are back on the track and contribute unity to the paragraph.

The most common place for an inexperienced writer to get sidetracked is at the end of his paragraph. Usually the error occurs because the writer, in an attempt to find closure, introduces a new topic sentence that should be either deleted or developed in a new paragraph. Notice the example below:

> In America the car has taken on some distinctly religious overtones. For instance, the family station wagon is a type of chapel where the family can commune with nature and each other; the weekly car wash is a baptismal ritual or cleansing rite; and the periodic trade-in for a better model is like a pilgrimage to find renewal, rebirth, and reaffirmation. The recent crop of religious bumper stickers ("Honk If You Love Jesus," "Have the Holy Spirit, Will Share," "Guess Who's Coming Again," "Smile, God Loves You") is undeniable evidence that religion has invaded the automobile. *However, the religious bumper sticker is not necessarily a sign of true religion. It takes more than hot slogans to be a real Christian.*

The italicized portion of this paragraph is not related to the announced topic sentence "In America the car has taken on some distinctly religious overtones." It should be left out or it should occupy a separate paragraph.

> **Gain unity by having all the sentences in your paragraph relate to the topic sentence.**

Coherence

Having unity in a paragraph is not enough. Even when all sentences in the paragraph relate strictly to the topic sentence, the *way* in which they are related to each other may be muddled. In other words, the sentences of a paragraph must cohere; they must be held together by more than sequence on the page. Four main devices can be used to insure coherence:

1. Transitional words and phrases
2. Pronoun reference
3. Repeated key terms
4. Parallelism

Coherence in a paragraph is achieved by the use of *transitional words and phrases*—words and phrases that point out the direction toward which the paragraph is moving. Here is an example:

In addition to the academic traditionalism in schools, there are other problems. *First,* there is the problem of coordinating education with the realities of the work world. *Second,* there is the question of how long the schooling period should be. Despite evidence to the contrary, a case can be made for the notion that we not only overeducate our children, but also take too long to do it.

The italicized words and phrases are there to add coherence to the passage. They help to lead the argument continuously from one sentence to the next. Other common transitional words and phrases are:

after all   in addition
also   in contrast
and   in fact
as a consequence   in spite of
but   moreover
finally   nevertheless
for example   next
however   therefore

Coherence is also achieved by the use of *pronoun reference*. A noun is used in one sentence or clause, and a pronoun to refer to it is used in the next sentence or clause.

Women are a majority of the population, but *they* are treated like a minority group. The prejudice against *them* is so deep-rooted that, paradoxically, most persons continue to pretend that it does not exist. Indeed, most women prefer to ignore the situation than to rock the boat. *They* accept being paid less for doing the same work as a man. *They* are as quick as any male to condemn a woman who ventures outside the limits of the role men have assigned to females: that of toy and drudge.

A noun is used in one sentence, and a pronoun is used in its place in the following sentences. The reader's attention is therefore directed from the sentence he is reading to the one before, thereby establishing a link between them.

Key terms may be repeated throughout the paragraph to help link its sentences together.

Fantasy is not restricted to one sector of the Southern California way of life; it is all pervasive. Los Angeles restaurants and their park-

> ing lots are such million-dollar structures because they are palaces of *fantasy* in which the upward-moving individual comes to act out a self-mythology he or she has learned from a hero of the mass media. Often enough, the establishments of La Cienega Boulevard's Restaurant Row are *fantasies* of history in their very architecture.

Here, the repeated use of the word *fantasy* provides a link between the sentences.

A final way of achieving coherence is through the use of *parallelism*. A similar grammatical pattern is used in various sentences throughout the paragraph to help link them together.

> The war in Vietnam had its admirers and its detractors. *To some* it was a shoddy affair, ill-conceived from the beginning, mismanaged along the way; *to others,* it was an example of America's commitment to its word. *To some* it was a sinful waste of our resources; *to others,* it was money well spent to turn back communism. However the war is viewed and in whatever light, almost everyone is glad that it is finally over.

or

> Besides *the grimy clothes on her back* and *the twenty-six cents in her pocket,* that jug of "musky" is her only possession. She needs its warm sweetness before the night is out to escape *her fears, her guilt, her remorse.* That is where she will find *the peace to quiet her nerves, the strength to keep from screaming.*

In both above examples, the link between sentences is the repetition of similar grammatical patterns.

Your sentences must contain one or more of these devices if they are to cohere in any fashion.

> **Make your paragraphs cohere by using:**
> **Transitional words and phrases**
> **Pronoun references**
> **Repeated key terms**
> **Parallelism**

Completeness

A good paragraph promises content, then proceeds to supply it with ideas, facts, or illustrations. Conversely, a bad paragraph is often one that

promises content but fails to deliver. Since every paragraph essentially consists of a topic sentence that needs to be proved, failure to deliver content
has two primary causes: either the topic sentence is not developed at all, or
it is merely extended through repetition. In either case, the reader is saddled
with useless generalizations. The following student paragraph is an example
of incompleteness:

> Withholding tax is a bad way to go about collecting taxes from the
> people in our country because this system assumes that the American
> people are incompetent.

This is a bankrupt paragraph. It hints at an argument, but then comes to a
dead stop. Automatically we ask, In what way or by what means does tax
withholding assume that the American people are incompetent? Without further evidence, the paragraph goes nowhere. The paragraph below, although
longer, leaves us just as dissatisfied:

> Withholding tax is a bad way to go about collecting taxes from the
> people in our country because this system assumes that the American
> people are incompetent. By withholding taxes, the federal govern-
> ment is acting as if the American people were a pack of irresponsible
> children who lack any sense of accountability. Tax withholding is a
> way of showing distrust. How can individuals become dependable citi-
> zens when their own government treats them as if they were incapa-
> ble of doing their duty?

Here the student has created a stagnant paragraph. He has expanded his
topic sentence by adding words, but he has not added any real content.
Every sentence repeats the original topic sentence, yet does not drive the
argument forward with convincing support. Now read the paragraph below:

> Withholding is a bad way to go about collecting tax money, even
> though the figures may show that it gets results. It is bad because it
> implies that the individual is incapable of handling his own affairs. The
> government as much as says, We know that, if left to your own de-
> vices, you will fritter away your worldly goods, and tax day will catch
> you without cash. Or it says, We're not sure you'll come clean in your
> return, so we will just take the money before it reaches you, and you
> will be saved the trouble and fuss of being honest. This implication is
> an unhealthy thing to spread around, being contrary to the old Ameri-
> can theory that the individual is a very competent little guy indeed.
> The whole setup of our democratic government assumes that the citi-
> zen is bright, honest, and at least as fundamentally sound as a com-

mon stock. If you start treating him as something less than that, you are going to get into deep water. The device of withholding tax money, which is clearly confiscatory, since the individual is not allowed to see, taste, or touch a certain percentage of his wages, tacitly brands him as negligent or unthrifty or immature or incompetent or dishonest, or all of those things at once. There is, furthermore, a bad psychological effect in earning money that you never get your paws on. We believe this effect to be much stronger than the government realizes. At any rate, if the American individual is in truth incapable of paying his tax all by himself, then he should certainly be regarded as incapable of voting all by himself, and the Secretary of the Treasury should accompany him into the booth to show him where to put the X.

—E. B. White, "Withholding"

While all of us may not agree with the ideas presented above, at least we feel that the writer has fulfilled his promise to show us why he does not like withholding tax. He has provided clear examples for his opinion, and he has moved from the general to the specific, always keeping in mind the direction of his topic sentence. His paragraph is complete.

Make your paragraphs complete by providing enough evidence to prove your topic sentence.

JOURNALISTIC VERSUS LITERARY PARAGRAPHS

Our own age, which values instantaneousness in its communications, has evolved a distinctive paragraph form—the short journalistic paragraph. Newspapers and popular magazines serve up their articles and stories in these skimpy paragraphs of two or three sentences. Serious magazines and books, however, continue to use the literary paragraph, which is longer, more complex, and more supportive of the topic sentence. The following passage is made up of typical journalistic paragraphs:

Andreas Alrea is a name that will live in legend on the Yale campus for many years.

Not as a great scholar, not as a great football hero—but as possibly the greatest hoaxer in the history of the 275-year-old Ivy League University.

In fact, "Andreas Alrea" is actually 21-year-old Patrick Michael McDermott of Los Angeles.

But, as the university's embarrassed dean of admissions admitted Friday, McDermott convinced everyone on campus that he was a precocious self-made millionaire whose greatest ambition was to become a Yale man.

Worth David, dean of admissions at the New Haven, Conn., university, said McDermott confessed Friday that all the documents and all the stories he had used to gain admittance to Yale last April were faked.

Among the documents were transcripts and letters of recommendation from Birmingham High School in Van Nuys showing "Alrea" as a straight-A graduate of the class of '73.

And among the stories were tales that "Alrea" had made $30 million before he was 21 by wheeling-dealing business deals in the hotel business in Alaska and the heavy equipment business in South America.

In a telephone interview from New Haven, McDermott admitted that "Alrea" is his pseudonym, that he was only a B-student at Birmingham High, and that he'd never been to Alaska or South America.

Nor, as he told Yale in his application, does he speak five languages.

All of it, he said, was sort of a joke.

"I am a writer," said McDermott-Alrea, "and I am interested in having new and varied experiences. I did this on a dare. It was just a practical joke, just for the fun of it."

—Jerry Belcher, *Los Angeles Times,* 23 Jan. 1977.

Notice that the article contains the bare essence of an idea presented in separate paragraphs so that the reader can skim down the page with the greatest speed. The value of this kind of paragraph is its accessibility, acquired, however, at the expense of detail.

The literary paragraph, as distinguished from the journalistic paragraph, is characterized by its thorough development. It will present a topic sentence, which it will then support at length, with balance, and, in the best cases, with grace. Following is a typical literary paragraph:

There may have been better priests, in some ways, than Father Adolf, but there was never one in our commune who was held in more solemn and awful respect. This was because he had absolutely no fear of the Devil. He was the only Christian I have ever known of whom that could be truly said. People stood in deep dread of him on that account; for they thought that there must be something supernatural about him, else he could not be so bold and so confident. All men speak in bitter disapproval of the Devil, but they do it reverently, not flippantly; but Father Adolf's way was very different; he called him by every name he could lay his tongue to, and it made everyone shudder that heard him; and often he would even speak of him scornfully and scoffingly; then the people crossed themselves and went quickly out of his presence, fearing that something fearful might happen.

—Samuel L. Clemens, *The Mysterious Stranger*

Notice that in the preceding paragraph the author uses his opening sentence as the pivotal center of his paragraph and from it he organizes and connects his subideas.

In the course of your college studies you will doubtless have occasions to use both the journalistic and the literary paragraph, but in this book we wish to stress the literary paragraph because, being an essay in miniature, it requires the particular skill of connecting a number of sentences to a central idea and making that connection immediately clear to the reader. Whereas you may want to use journalistic paragraphs in private correspondence and in certain essay examinations, you will find that the literary paragraph will be the staple of most research papers or essays.

INTRODUCTORY PARAGRAPHS

The opening paragraph should beguile and tantalize readers with a hint of splendid things to come. If you don't capture the attention of readers immediately, they may not linger to savor the wisdom of your essay. Usually, it is unwise to blurt out your thesis in the first sentence. Instead, use the first few sentences to lead readers to your thesis and to whet their appetite.

Here are some suggestions for good opening paragraphs:

1. Open with a provocative question.

> Do we know who our children really are? We stand before them the way a hen faces a duck she has hatched by mistake. It is our responsibility to bring up our children; yet, how is this to be accomplished? Should we threaten them with punishment if they are bad? Or, should we promise them a reward if they are good?
> —Bert Beach, "Training for Morality"
>
> *Thesis: The truth is that no system of training based on sanction builds morality because true morality is the capacity to judge and to choose between good and evil.*

2. Open with a narrative.

> In the local newspaper of my community recently, there was a story about a man named Virgil Spears. He lived in a small town about 40 miles from my home. He had served five years in the Missouri State Penitentiary for passing bogus checks. When he returned to his family, Mr. Spears couldn't find a job. Everyone knew he was an ex-con and everyone knew that ex-cons aren't to be trusted. Finally, in what was described as calm desperation, he walked into a local barbershop where he was well known, pulled a gun, and took all the money the

barber had. Up to this point it had been a fairly routine robbery, but then something unusual happened. Mr. Spears didn't try to get away. He got into his car, drove slowly out of town, and waited for the highway patrol. When they caught him, he made only one request. He turned to the arresting patrolman and said: "Would you please ask that the court put my family on welfare just as soon as possible?"
—Sally Webb, "On Mouse Traps"

Thesis: Stereotyping is often a destructive system of classification.

3. Open with an appropriate quotation.

Theodore Parker once said, "Democracy means not 'I am as good as you are,' but 'You are as good as I am.'"This quotation reaches to the core of the bilingual problem in America today.

Thesis: Democracy demands that we allow Americans with a Hispanic or Chinese heritage to preserve their cultures.

4. Open by focusing on a serious problem.

To judge from the recent, bitter example given us by the good folks of a respectable New York residential area, Samaritans are very scarce these days. In fact, if the reactions of the 38 heedless witnesses to the murder of Catherine Genovese provide any true reflection of a national attitude toward our neighbors, we are becoming a callous, chicken-hearted and immoral people.
—Louden Wainwright, "The Dying Girl That No One Helped"

Thesis: People are afraid to get involved in the troubles of others.

5. Open with a titillating observation.

The last thing that can be said of a lunatic is that his actions are causeless. If any human acts may loosely be called causeless, they are the minor acts of a healthy man; whistling as he walks; slashing the grass with a stick; kicking his heels or rubbing his hands. It is the happy man who does the useless things; the sick man is not strong enough to be idle. It is exactly such careless and causeless actions that the madman could never understand; for the madman (like the determinist) generally sees too much cause in everything.
—G. K. Chesterton, "Madness"

Thesis: A madman has lost everything except his reason.

81

6. Open with a purpose statement.

> In this paper I should like to discuss the three most irritating faults of public speakers: mumbling, repeating oneself, and lack of preparation.

(Purpose statements are mostly restricted to research papers.)

Here are some introductions to avoid:

1. Vague introductions that leave the reader wondering how they relate to the rest of the essay.
2. Long, rambling introductions. Most short essays require only a crisp, one-paragraph introduction.
3. Trite introductions, such as "I have been asked to write an essay on friendship," or "Friendship is a wonderful thing."
4. Apologetic introductions, such as "Although I am not an expert on prison reform, I belive that we must make sure that prisoners live in a decent environment."

TRANSITIONS BETWEEN PARAGRAPHS

Paragraphing is the accepted method of blocking off major ideas into separate and indented units. The major ideas of the essay are separately stated and developed in unified, coherent, and complete paragraphs. But if the essay is to flow smoothly from one major idea to another, it is necessary to have transitions between its paragraphs.

The paragraph break alone is not usually enough to signal that the writer will now deal with a new idea or at least a new phase of the previous idea. Like sentences, paragraphs too must be held together with phrases and words that make the transitions from one idea to the next smooth and logical. In the following short essay, notice how each new paragraph begins with enumeration. Words like *first, second,* and *third* make it easy for the reader to follow the writer's argument.

> ### TYPES OF CORAL REEFS
>
> There are three main types of coral reef. The first is the fringing reef which lies just off the main shore, separated from it by a narrow and shallow lagoon. It is this kind of reef which encircles Mauritius like a girdle, leaving between itself and the coast of the island a shallow stretch of water, in places only a few hundred yards wide but in others, as at Grand Port, expanding to a width of two miles or more.

Fringing reefs, too, encircle many of the islands that we visited such as Coetivy and Agalega and, though irregular and broken in places, lie off parts of the coasts of Mahe and Praslin in the Seychelles. Down the east coast of Africa from Cape Guardafui to the coast of Portuguese East there runs an almost continuous coral reef which is mostly of the fringing type.

The second type is the barrier reef, which lies at a much greater distance from the coast than the fringing reef and may be several miles wide with many channels through it, and is separated from the mainland by a wide lagoon. The most famous example of this type is the Great Barrier Reef off the eastern coast of Australia. It is over a thousand miles long. In its northern half the barrier may not be more than 20 or 30 miles from the Queensland coast, but in its southern half it is as much as 50 or 100 miles from the coast and consists of several parallel reefs with channels between them.

The third type of reef is the atoll, a ring of growing corals crowned with palm trees, often hundreds of miles from any true land and rising abruptly in the ocean from a depth of thousands of fathoms. In the Chagos Islands we found true atolls at Diego Garcia and Peros Banhos, irregular rings of coral rock and sand on which a lush vegetation has taken root, and on which plantations have long been cultivated by man. In the Aldabra group also, 700 miles south-west of the Seychelles, we found coral reefs of varying degrees of perfection.

—F. D. Ommanney, *The Shoals of Capricorn*

Transitions from one paragraph to the next are not always as obvious as in the above example. Sometimes the connecting link is so subtle that you really hardly notice it. In the essay below, for example, the main thread that strings the paragraphs together is the repeated mention of the evil involved in killing for sport. The first paragraph states the thesis: *Killing for sport is pure evil*. The second paragraph is connected to the first by advancing the argument and showing how most other wicked deeds are different from killing for sport. The final paragraph clinches the argument by introducing the difference between killing for profit and killing for sport.

KILLING FOR SPORT IS PURE EVIL

To me it is inconceivable how anyone should think an animal more interesting dead than alive. I can also easily prove to my own satisfaction that killing "for sport" is the perfect type of pure evil for which metaphysicians have sometimes sought.

Most wicked deeds are done because the doer proposes some good to himself. The liar lies to gain some end; the swindler and the thief want things which, if honestly got, might be good in themselves. Even the murderer may be removing an impediment to normal desires or gaining possession of something which his victim keeps from him. None of these usually does evil for evil's sake. They are selfish or unscrupulous, but their deeds are not gratuitously evil. The killer for sport has no such comprehensible motive. He prefers death to life, darkness to light. He gets nothing except the satisfaction of saying, "Something which wanted to live is dead. There is that much less vitality, consciousness, and, perhaps, joy in the universe. I am the Spirit that Denies." When a man wantonly destroys one of the works of man we call him Vandal. When he wantonly destroys one of the works of God we call him Sportsman.

The hunter-for-food may be as wicked and as misguided as vegetarians sometimes say; but he does not kill for the sake of killing. The rancher and the farmer who exterminate all living things not immediately profitable to them may sometimes be working against their own best interests; but whether they are or are not they hope to achieve some supposed good by their exterminations. If to do evil not in the hope to gain but for evil's sake involves the deepest guilt by which man can be stained, then killing for killing's sake is a terrifying phenomenon and as strong a proof as we could have of that "reality of evil" with which present-day theologians are again concerned.

—Joseph Wood Krutch, "Killing for Sport Is Pure Evil"

Keep your paragraphs properly linked by using clear, logical transitions between them.

CONCLUDING PARAGRAPHS

Your final paragraph should not simply sputter to a stop but should round out the essay and draw a convincing conclusion. The reader should be left fully convinced of the truth and wisdom of your essay. This is not the time to ramble or wander off; rather, every word should be fraught with meaning. Give particular thought to the phrasing of your last sentence. Intend it to be remembered and banish all doubt, hesitancy, or reticence from your conclusion.

The following are some suggestions for good last paragraphs:

1. End by reasserting your thesis.

If you care, boycott Japanese and Russian imports, write your senator and congressmember a letter, or send a dollar to the Blue Whale Fund. Do this for the people of earth a generation from now who may never experience the magnificent, raw, breathtaking beauty of the Lord of the Fishes, the blue whale.

2. End with an appropriate quotation.

From an essay on the need for prison reform:

If we leave our prisons the way they are—caves of corruption where first-time offenders mingle with hardened murderers and rapists—then we can expect that all offenders will end having their minds forever twisted. Society's obligation is not only to confine a criminal, but also to return him to society as a rehabilitated human being. Oscar Wilde's poem "Ballad of Reading Gaol" tells a world of truth:

> The vilest deeds like poison weeds,
> Bloom well in prison air,
> It is only what is good in Man,
> That wastes and withers there.

3. End by stating your final point.

From an essay delineating reactions to the Great Depression on the part of farmers:

Finally, the farmers took their most radical action. They burned their crops instead of shipping them to the market at a transportation cost that would have been even higher than the revenue from their products. This dramatic action was a way of forcing city people into giving the farmers a square deal. It was a shocking act, but it focused on the farmers' desperate plight and was one of the steps that eventually led our country out of its demoralized state of depression.

4. End by restating the main points of your essay.

From an essay on the uniqueness of the U.S. Constitution:

Thus our Constitution contains four unique features: First, it is written in a single document; second, it is supreme over the legislature; third, it divides authority into three coordinate branches none of which has supremacy over the other; fourth, it provides an independent judiciary. All of these unique features, of course, have as their purpose to assure a limited government in which all officials are compelled to exercise their powers within strictly defined boundaries. It is this balance of power that allows Americans to have confidence in their government.

Here are examples of endings that you should avoid:

1. Endings that apologize for your shortcomings:

While I am not an expert on this subject, I feel that we didn't treat the Japanese right during the Second World War.

2. Endings that bring up an entirely new major point:

   Whereas my essay deals only with a definition of *free enterprise,* the effects of this system must also be considered.

3. Endings that announce that you have ended:

   In conclusion, I wish to state that earthquakes are a major problem of our nation's future.

4. Endings that stop rather than conclude:

   Most of Hemingway's novels reflect this ethical code. Some characters live up to the code; some fail to live up. In *Farewell to Arms* the main character, who is Frederick Henry, is a nihilistic Hemingway hero.

5. Endings with a platitude:

   This problem deserves the serious attention of every right-thinking American who loves our wonderful land.

EXERCISES

1. In order to help you better understand the idea of a visually shaped paragraph, fill in the space on page 87 with a topic sentence about yourself, then three other sentences to support the topic sentence, and finally a sentence to clinch the main idea. A sample topic sentence might be: "I am a jealous person," or "I feel insecure in public," or "Snow skiing is my way of getting close to nature." Regardless of your choice of topic sentence, remember that your supporting sentences must be narrower and more specific than the topic sentence. Also, your final sentence must be as broad as the topic sentence.

2. Divide the following paragraph into its proper levels of generality by numbering each sentence.

   No discussion of maternal fatigue would be complete without mentioning the early evening hours—unquestionably the toughest part of the day for the mother of small children. Much has been written lately about the international "energy crisis," but there is nothing on the globe to parallel the shortage of energy in a young mother between 6:00 and 9:00 P.M.! The dinner is over and the dishes are stacked. She is already tired, but now she has to get the troops in bed. She gives them their baths and pins on the diapers and brushes their teeth and puts on the pajamas and reads a story and says the prayers and brings them seven glasses of water. These tasks would not be so difficult if the children *wanted* to go to bed. They most certainly do not, however, and develop extremely clever techniques for resistance and postponement. It is a pretty dumb kid who can't extend this ten-minute process into an hour-long

tug of war. And when it's all finished and Mom staggers through the nursery door and leans against the wall, she is then supposed to shift gears and greet her romantic lover in her own bedroom. Fat chance!

—James Dobson, *What Wives Wish Their Husbands Knew About Women*

3. Create a paragraph based on the topic sentence provided and following the levels of generality as listed.

  1 Fashion designers force consumers to spend unnecessary money on clothes by declaring last year's fashions outmoded every new season.
     2
        3
        3
           4
     2
     2

4. In the following paragraphs, draw a line through any sentence that weakens paragraph unity.

a. I agree with Thomas Jefferson that there is a natural aristocracy among human beings, based on virtue and talent. A natural aristocrat is a person who shows genuine concern for his fellow human beings and has the wisdom as well as ability to help them improve the quality of their lives. He is the kind of person to whom you would entrust your most important concerns because his decisions would be honest rather than self-serving. A natural aristocrat cannot be bought or manipulated. He will not promise what he cannot deliver. But when he makes a promise, he has virtue backed up by talent to fulfill it. Unfortunately, few political leaders today are natural aristocrats because early in their ambitious careers they get beholden to those powers that helped them up the political ladder.

b. In medieval society physical strength and animal cunning were the most admired characteristics of human beings, but since the invention of gun powder, we have come to value other qualities more highly. Now that even a physically weak person can be made strong by carrying a gun, other ingenuities have become the marks of heroic people. Of course, boxing requires physical strength and animal cunning; yet many people today admire good boxers. The qualities most admired today are intellectual acumen, leadership ability, artistic talent, and social adjustment. I find it distressing that we do not prize goodness as much as we should. After all, Lincoln's outstanding feature was goodness. If a person is not good, he is not admirable. The tournament and personal combat have been replaced by the university, the political arena, the stage, and the personality inventory as testing grounds for heroes.

5. Identify the most obvious means used to gain coherence in the following paragraphs.

a. In general, relevancy is a facet of training rather than of education. What is taught at law school is the present law of the land, not the Napoleonic Code or even the archaic laws that have been scratched from the statute books. And at medical school, too, it is modern medical practice that is taught, that which is relevant to conditions today. And the plumber and the carpenter and the electrician and the mason learn only what is relevant to the practice of their respective trades in this day with the tools and materials that are presently available and that conform to the building code.
—Harry Kemelman, *Common Sense in Education*

b. The extent of personal privacy varies, but there are four degrees that can be identified. Sometimes the individual wants to be completely out of the sight and hearing of anyone else, in solitude; alone, he is in the most relaxed state of privacy. In a second situation the individual seeks the intimacy of his confidants—his family, friends, or trusted associates with whom he chooses to share his ideas and emotions. But there are still some things that he does not want to disclose, whether he is with intimates or in public. Either by personal explanation or by social convention, the individual may indicate that he does not wish certain aspects of himself discussed or noticed, at least at that particular moment. When his claim is respected by those around him, he achieves a third degree of privacy, the state of reserve. Finally, an individual sometimes goes out in public to seek privacy, for by joining groups of people who do not recognize him, he achieves anonymity, being seen but not known. Such relaxation on the street, in bars or movies or in the park constitutes still another dimension of the individual's quest for privacy.

—Alan F. Westin, "Privacy"

c. The motor car is, more than any other object, the expression of the nation's character and the nation's dream. In the tree billowing fender, in the blinding chromium grills, in the fluid control, in the everwidening front seat, we see the flowering of the America that we know. It is of some interest to scholars and historians that the same autumn that saw the abandonment of the window crank and the adoption of the push button (removing the motorist's last necessity for physical exertion) saw also the registration of sixteen million young men of fighting age and symphonic styling. It is of deep interest to me that in the same week Japan joined the Axis, De-Soto moved its clutch pedal two inches to the left—and that the announcements caused equal flurries among the people.

—E. B. White, *An E. B. White Reader*

6. Write a provocative introductory paragraph for an essay on one of the following topics:

   a. The admittance of women into military schools
   b. Crash diets
   c. Hair transplants for balding men
   d. Rationing of water or gasoline
   e. Automatic capital punishment for terrorist hijackers

7. Improve the coherence of the following paragraph through better transitions.

   My most prized possession is my Zenith stereo. I have been well pleased with its performance in the three years that I have owned it. It is not a big set. The main base of the set is two feet long, one-and-a-half feet wide, and seven inches high. I derive pleasure from this instrument for several reasons. First, it has an AM/FM radio and five tuning dials that allow me to hear lovely tones from numerous stations. I particularly like the fact that it has a jack for headphones. When I curl up in my comfortable bean bag with my headphones over my ears, I feel as though I were in a magic world of melody, far removed from the cacophony of my city. My stereo is constructed so I can tape my own music. Whenever I hear a new symphony on the radio, I can tape it and listen to it again later. I would give up my car before I would give up my stereo.

8. Combine the sentences below into a coherent paragraph, using any one of the four devices suggested at the beginning of this chapter.

   a. The crisis of doubt about education as the great leveler of society began in the 1960s after it became clear that the schools were not giving equal education to black and Spanish-speaking Americans.

b. Most educators believed that all that was needed was a series of reforms.

c. Schools should be integrated to wipe out unequal facilities.

d. Compensatory programs like Head Start were to help poor children do as well as middle-class children.

e. Billions of dollars were spent in the name of these reforms.

f. Little concrete evidence of success could be found.

g. One side felt that the programs were good, but needed to be run better.

h. The other side felt that the fault lay in expecting too much from education.

i. The Coleman report concluded that family-background differences account for much more variation in achievement than do school differences.

j. Many educators and policy-makers now no longer view education as the "balance-wheel of the social machinery."

6

What's the best way of following through?

NARRATION

   Setting
   Point of View
   Character
   Pacing

DESCRIPTION

EXAMPLE

DEFINITION

COMPARISON AND CONTRAST

CAUSAL ANALYSIS

DIVISION

COMBINATION OF METHODS

EXERCISES

After you have honed your ideas into a thesis and mapped out a plan of how you intend to proceed, you have to select a method of development. The seven major methods of development are:

1. Narration
2. Description
3. Example
4. Definition
5. Comparison and contrast
6. Causal analysis
7. Division

Most if not all the writing you will be required to do in college will use one or a combination of these methods. This chapter discusses each of them.

NARRATION

To narrate means to recount an incident or to tell a story. Narration, however, is not limited to simple story-telling. You are using a form of narration whenever you relate an experience or present information in a definite sequence. A short story or a novel is written in the narrative form but so are the minutes of a chamber of commerce meeting.

Here is an example of a narrative passage that follows a chronological order:

> Our life in the sanatorium was like that of hogs, nothing but eating and sleeping. At seven a bell rang for breakfast. We had to bathe at eight and at nine we had to go back to sleep until eleven, which was lunchtime. From twelve to three we had to sleep again. From three until four, which was dinner time, we were allowed to be awake, and after eating we had to sleep once more. They didn't allow us to walk around much, and an asthmatic like me needs to walk.
> —Oscar Lewis, "One Can Suffer Anywhere"

This paragraph, which recounts the schedule of an inmate's day in a sanatorium, exemplifies narration at a rather simple level. More complex narrative writing requires setting, a point of view, lifelike characters, and pacing.

Setting

Setting refers to the physical locale in which the narrative takes place, and the description of it is primarily responsible for generating a dominant mood or atmosphere. Dramatic appropriateness is the ruling principle behind narrative setting. If the story concerns a visitation by some unspeakable horror, such as a vampire, a zombie, a werewolf, or a Martian, the setting must be manipulated to evoke a suitably gloomy mood. Hollywood, in its infinite wisdom, has been slavishly obedient to the setting needs of its monsters. When the vampire is about to appear, dark clouds float overhead; a misty drizzle falls; jagged streaks of lightning flash across the movie screen, and thunder shakes the roof of the theatre in which the audience huddles, clinging nervously to cardboard cups of popcorn. Similarly, the sun shines, animals romp, and birds sing when Snow White consorts with her dwarfs.

In the following example of setting, a mood of evil is evoked through the description of a haunted house:

> No human eye can isolate the unhappy coincidence of line and place which suggests evil in the face of a house, and yet somehow a maniac juxtaposition, a badly turned angle, some chance meeting of roof and sky, turned Hill House into a place of despair, more frightening because the face of Hill House seemed awake, with a watchfulness from the blank windows and a touch of glee in the eyebrow of a cornice. Almost any house, caught unexpectedly or at an odd angle, can turn a deeply humorous look on a watching person; even a mischievous little chimney, or a dormer like a dimple, can catch up a beholder with a sense of fellowship; but a house arrogant and hating, never off guard, can only be evil. This house, which seemed somehow to have formed itself, flying together into its own powerful pattern under the hands of its builders, fitting itself into its own construction of lines and angles, reared its great head back against the sky without concession to humanity. It was a house without kindness, never meant to be lived in, not a fit place for people or for love or for hope. Exorcism cannot alter the countenance of a house; Hill House would stay as it was until it was destroyed.
>
> —Shirley Jackson, *The Haunting of Hill House*

Like proverbs and the saws of an earlier generation, overused setting ages badly, eventually becoming insipid and flat. The vampire setting of the typical horror movie, for instance, has become so hackneyed in the public mind that it is now used in comedy skits on television. Likewise, poor

Snoopy from *Peanuts* has been forever trying to write a novel that begins, "It was a dark and stormy night," a setting as stale as a mummified Pharaoh. Establish suitable dramatic backdrops for your own narrative, but beware of the hackneyed.

Point of view

Point of view is the angle from which the events in a story are observed. A story may be written from a subjective point of view—with the narrator referring to himself or herself as "I"—or from an objective point of view—with the author successively narrating events from the viewpoints of different characters referred to as "he," "she," or "they." In either case, the language of the narrative must reflect the world view of the character from whose point of view it is told. The novel *The Catcher in the Rye*, for instance, is written from the viewpoint of a rebellious adolescent and the language appropriately reflects his personality:

> If you really want to hear about it, the first thing you'll probably want to know is where I was born, and what my lousy childhood was like, and how my parents were occupied and all before they had me, and all that David Copperfield kind of crap, but I don't feel like going into it, if you want to know the truth. In the first place, that stuff bores me, and in the second place, my parents would have about two hemorrhages apiece if I told anything pretty personal about them. They're quite touchy about anything like that, especially my father. They're nice and all—I'm not saying that—but they're also touchy as hell. Besides, I'm not going to tell you my whole goddamn autobiography or anything.
>
> —J. D. Salinger

"The Catbird Seat," on the other hand, is a story narrated from the point of view of Mr. Martin, a fussy clerk, whose fastidious personality is mirrored in the language:

> It was just a week to the day since Mr. Martin had decided to rub out Mrs. Ulgine Barrows. The term "rub out" pleased him because it suggested nothing more than the correction of an error—in this case an error of Mr. Fitweiler. Mr. Martin had spent each night of the past week working out his plan and examining it. As he walked home now he went over it again. For the hundredth time he resented the element of imprecision, the margin of guesswork that entered into the business. The project as he had worked it out was casual and bold, the risks were considerable. Something might go wrong anywhere along the line. And therein lay the cunning of his scheme. No one would

ever see in it the cautious, painstaking hand of Erwin Martin, head of the filing department at F & S, of whom Mr. Fitweiler had once said, "Man is fallible but Martin isn't." No one would see his hand, that is, unless it were caught in the act.

—James Thurber

The range of voices that can be projected into a narrative is limited only by the writer's imagination, with dramatic consistency being the principal requirement. For instance, if you begin a story from the viewpoint of a child, you should not suddenly make her sound like an adult as the following paragraph does:

We went for a walk and I got hungry. I asked my mommy for some candy. My mommy bought me candy. We sat down on a park bench and ate it. Pigeons came right up to my toes. *But because my doctor has repeatedly cautioned me against the abnormally high level of triglycerides in candy, I decided only to nibble it.*

Obviously, the final sentence destroys the illusion of the child character from whose viewpoint the passage was supposedly being narrated.

Character

Narrative writing as it is practiced in the classroom never requires the student to write full-blown novels peopled with intricate, knotty personalities. But occasionally an instructor will ask students to write about a memorable acquaintance or to recount some experience that requires the depiction of characters. Character is indeed the lifeblood of narration. The world of fiction is crowded with a fascinating array of sour spinsters, corrupt fathers, powerful businessmen, gracious ladies, and thousands of other people who jump stunningly to life from the printed page. Good character portrayal comes from writing about a person not as a statistic, stereotype, or faceless wanderer in an enormous crowd, but as a unique individual with specific mannerisms, looks, desires, and habits. The Reverend Obadiah Slope, villain of the nineteenth-century British novel *Barchester Towers*, comes vividly to life in this portrayal of him:

Mr. Slope is tall, and not ill made. His feet and hands are large, as has ever been the case with all his family, but he has a broad chest and wide shoulders to carry off these excrescences, and on the whole his figure is good. His countenance, however, is not specially prepossessing. His hair is lank, and of a dull pale reddish hue. It is always formed into three straight lumpy masses, each brushed with admirable precision, and cemented with much grease; two of them adhere closely to the sides of his face, and the other lies at right angles above them. He wears no whiskers, and is always punctiliously shaven. His face is nearly of the same colour as his hair, though perhaps a little redder; it is not unlike beef,—beef, however, one would say, of a bad quality. His forehead is capacious and high, but square and heavy, and unpleasantly shining. His mouth is large, though his lips are thin and bloodless; and his big, prominent, pale brown eyes inspire anything but confidence. His nose, however, is his redeeming feature: it is pronounced straight and well-formed; though I myself should have liked it better did it not possess a somewhat spongy, porous appearance, as though it had been cleverly formed out of a red coloured cork.

I never could endure to shake hands with Mr. Slope. A cold, clammy perspiration always exudes from him, the small drops are ever to be seen standing on his brow, and his friendly grasp is unpleasant.

—Anthony Trollope

Notice the painstaking attention to detail—Mr. Slope's porous nose, bad complexion, greasy hair, and clammy handshake being all carefully documented with appropriate images and metaphors. Similar attention to detail in your narratives will result in a successful depiction of your characters.

For further discussion of point of view, character, and setting in fiction, drama, and poetry, see Chapter 11, "Writing about Literature."

Pacing

Narrative writing must be paced to highlight and develop significant episodes, scenes, and incidents, while glossing over those that are insignificant or uneventful. Here, for example, is how Samuel Butler dismisses an entire uneventful month in his satirical novel, *Erewhon:*

Another month flew by, during which I made such progress in the language that I could understand all that was said to me, and express myself with tolerable fluency. My instructor professed to be astonished with the progress I had made; I was careful to attribute it to the pains he had taken with me and to his admirable method of explaining my difficulties, so we became excellent friends.

—Samuel Butler

It's neither necessary nor desirable for a writer to expend equal numbers of words and pages on unequal incidents and events. Some episodes and occurrences are intrinsically more important to the narrative than others and must be developed in finer detail. Later on in *Erewhon*, Butler spends an entire chapter describing a court trial that lasted only a few minutes, but which was dramatically more significant to the plot of the novel than the month spent learning the Erewhonian language.

> In writing a narration, establish a dominant mood through setting; keep the point of view consistent; be detailed in the depiction of character; and pace the story to focus on significant episodes and events.

DESCRIPTION

Suppose you are writing an essay about a fight between a gopher and a weasel that you observed. Your key thought is: "The fight between the gopher and the weasel was a fierce struggle." Here is how one writer wrote on this subject:

> The weasel's three good feet gathered under it and it circled, very slowly, along the wall, its lips still lifted to expose the soundless snarl. The abject gopher crowded against the boards, turned once and tried to scramble up the side, fell back on its broken leg, and whirled like lightning to face its executioner again. The weasel moved carefully, circling, its cold eyes hypnotically steady.
> Then the gopher screamed, a wild, agonized, despairing squeal that made the boy swallow and wet his lips. Another scream, wilder than the first, and before the sound had ended the weasel struck. There was a fierce flurry in the straw before the killer got its hold just back of the gopher's right ear, and then there was only the weasel looking at him over the dead and quivering body. In a few minutes, the boy knew, the gopher's carcass would be as limp as an empty skin, with all its blood sucked out and a hole as big as the ends of his two thumbs where the weasel had dined.
> —Wallace Stegner, *Big Rock Candy Mountain.*

The secret of a good description is focus and concentration. You focus on a dominant impression and concentrate on it, leaving out anything that is not directly connected. In the above example, the dominant impression is fierce struggle. Every phrase in the description relates to this dominant impression. Nothing irrelevant is thrown in, nothing that would distract from the setting of ferocity. There is a "soundless snarl," a lightning whirl, a "wild, agonized, despairing squeal," more screaming, then a "fierce flurry in the straw," and finally the "dead and quivering body." What you notice is a sense of meticulous observation. Henry James once claimed that a good writer is one on whom nothing is lost. For practice, go to the main street in your town. Stand on a corner and observe your surroundings until you can put into words a dominant impression. An example of such an impression might be, "Brand Street is a thoroughfare marked by contrasts." Now set down only those details that stress the dominant impression, which is "marked contrasts." Make up a list of those details that illustrate contrast. Your list might be as follows:

1. A little gray pigeon cocking its head at a burly policeman
2. A deserted ice-cream parlor next to a thrift shop crammed with junk
3. A young girl in red shorts skipping by an old woman, wrinkled and bent over with age
4. The sound of sentimental juke box music mingling with the sound of screeching, swishing traffic
5. The smell of stale tobacco emanating from a bar and the smell of warm, buttery popcorn drifting from a movie house

From this list you can develop an effective description. If you have the ability to see likeness between unlike objects, you may heighten the sensory quality of your description by introducing figurative language, as in the following description of a dreamy summer day:

The sun was a hot caress between his shoulder blades, and on the bare flesh where his overalls pulled above his sneakers it bit like a burning glass. Still he was comfortable, supremely relaxed and peaceful, lulled into a half trance by the heat and the steamy flower smells and the mist of yellow from the buttercup coulee below him.
—Wallace Stegner, *Big Rock Candy Mountain*

Notice how the author compares the heat of the sun to a "hot caress" and to a bite from "a burning glass." Comparisons such as these make your description come to life. You could say, for instance, in your description of Brand Street:

1. "People's shadows on the sidewalk melted in and out of each other like projections in a phantom movie."
2. "The sidewalk seemed to sweat oil and tar."
3. "The traffic stopped and flowed in abject obedience to the giant eyes blinking red or green at each cross street."

You should also make your description appeal to your readers' senses. Do not just tell them that the football coach was angry. Let them *see* anger flaming in the coach's face. Do not just comment that the coffee was freshly brewed. Let them *smell* the delicious odor of those freshly ground roasted beans. Do not just inform them that it snowed. Let them *feel* the way the white ice flurries hit your cheek, melted, and ran down your face. Do not just state that the lemon was sour. Make them *taste* the tangy acidity that makes your mouth pucker and your brows draw together. Do not just state that the leaves are rustling. Let them *hear* them in the sycamore tree as they whisper like old men and women divulging local gossip.

Avoid words that tell how you feel about the subject you are describing rather than what the subject is like. For example, in the sentences,

> Cathedral Peak was awe-inspiring.
> The old miner looked frightening.

awe-inspiring and *frightening* reveal little about the peak or the miner. If you supply the right details (the peak stands tall against the sky, its jagged cliffs massive and indestructible), your reader will infer the proper effect.

> **Make your reader see, hear, taste, smell, and feel what you are describing.**

EXAMPLE

You can develop a key thought by supplying one or more apt examples. Good examples are always welcome. Who are the best teachers, the best preachers, the best politicians you can remember? Most likely they are those who could illustrate a point with a fitting example.

Essays should not consist of big generalities or sweeping statements without supplying specific detail. Education prevents prejudice, love is the universal thirst for communion, the family provides a framework for child development, abortion should be legalized, everyone needs Christ in his life—all are fine generalizations, but must be supported with specific detail to be believable.

The simplest way to go about supporting a key thought is by supplying concrete examples. Take the statement, "Education prevents prejudice." The readers will want to know specific ways in which education prevents prejudice; their curiosity will not be satisfied by mere repetitions of the same thought. It is useless to write, as one student did,

> Education broadens a person's sympathies and makes fanaticism unattractive. The educated person learns to stand on his own two feet without making arrogant or uncompromising assertions. The truly educated person will not become a follower of any party or creed

> because his learning has taught him that no thoughtful person can be intractably wedded to any opinion.

This writer is circling the key thought without penetrating it.

A better way to develop this idea is to ask, "What are some specific examples of how education prevents prejudice?" You may remember, for example, how your political science instructor destroyed one of your favorite prejudices—that the poor are poor because they do not practice the Puritan virtues of thrift, piety, and hard work. You had firmly believed in the Horatio Alger myth of any American's being able to pull himself up by his own bootstraps until this professor proved the opposite was true. You were shocked to learn that 15 percent of the population today—no matter how hard working or how thrifty and pious—are doomed to remain poor because they are nonskilled workers, migrant laborers, the aged, and female heads of households. This could be one specific example of how education (in the form of a political science class) helped to prevent prejudice. By using such examples, you avoid both vagueness and repetition.

An example can be one sentence long, or it can fill a whole paragraph—maybe even a whole book. The following passage consists of one key thought supported by three examples, all in a single sentence:

> Almost everything you need to know about a man is in his hand-shake—his decisiveness, his virility, his integrity.

The writer of the following uses an entire paragraph to supply examples for her key thought that middle-aged and old people make life seem commonplace:

> When I was young I could not bear to have anyone make life seem commonplace, and yet that was the thing that nearly all the middle-aged and old people did. I could not bear to hear droning middle-aged women tell about their stomachs and the gas that was or had been on their stomachs and about their constipated bowels. It was even worse when they talked about other subjects because they spoke of such things as childbirth and death in the same familiar and gossipy tone in which they talked about their stomachs and bowels. Such an absence of Awe toward these miraculous things struck me when I was young as a horrible blasphemy against life. I could not endure it. I was shocked not only by their tone but by all the subjects which most of the old people spent their time thinking and worrying about—these subjects were not love and forgiveness and death and night and the

stars, but sinks that had to be cleaned, the stock market, and that mysterious important monster whose name was Business, and whose health had to be inquired about and reported upon every day, as if he were a terrible old god whose good humor could make us all happy and whose bad days could plunge us into gloom. I despised the old people for allowing the mood of their immortal souls to be dependent on the whims of this monster. I said to myself that I would never submit to it.

—Katherine Butler Hathaway, *The Little Locksmith*

One example is cited by the writer of the following paragraph in support of his view that the ideals of physical beauty change from generation to generation:

It looks as though the physical characteristics of a race, and with them the ideal of beauty, can change within a generation or two. The beautiful Englishwoman of my youth had an ample bosom, a small waist and massive hips. She gave the promise of having many children. Now she is slim, her hips are slender, her breasts small and her legs long. Is it possible that she is admired for these traits because economic circumstances have made large families undesired, and that her approximation to the male figure pleases owing to its suggestion of sterility?

—W. Somerset Maugham, *A Writer's Notebook*

In the following paragraph, the writer illustrates "romantic recognition" with two examples:

Romantic recognition. Two examples will do. When we were flying from Erivan, the capital of Armenia, to Sukhum, on the Black Sea, a Soviet scientist, who spoke English, tapped me on the shoulder and then pointed to a fearsome rock face, an immeasurable slab bound in the iron of eternal winter. "That," he announced, "is where Prometheus was chained." And then all my secret terror—for a journey among the mountains of the Caucasus in a Russian plane is to my unheroic soul an ordeal—gave way for a moment to wonder and delight, as if an illuminated fountain had shot up in the dark. And then, years earlier, in the autumn of 1914, when we were on a route march in Surrey, I happened to be keeping step with the company commander, an intelligent Regular lent to us for a month or two. We were passing a little old woman who was watching us from an open carriage, drawn up near the entrance to a mansion. "Do you know who that is?" the captain asked; and of course I didn't. "It's the Empress

Eugenie," he told me; and young and loutish as I was in those days, nevertheless there flared about me then, most delightfully, all the splendor and idiocy of the Second Empire, and I knew that we, every man Jack of us, were in history, and knew it once and for all.

—J. B. Priestley, "Romantic Recognition"

These examples are effective because they are vivid and allow us to relive the circumstances exemplified—to imagine ourselves in Priestley's place as he encounters the mysteries of the past. Vivid writing is not—as much writing is—crammed with mushy generalizations; it is concrete, specific, and shows rather than tells.

Some examples appear in the form of little narrations, as in this argument by Ambrose Wilson.

Jonah could have been swallowed whole by a sperm whale. . . .

A ship in the South Seas in 1771 had one of her boats bitten in two by a sperm whale. The beast seized one unlucky crew member in her mouth and went down with him. On returning to the surface the whale ejected him on the wreckage of the broken boat, much bruised but not seriously injured. . . .

A worse fate befell another victim in 1891. The *Star of the East* was in the vicinity of the Falkland Islands and the lookout sighted a large sperm whale three miles away. Two boats were launched and in a short time one of the harpooners was enabled to spear the fish. The second boat attacked the whale but was upset by a lash of its tail and the men thrown into the sea, one man being drowned, and another, James Bartley, having disappeared, could not be found. The whale was killed and *in a few hours* was lying by the ship's side and the crew were busy with axes and spades removing the blubber. *They worked all day and part of the night.* Next morning they attached some tackle to the stomach which was hoisted on the deck. The sailors were startled by something in it which gave spasmodic signs of life, and inside was found the missing sailor, doubled up and unconscious. He was laid on the deck and treated to a bath of sea water which soon revived him.

—quoted in Victor B. Scheffer, *The Year of the Whale*

Examples in the form of short statements providing objective information are called *facts* and are a common ingredient to the development of a paragraph. When you write a topic sentence, you may wish to support it with facts. In the following paragraph, notice how a quick succession of facts supports the topic sentence that "Palestine was, in biblical times, small in size and poor in natural resources":

> Palestine was, in biblical times, small in size and poor in natural resources. The ancient Land formed a narrow strip stretching along the Levant; in the east it was bordered by the western fringe of the great Syrian-Arabian desert; in the south the wilderness of Sinai separated it from Egypt; in the north the country's extreme was marked by the city of Dan, near the main source of the river Jordan at the foot of Mount Hermon. The total distance from the northernmost point of Dan to Beersheba in the south (where sendentary habitation generally ended) is approximately 140 miles, and nowhere—from sea to steppe—was the country more than 80 miles wide, making a total area of about 11,340 square miles. (Modern Israel has an area of 7,992 square miles.)
>
> —David Ben-Gurion, *The Jews in Their Land*

These facts are effective because they are immediate; needing no long introduction or context, they instantly connect to the point being made. If you are going to use long examples, short facts, or a combination of the two, you must observe three rules:

1. The examples or facts must be vivid (specific and concrete).
2. The examples or facts must prove a point.
3. The examples or facts must be immediate.

DEFINITION

Say you wanted to write on the idea, "A politician's success is often due to charisma." *Charisma* is a vague word with multiple meanings, and you had better develop this idea by first defining *charisma. Webster's New World Dictionary* defines *charisma* as follows:

charisma: a special quality of leadership that captures the popular imagination and inspires unswerving allegiance and devotion.

A *dictionary definition* first places a term in the general group to which it belongs and then states how the term differs from other members of that particular group. The following definitions illustrate this point:

Term	General Group	How the term differs
bed	a piece of furniture	to sleep on
psychiatry	the study, treatment, and prevention	of mental disease

poor	the condition	of having little or no wealth
(to) marry	to act	in order to acquire a husband or wife

But although a dictionary definition is a good way to start defining an ambiguous term, the above definition of *charisma* adds nothing to our understanding of a particular politician's charisma. We are in need of an *extended definition*, such as the following:

Charisma is convincing thousands of college students all over the country that the time has come for a new age of innocence in government. Charisma is appealing to a lettuce boycotter in California, a bank clerk in Nebraska, a political science professor at Harvard, and a rich ranch owner in Texas—all through the same speech. Charisma is stepping in front of an angry group of yippies hurling vicious epithets and calming them down, or, with a single handshake, reassuring the middle American that grassroots America has found its Messiah.

Some definitions are not technical, but poetic, as is the following definition of *home:*

Home is where you hang your hat. Or home is where you spent your childhood, the good years when waking every morning was an excitement, when the round of the day could always produce something to fill your mind, tear your emotions, excite your wonder or awe or delight. Is home that, or is it the place where the people you love live, or the place where you have buried your dead, or the place where you want to be buried yourself? Or is it the place where you come in your last desperation to shoot yourself, choosing the garage or the barn or the woodshed in order not mess up the house, but coming back anyway to the last sanctuary where you can kill yourself in peace?
—Wallace Stegner, *Big Rock Candy Mountain*

Other definitions emphasize technical precision, as the following definition of *palimpsest:*

Palimpsest is a writing surface, whether of vellum, papyrus, or other material, which has been used twice or more for manuscript purposes. Before the invention of paper, the scarcity of writing material made such substances very valuable and the vellum surfaces were often scraped or rubbed or the papyrus surfaces washed. With material so

used a second time it frequently happened that the earlier script either was not completely erased or that, with age, it showed through the new. In this way many documents of very early periods have been preserved for posterity. In one instance, for example, a Syriac text of St. Chrysostom of perhaps the tenth century was found to be superimposed on a sixth-century grammatical work in Latin, which again had covered some fifth-century Latin records. Modern chemical methods make it possible today to recover many of the original texts.
—William Flint Thrall and Addison Hibbard, *A Handbook to Literature*

Sometimes it is helpful to define a term by stating what it is not. For instance,

A felony is not a misdemeanor, such as rioting, being a public nuisance, committing libel, or perjuring oneself under oath. Rather it is a more serious crime, such as arson, burglary, conspiracy, rape, or murder, which is punishable by a term in the state penitentiary or by death.

Many definitions have been known to cause arguments. The definition of *obscenity*, for instance, has been the target of censorship battles ever since the beginning of this nation. At first, its definition was often circular (*obscene* means *dirty, lewd, lascivious, scurrilous*). Nor did the Supreme Court's 1957 definition of obscenity as material that deals with sex in a manner appealing to "prurient interest" really clarify the issue, since the term *prurient* demands further definition in order to be interpreted accurately. Howard Moody has suggested a new definition: "Obscenity is that material which has as its dominant theme and purpose the debasement and depreciation of human beings—their worth and their dignity." Moody extends his definition:

Such a definition might include some material dealing with sex but this would be a minor aspect of pornography. The "words" that would offend us and from which we want our young protected would not be "Anglo-Saxon" but English, French, German, which carried within their etymology and meaning outrages against human individuals and groups.

The pornographic pictures would be those that showed humans being violated, destroyed, physically beaten. (The prize obscene film might be a three-minute documentary of a fully clothed man, twitching and writhing as the shock of electricity applied by our officials burns through his body.)

All the resources of our Christian teaching and tradition, all the theological armament in the Church could be called up in the warfare against "the new obscenity." The significant concomitant of this is that it would lessen the distortion and perversion of sex in our society that the present definition of obscenity has created. A further advantage to this new understanding would be that the Church and many literary critics would be saved the embarrassment of having to defend every mediocre form of literature and art against the wild attacks of the book-banners.

—Howard Moody, *Christianity and Crisis*

In philosophy, theology, and politics people have argued over the definition of such terms as *existence, God,* and *freedom* without agreeing. Those arguments are partly what keeps language alive. What is important to remember is that a good definition is always an answer to the question, What is it? You can extend your definition by description, example, or any other method necessary to clarify what a term is.

A definition must answer the question, What is it?

COMPARISON AND CONTRAST

The odds are that you will not get through college without sometime having to compare or contrast two items, either in an essay exam or in a research paper. For instance, your English exam may read, "Contrast the tragic flaw in the character of Oedipus with that of Othello." Or in your sociology report you may have to "compare the basic demands of the feminist movement with those of the civil rights movement." Similar questions are asked not only in liberal arts studies but also in the sciences.

To compare means to point out how two things are alike, while to contrast means to point out how they are unlike. When you say that both Mark and Allen are wearing purple socks with yellow jumpsuits, you are *comparing* their clothing. When you say that Alice is attired in a flimsy summer dress whereas Martha is sporting an ankle-length fur coat, you are *contrasting* their clothing. Many students do not recognize the difference between these two techniques.

A well-developed comparison or contrast is a study in logic and in composition. Suppose you want to develop the key thought, "My college experience is teaching me that good instructors are a different breed from bad ones." You must first decide on your bases for contrast. You must ask yourself in which areas of instruction you wish to contrast the activities of good teachers with bad teachers. The following three could be your choice: 1. time spent on lesson preparation; 2. willingness to tolerate dissent; 3. personal relationship with students. Having chosen your bases, write down the three areas under consideration on the left side of a sheet of paper and then create two columns (one for good instructors, the other for bad instructors) in which you will place comments, as follows:

	Good instructors	Bad instructors
1. Time spent on lesson preparation	Instructor constantly revises lessons, including up-to-date reviews, newspaper clippings, research results, and other relevant material. Instructor alludes to more than one source work and gives suggestions for further reading. Lectures and discussions are the result of clear objectives.	Instructor gives same lectures year in and year out, including the same dead jokes. Only rudimentary facts are spelled out, to be memorized verbatim for final tests. Class time is often spent on dull workbook assignments. Instructor shows as many movies as possible, during which he naps.
2. Willingness to tolerate dissent	Instructor welcomes arguments as a way of bringing life into the classroom and of pointing up alternatives. Like Socrates, instructor believes that the classroom dialectic is a valid learning method.	Instructor sees dissent or discussion as a threat to discipline and to his authority, so avoids both. He feels safe only when he is parroting himself or his textbook.
3. Personal relationship with students	Instructor spends time beyond his office hour listening to student questions or complaints. He willingly clarifies difficult problems. Never embarrasses or patronizes students.	Instructor is usually too busy off-campus to spend time in personal consultation with students. He delivers his lecture and disappears. The student is made to feel inferior if he asks for special help.

Cnce you have made this preliminary sketch, you can develop it simply by adding a few transitional words and phrases, as has been done in the following passage (transitions are in italics).

$\digamma$

My college experience is teaching me that good instructors are a different breed from bad ones. *In terms of time spent on lesson preparation*, the good instructor constantly revises his lessons, including such items as up-to-date reviews, newspaper clippings, research results, or any other related material. He alludes to more than one source work and gives suggestions for further reading. His lectures and discussions are the obvious result of clear objectives. *In contrast*, the bad instructor gives the same lectures year in and year out, including the same dead jokes. Only the rudimentary facts are spelled out in class, to be memorized verbatim and regurgitated on final tests. Classroom time is often spent on dull workbook assignments. As often as possible the instructor shows a movie, during which he takes a nap.

Another big difference between good and bad instructors is in their willingness to tolerate dissent. The good instructor welcomes arguments as a way of bringing life into the classroom and of pointing up alternatives. Like Socrates, he believes that the classroom dialectic is a valid learning method. *The bad instructor, however, takes the opposite tack.* He sees dissent or discussion as a threat to his discipline and to his authority, so he avoids both. He feels safe only when he is parroting himself or his old textbook.

Good and bad instructors differ markedly in their relationship to students. The good instructor spends time beyond his office hour listening to student questions or complaints. He willingly clarifies difficult problems, and he never embarrasses or patronizes his students. The bad instructor, *on the contrary*, is usually too busy off-campus to spend time in personal consultation with students. He delivers his lecture and disappears. The student who asks for special help is made to feel inferior.

The example just cited demonstrates the *alternating* method of comparison/contrast. The paragraph is written to alternate back and forth from one side of an issue to the other. Another system—called the block method—expends separate paragraphs for each side of the issue, as illustrated in the following passage that contrasts two differing views of Jewish history:

On the one hand, the Diaspora* Jews can say that this talk of a predestination drama is a lot of nonsense. What has happened is only an interesting constellation of accidental, impersonal events, which some people have distorted out of all proportions to reality. We were defeated in war, they could say, we lost our land, we were exiled, and

* Term used for the dispersion of the Jews throughout the world.

now it is our turn to disappear, just as under similar circumstances the Sumerians, the Hittites, the Babylonians, the Assyrians, the Persians—yes, even the Jews in the Kingdom of Israel—disappeared.

On the other hand, they can say that their ancestors could not have been pursuing a mere illusion for 2,000 years. They could say that if we are God's Chosen People as our forefathers affirmed, if we have been placed in an exile to accomplish a divine mission as our Prophets predicted, and since we did receive the Torah, then we must survive to fulfill our Covenant with God.

—Max I. Dimont, *The Indestructible Jews*

The alternating and block methods of comparison/contrast are further clarified in the following two outlines contrasting the Datsun and Volkswagen on the basis of cost, performance, and looks:

Alternating outline

I. Cost
   A. Datsun
   B. Volkswagen   first paragraph

II. Performance
   A. Datsun
   B. Volkswagen   second paragraph

III. Looks
   A. Datsun
   B. Volkswagen   third paragraph

Block outline

I. Datsun
   A. Cost
   B. Performance   first paragraph
   C. Looks

II. Volkswagen
   A. Cost
   B. Performance   second paragraph
   C. Looks

Three rules must be observed in the development of a comparison/contrast.

1. *The items to be compared/contrasted must belong to the same class.*

Some common ground must exist between items being compared/contrasted or the attempt at comparison will be meaningless. For example, no conceivable good can come from a comparison between a hummingbird and a cement mixer, or between backgammon and Dutch Cleanser. On the other hand, some usefulness may be derived from a comparison between the Chinese and Japanese languages, or between golf and tennis—pairings that respectively belong to common groups: Oriental languages and sports. Moreover, the expression of the comparison/contrast must be grammatically accurate:

Wrong: Our telephone system is better than Russia.
            (Here a telephone system is contrasted with all of Russia.)
Better: Our telephone system is better than *that* of Russia.
Wrong: Ed's income is less than his wife.
            (Here Ed's income is contrasted with his wife.)
Better: Ed's income is less than *that* of his wife.

2. *Both sides of the question must be dealt with.*

All comparisons and contrasts are concerned with two sides, and you must deal equally with both sides of the question. Do not mention one side and assume that your reader will fill in the other side. If you are contrasting the summer weather in Death Valley with the summer weather at Donner Pass, *do not* say,

> In Death Valley the heat is so intense that even lizards wilt.

and assume that your reader will fill in, "but at Donner Pass the summers remain cool." You must draw the contrast fully, as the following:

> *Rewrite:* In Death Valley the heat is so intense that even lizards wilt, *whereas* at Donner Pass a cool breeze freshens even the hottest season.

3. *Expressions indicating comparison/contrast should be generously used.*

Although comparison requires less back and forth movement than contrast, you must nevertheless take both sides into account by stating exactly what traits they have in common. For instance, in pointing out that in some ways high schools are like prisons, you cannot restrict yourself to discussing the domineering principal, the snoopy truant officer, the pass required to leave campus, or the punitive grading system. You must mention both sides, indicating that the domineering principal in high school is *like* the stern warden in prison; that the snoopy truant officer who makes sure that students attend school has much *in common with* the prison guards who make sure that inmates stay in prison; that the pass required to leave campus is *similar to* the formal permission required to leave a locked ward; and that the punitive grading system of high schools is *like* the demerit system of prisons. These expressions serve as signposts in your text, telling your reader how your different points relate.

The following expressions indicate *comparison:*

also	like
as well as	likewise
bears resemblance to	neither . . . nor
both . . . and	similar
in common with	too
in like manner	

The following expressions indicate *contrast:*

although this may be true	on the contrary
at the same time	on the one hand . . . on the other hand
but	otherwise
for all that	still
however	unlike
in contrast to	whereas
in opposition to	yet
nevertheless	

Contrast attempts to emphasize separate sides of an issue by pulling them apart as much as possible in order to expose differences. Comparison is less two-sided because it tries to draw together both sides of an issue in order to expose what they have in common. In short, *contrasts diverge* while *comparisons converge.* In the following passage, note how the Egyptian world and the Greek world are placed far apart so that their ideological differences stand out. Note also how the italicized expressions indicating contrast clarify the shift from one side to the other:

A brief consideration of Egyptian mythology *contrasted* with the mythology of the Greeks is enough to convince us of the revolution in thought that must have taken place from one age to the other. The Egyptian gods had no resemblance to anything in the real world, *whereas* the Greek gods were fashioned after real Greek people.

In Egypt the gods that were typically worshiped consisted of: a towering colossus, so immobile and so distorted that no human could imagine it alive; or a woman with a cat's head, suggesting inflexible, inhuman cruelty; or a monstrous mysterious sphinx, aloof from anything we might consider human. The Egyptian artists' interpretations of the divine were horrid bestial shapes that combined men's heads with birds' bodies or portrayed lions with eagle wings—creatures that could inhabit only terrifying nightmares. The monstrosities of an invisible world were what the Egyptians worshiped.

The Greek interpretation of divinity stands *in opposition to* this dark picture. The Greeks were preoccupied with the visible world. *Unlike* the Egyptians, they found their desires satisfied in what they could actually see around them. The ancient statues of Apollo, for instance, resemble the strong young bodies of athletes contending in the Olympic games. Homer describes Hermes as if he were a splendid Greek citizen. Generally the Greek artists found their gods in the idealized beauty or intelligence of actual human counterparts. *In direct contrast to* the Egyptians, they had no wish to create some hideous fantasy that they then called god.

In the next passage, note the funneling effect that emphasizes what whales and human beings have in common. Note how the italicized expressions indicating comparison draw together these two seemingly divergent animals:

Whales and human beings are *like* two nations of individuals who have certain characteristics in common. As mammals they *both* are warm-blooded, giving milk, and breathing air. As social creatures they *both* have basic urges for privacy as well as for fraternization. As species bent on reproduction they *both* show similar patterns of aggression during courtship, the male trying to gain the female's attention and the female responding. Finally, as mystical beings they *both* are caught in the net of life and time, fellow prisoners of the splendor, travail, and secrets of earth.

Comparisons are often used to clarify abstract or complex ideas. For example, in the Bible Jesus remarks (Matthew xiii.32–33):

The kingdom of heaven is like to a grain of mustard seed, which a man took, and sowed in his field: Which indeed is the least of all seeds; but when it is grown, it is the greatest among herbs, and becometh a tree, so that the birds of the air come and lodge in the branches thereof.

In this comparison, the complicated idea of God's kingdom is made understandable to the Jewish people by being compared to a mustard seed, something simple and familiar to agrarian Jewish life. Through this comparison Jesus explains to his listeners something about the power of growth and the spread of influence that a life dedicated to God can exert on those who commit themselves to it.

Use comparison to emphasize what two sides have in common. Use contrast to emphasize opposing sides of an issue.

CAUSAL ANALYSIS

Causal analysis involves the ability to see cause and effect relationships between two elements. When you investigate the reason for something, you are either answering the question, Why did this happen? or, What will this do? The answer to the first question we label *cause;* the answer to the second we label *effect*. When you say, "Harold has lost one friend after another because he wears dirty clothes, uses obscene language, and is moody," you are dealing with cause. When you say, "Harold's dirty clothes, obscene language, and moodiness will make lasting friendships impossible," you are dealing with effect. *Cause* explains what has happened in the past; *effect* predicts what will happen in the future.

A student of psychology, for instance, may wish to examine the question, "Why are so many couples unable to discuss their marital problems?" The answer quite naturally leads him to causal analysis. He may come up with the key thought, "Barriers between husbands and wives have two major causes." Such a key thought could be developed as follows:

Barriers between husbands and wives have two major causes. The first is timidity. Many couples are embarrassed to discuss intimate problems, such as sexual maladjustment, personal hygiene, or religious beliefs. They prefer to let their discontent ulcerate rather than to confront it openly. A wife says, "I wouldn't hurt my husband by telling him that his dirty hands offend me." A husband says, "I dislike the way my wife compares me to her father in everything I do, from mowing the lawn to smoking my pipe, but I could never tell her so." Guilt feelings can reinforce this sort of timidity. If a wife or husband knows that a frank talk about sex, for instance, will uncover some past indiscretion, he or she will avoid the confrontation out of guilt on one partner's part or fear of knowing on the part of the other partner. The longer this silence is kept, the stronger it becomes.

The second major cause is pride. Many couples are too proud to admit that they have problems. Their Hollywood view of marriage does not provide for unpleasantness or failure, so they fantasize married bliss instead of admitting and discussing problems that cause pressure and pain. Many wives, for example, whose husbands escape into work because they have lost interest in the home, will give elaborate excuses for this escape in order to avoid the humiliation of friends finding out that the marriage is not idyllic. Similarly, many partners refuse to share such worries as financial losses or job decline, thinking that admitting to such worries somehow makes them look weak. One marriage counselor claims that many divorces could be prevented if only the couples involved would drop their sense of false pride and discuss whatever is making the marriage miserable.

Strange as it may seem, two people can live under the same roof, joined together in life's most intimate relationship, while their timidity or their pride keeps them from discussing problems that vitally affect the quality of their union.

A slight shift in approach could lead the same psychology student to a discussion of effect rather than cause. If he asks the question, "What happens when two people no longer discuss their marital problems?" he is not interested in the cause of lack of communication, but in its effect. He might develop the key thought, "Barriers between husband and wife result in a tension-filled home," as in the following paragraph:

Barriers between husband and wife result in a tension-filled home. When marriage partners constantly overlook a problem or pretend it does not exit, they eventually become frustrated and angry. They develop feelings of isolation and rejection as their unfulfilled yearnings become a gnawing hunger. Lacking communication, the marriage is left without an emotional safety valve to let off pent-up frustration. The ensuing strain increases as the angry partners take out hidden, unexpressed resentments on their children, using them as scapegoats for their own great void. In the beginning the tension may show itself only in minor misunderstandings or brief pout sessions, but as the barriers remain, these little hurts turn into wounds. The husband may become belligerent toward the wife, belittling her in front of friends or ignoring her until she retreats in cold indignation. The wife may feel so rejected and worthless that she seeks another man to comfort her or to treat her with sensitivity. The tension grows. Soon the home has become a place of bitter hostility, where love and warmth are impossible. The cause is their unwillingness to talk and listen.

In pinning down causes, you need to distinguish among three kinds: *necessary, sufficient,* and *contributory*.

A *necessary* cause is one that *must* be present for the effect to occur, but it alone cannot make the effect occur. For instance, irrigation is necessary for a crop of good grapes, but irrigation alone will not cause a good crop. Other factors have to be present, such as enough sunshine, correct pruning, proper pesticides, and good soil.

A *sufficient* cause is one that *can* produce a given effect by itself. For instance, an empty gasoline tank alone can keep a car from running, even though other problems, such as a bad spark plug, a leaking hose, or ignition trouble may be present also.

A *contributory* cause is one that *may* produce an effect, but cannot produce the effect by itself. For instance, vitamin E may help a long-distance runner to win a race, but other factors have to be present also, such as the correct time count, judges to observe the event, and so forth. The runner may also win the race without the help of vitamin E.

Understanding the difference among these three causes will help you in your investigations of cause and effect. First, it will keep you from careless assertions. For example, you will know better than to make either of the following statements.

Busing will provide equal education and social integration.
Busing will not provide equal education and social integration.

Both of these assertions are wrong because they treat busing as a sufficient cause for equal education and social integration. In reality, busing may be a necessary cause or a contributory cause, but busing alone can provide neither equal education nor social integration. Other factors are necessary, such as enlightened students, teachers, and parents.

Second, understanding the difference among the three causes will keep you from making dogmatic statements, such as:

A vegetarian diet will prevent cancer.
Acupuncture is the answer to anesthesiology problems in America.
Violence on television is the cause of today's growing criminal violence.

Rather, you will soften your statements by inserting such phrases as "may be," "is a contributing factor," "is one of the reasons," or "is a major cause." A careful study of cause and effect teaches that few causes are sufficient; most are merely necessary or contributory.

In looking for correct cause-effect relationships, check yourself for the following errors:

1. Mistaking an effect for a cause. If you claim that a sour taste in your mouth gave you a stomach upset when in fact the sour taste resulted from a stomach upset in the first place, you are mistaking an effect for a cause. Often cause and effect are difficult to separate. For instance, is the new sexual freedom among teenagers the result of permissiveness on the part of society, or has the new sexual freedom caused a growing permissiveness? Answering this question is like trying to answer the proverbial question, Which came first, the chicken or the egg?

2. Assuming that because one event followed another, the first event caused the second event. If you assume that because Peggy drank milk as a child she smokes marijuana as a teenager, you are making this mistake. You must be able to prove a relationship between two events in order to assert that one caused the other.

3. Mistaking a contributory cause for a sufficient cause. If you assert that your father's temper was the cause of your parents' divorce when in actuality his temper was merely a reaction to deeper causes of dissatisfaction with the marriage relationship that eventually led to the breakup, you are mistaking a contributory cause for a sufficient cause.

Most writers do not pay rigid obedience to these principles of causal analysis except when they argue a highly technical question that must be explained according to the strict rules of logic. The following passage is an example of the free use of the principles of causal analysis:

> The association of love with adultery in much of medieval love poetry has two causes. The first lies in the organization of feudal society. Marriages, being matters of economic or social interest, had nothing whatever to do with erotic love. When a marriage alliance no longer suited the interests of the lord, he got rid of his lady with as much dispatch as he got rid of a horse. Consequently, a lady who might be nothing more than a commodious piece of property to her husband, could be passionately desired by her vassal. The second cause lies in the attitude of the medieval Christian church, where the desire for erotic, romantic love was considered wicked and a result of Adam's sin in the Garden of Eden. The general impression left on the medieval mind by the church's official teachers was that all erotic pleasure was wicked. And this impression, in addition to the nature of feudal marriage, produced in the courtly poets the perverse desire to emphasize the very passion they were told to resist.

The student who wrote the above paragraph does not demonstrate cause according to precise rules, but rather shows the common-sense result of his research into why medieval poetry emphasized adulterous love. It is important to be careful in asserting causal connections between events. If a connection is not there, you should not create one. If a cause appears possible but not certain, use a word like *probable* to protect your credibility, as

Nervous exhaustion is the *probable* reason for Michael's depressions.

If a cause is not sufficient, but merely contributory, make this clear, as in the statement,

Motorcycles are *one of the reasons* for a dramatic increase in noise pollution.

In developing an idea by causal analysis, carefully scrutinize the relationship between two events.

DIVISION

Some key thoughts require that you divide a subject into smaller units, such as the following:

My *library* consists of three kinds of books.
Four varieties of *beer mugs* decorate the Mother Hubbard Coffee Shop.
Mark Twain's *humor* contains four elements.

In each of these cases, the italicized subject will be developed by breaking it into smaller parts. The purpose, of course, is to discover the nature of the parts that make up the whole. In order to divide a subject, you must examine all the items contained in it and decide how these items can be grouped into distinct categories. The process is somewhat like sorting clothes from a laundry basket—according to color—whites in one pile, coloreds in another, and darks in a third. The passage below is an example of development by division.

There are three main methods of communicating knowledge from instructor to student: the lecture, the dialog, the recitation.

In a lecture, the instructor is the main performer. He does all of the talking except for an occasional question from a student wanting clarification or repetition. The students listen and take notes on what they consider the highlights of the lecture; then they go home and ponder what was said. The main advantage of the lecture is that it allows for a steady flow of information between instructor and student. Certain subjects need this steady flow. The surgeon demonstrating a surgical procedure, the physicist expounding a theory, the lawyer analyzing a court case, do so best without interruption.

In a dialog, also called "Socratic dialog" because Socrates used this method, the instructor does not give an organized talk; he merely repeatedly questions his students in an effort to elicit proper answers, which he assumes to be implicit in all rational thinkers. His questions are designed to pierce the heart of a problem or fact, and they are so arranged as to make a student aware that glib answers are not always right, but that sometimes he must consider and weigh a question before finding the answer. When properly used, the dialog method will make a student conscious of his own ignorance, but at the same time it will lead him to find answers to the questions asked, and he will remember these answers because they were not handed to him ready-made, but drawn out of his own mind. This method is effective for classes in philosophy and problem-solving.

In a recitation, the instructor assigns a lesson for the students to study on their own. The students struggle through, soaking up the material as best they can. Then, at the next class meeting, the instructor confronts the class and goes over the lesson with them, point by point. He examines them on the difficult passages to make sure that they have understood the assignment, and if he finds that in their answers they show vagueness or doubt, he will further clarify, expose, and emphasize until he is satisfied that the students have assimilated what they need to know. This is the standard way of teaching languages, literature, history, and the descriptive sciences.

This passage examines the field of teaching by subdividing it according to the various methods used by instructors. In so doing, it follows three rules. First, the division is based on a single principle—the methods instructors use to communicate knowledge to their students. Student preferences, the length of class periods, or the subject matter taught is not taken into consideration. Second, *all* main methods of teaching have been included. If the dialog method, for example, had been left out, the division would be incomplete. Third, each category of teaching methods is mutually exclusive. None overlap; each is separate and well-defined. Lecture is properly excluded from dialog and recitation; likewise, dialog is separated from lecture and recitation. When you develop a key thought through division, be sure to observe these rules:

1. Use a single principle.
2. Make the division complete.
3. Exclude each part from the others.

The writer of the following passage has broken one of the rules.

Mass production in American industry is made up of four distinct elements: division of labor, standardization through precision tooling, assembly line, and consumer public. First is the division of labor, which means that a complicated production process is broken down into specialized individual tasks that are performed by people or machines who concentrate on these tasks only. Second is the standardization of parts as a result of precision tooling. This means that each part can be produced by machines both for interchangeability and for assembly by semiskilled workers. Third is the assembly line, which is a method of moving the work from one person to another in a continual chain of progress until the item is completed. This is a way of moving the work to the person, instead of the person to the work. The last element is the consumer public. Without it mass production would be a futile endeavor, for it is the public that buys up all the mass-produced items as fast as they roll off the assembly line.

Clearly, the student who composed the above did not base his division on a single principle. His error shows up immediately. In his key thought, the first three divisions are distinctly elements of mass production, but the fourth division, the consumer public, is not part of the mass production process, but comes into the picture only after the item is already on the market. The student has not stuck to the principle of division, which was to identify the elements of mass production.

Development through division serves not only to depict parts of a whole, but also to trace steps in the course of a process, as in the following example:

The act of falling asleep is divided into two stages: drowsiness and unconsciousness. The first stage, drowsiness, involves a feeling of heaviness in the eyes, the head, and the limbs. The drowsy person finds it difficult to keep his eyes open or his head up. His tendency is to slump as his eyelids gradually close over his pupils. He yawns in order to relax his whole body, and he is unable to focus attention on what is happening around him. If he is at a movie, he loses track of the plot; if he is talking to a friend, he becomes incoherent. The second stage, losing consciousness, also begins with an emphasis on the body. The person who is beginning to lose consciousness will first feel his limbs becoming burdensome. Next, he may be acutely aware of his internal organs, such as his beating heart. Every little ache and pain are emphasized. Then his breathing deepens and becomes increasingly regular, like that of a child. Finally, the body seems to fade out, and all perceptions cease.

120

When dividing a subject, divide it completely, according to one consistent principle, making the divisions mutually exclusive.

COMBINATION OF METHODS

The methods taught in this chapter are intended as guidelines to help you write well, not as mutually exclusive prescriptions. Indeed, many essays are not written according to a single type of development but use, instead, a combination of these methods. An essay having as its prime purpose a definition, a contrast, or an analysis of cause may also employ strategies of narration, description, or any other method of development to achieve that purpose. The following annotated essay exemplifies this sort of blending:

THE POPULATION BOMB IN YOUR OWN BACKYARD

Introduction

Even as you read this paper you may be stroking or petting a time bomb that will tick the human race into mass famine. Yes, that cuddly ball of fluff on your lap is one of humanity's most unbelievable blunders. *Owning family domestic animals is a luxury we can no longer afford and a practice we must sharply curtail or discontinue completely within the next ten years.*

Thesis

Definition

Webster's Collegiate Dictionary defines a pet as, "an animal or bird that is cherished." Indeed, the family dog or cat has become as much a part of the American family unit as apple pie and Thanksgiving dinner. We find pets included in everything from family portraits to presents under the Christmas tree. But let's be serious and mature. If we discount our emotional ties to domestic pets, we are left with a personal liability and an economic drain without any redeeming social value.

Facts

Let us first explore some facts related to pet ownership. According to Carl Djerassi's article "Planned Parenthood for Pets," which appeared in the January 1973 *Bulletin for Atomic Scientists*, the United States has the highest ratio of pets to humans in the world, with between 70 and 110 million dogs and cats. Many of these pets receive a much better diet than 1 to 2 billion humans. Each year dogs in the United States alone consume enough protein to feed 4 million human beings. Americans spend an estimated $4.5 billion a year on pet shelters, health care (some pets have hospital-ization plans and a few even visit psychiatrists), waste clean-up (40 million pounds of dog dung are deposited each year in New York City alone), pet foods, collars, clothes, vitamins, li-censes, doggie and kitty hotels, and funerals. About $1.5 billion was spent in 1971 for pet food, almost four times the $390 million spent on baby food in that same year.

Transitional paragraph using contrast

One may argue strongly that we need pets as an important form of diversity, to alleviate feelings of loneliness and inadequacy, and as a child substitute, thus helping to limit popula-tion growth. It seems clear, however, that we have gone much too far. The massive popula-tion explosion of dogs and cats not only drains off valuable nutrients from less fortunate hu-mans, but ironically has resulted in a dramatic rise in abandoned pets.

Narration

An experience comes to mind that affirms my stand against domestic pets. While serving in the military, I was attached for training to the 651st desert warfare and survival school at Ed-wards Air Force Base, California, located ninety miles outside Los Angeles. During my duty there it was reported that a large pack of wild dogs was terrorizing the base housing area, schools, and shopping center, resulting in de-struction of property, several animal bites, and, as a consequence, series after series of painful antirabies vaccinations mandatorily adminis-tered to the bite victims. The problem came to a crisis when several men working to recover practice bombs from the bombing range were attacked by a pack of wild dogs. One man was severely bitten, and as the men took refuge in their vehicle, one large animal jumped and hit the driver's side window with such ferocity and velocity as to shatter it. Several other men of my squad and I were ordered to search out and destroy these animals. Armed with some of the finest combat-tested equipment in the U.S. ar-senal and assisted by helicopter gunships, the animals were located, trapped in a gully, and vaporized in a display of firepower that rivaled some of the fiercest fire-fights and perimeter defense actions I was to experience less than a year later in the rice paddies of Laos and South Vietnam. Closer inspection of the dead animals revealed that all sixty-one of them were abandoned pets with collars, innoculation marks and name tags proving beyond a doubt that this pack of wild, diseased, rabid dogs had not long ago been "man's best friend." Few Americans are aware that approximately 13.3 million pets are destroyed each year at public and private shelters, at an annual cost of about one hundred million dollars.

Examples

We must find a better way to limit pet population growth, preferably by sharply lowering the pet birth rate and decreasing our need for so many pets. In fact, all major pet food manufacturers in the United States have begun to diversify and produce food products for human consumption as a hedge against the "dog that may bite its master's hand." Two examples in the Los Angeles basin are Kal-Kan dog food and Ralston-Purina Corporation, both of whom now

Back to thesis

market frozen T.V. dinners for people. *It is becoming urgent that the family "Fido," "Muffin," or "Lassie" be, to a great extent, eliminated from the American scene.*

Conclusion

My dog Spot must go, and to the avid pet lover who would argue that "she saved my life," etc., etc., I suggest that a thirty-dollar smoke detector or an alarm in the car or house would serve just as well or even better. For the rhapsodizer who points to his doe-eyed Beagle puppy and asks, "How can you be so heartless?" I will immediately produce a picture of an eight-year-old doe-eyed, starving, ragged Appalachian coal miner's daughter and retort, "How can you be so insensitive and cruel?"

EXERCISES

1. Which is the most appropriate method for developing the following key thoughts? What information would you include in your development?

a. Since there is no clear-cut medical definition for depression, the term tends to be defined pragmatically by its symptoms.
b. The fact that most candidates for the office of United States Vice President are hastily chosen by only one man and his advisers could have tragic results for our nation.
c. Nothing is more pathetic than the sight of a man desperately trying to hang on to a lover when she is through with the relationship but he is not.
d. I agree with the aim of the feminist movement to abolish some of the unnecessary gallantries men are supposed to perform for women.
e. During the last few years vitamin E has become the focus of interest and attention in the scientific community.
f. The average American female spends more money on clothes than does the average European female.
g. A Leo man and a Scorpio woman have many personality traits in common.
h. Abortion clinics today consist of three main kinds: those run by qualified physicians in private practice, those run by the county government, and those run by quacks.
i. A drop of water viewed through a microscope presents a fascinating spectacle.
j. My favorite Christmas took place in Vermont when I was ten years old.

2. Relate a childhood experience that taught you an important lesson.

3. Write a one-paragraph description of your room based on a dominant impression.

4. In the following description, strike out those words that do not support the dominant impression.

Desolation and decay are the dominant manifestations of this Navajo wildland. Sound and movement seem to have no place here. As far as the eye can see, the view is one vast yellow and purple corrugated world of canyons and mesas void of citizenry. Only occasionally does the roar of an airplane streaking across the sky interrupt the eerie silence to remind me that another inhabited world exists. As I gaze out into this majestic expanse, I get an insight into the meaning of time as measured by ages. So much of the view is the result of slow corrosion and natural destruction. I can hardly believe my eyes when accidentally I discover two blue and white Hamm's beer cans wrapped in sandwich bags and dropped behind a withered bush. A picnic in this wasteland—how incongruous! The miles upon miles of canyon-gashed, billowing slickrock supporting a series of sculptured sandstone buttes are like the monuments of a splendid but vanished past.

5. Which of the following two passages makes better use of examples in developing a key thought? Give reasons for your choice.

a. When I was eleven, I became possessed of an exaggerated fear of death. It started one quiet summer afternoon with an explosion in the alley behind our house. I jumped up from under a shade tree and tailed Poppa toward the scene. Black smoke billowed skyward, a large hole gaped in the wall of our barn, and several maimed chickens and a headless turkey flopped about on the ground. Then Poppa stopped and muttered, "Good Lord." I clutched his overalls and looked. A man, or what was left of him, was strewn about in three parts. A gas main he had been repairing had somehow ignited and blown everything around it to bits.

Then once, with two friends, I had swum along the bottom of the muddy Marmaton River, trying to locate the body of a Negro man. We had been promised fifty cents apiece by the same white policeman who had shot him while he was in the water trying to escape arrest. The dead man had been in a crap game with several others who had managed to get away. My buddy, Johnny Young, was swimming beside me; we swam with ice hooks which we were to use for grappling. The two of us touched the corpse at the same instant. Fear streaked through me, and the memory of his bloated body haunted my dreams for nights.

b. Adultery can strengthen a marriage. For an example of this strengthening, I think of the movie *Bob and Carol and Ted and Alice*. Here an upper-middle-class couple dabble with group sex and extramarital affairs, but this adultery leads them in the end to a greater appreciation of each other because they realize that adultery is really boring and unfulfilling while the richest relationship lies in a marriage where the two partners form a close-knit unit and remain faithful to each other. But they had to learn this truth through adultery.

Another example of this strengthening is a thirty-five-year-old mother of three who once said that when her husband had an affair, he found out that the woman he was going with was far more jealous and tied him down much more than she did. So he came back to being a faithful husband, and their marriage now is better than ever. The husband found out that the grass is not always greener on the other side of the fence.

6. Pick out one outstanding trait in your personality (for example, shyness, generosity, jealousy, temper) and give three specific examples of how this trait has shown up in your life.

7. Develop a 300–500-word definition of one of the following terms. Begin with the lexical definition; then extend the definition in any way that best explains the term.

a. Diplomacy	e. Panache
b. Adolescence	f. History
c. Tyranny	g. Black humor
d. Imagination	h. Miracle

8. Using the example on page 108 as a pattern, set up a sketch in which you contrast one of the following:

   a. Teachers and students
   b. Alcohol and marijuana
   c. American cars and foreign cars
   d. Reformers and revolutionaries
   e. Academic learning and practical experience
   f. Believers and atheists
   g. Socialists and communists

9. List several ways in which the following are alike:

   a. First love and a spring thunderstorm
   b. Psychology and religion
   c. A boy locked in a room and a boy dominated by his mother
   d. Senility and childhood
   e. All wars

10. Classify the following causes as either *sufficient, necessary,* or *contributory.* (Use a common-sense approach rather than a technical one.)

   a. A ruptured artery causes heart failure.
   b. A drop in temperature causes water to freeze.
   c. Overwork causes a divorce.
   d. Birth control causes a drop in college enrollment.
   e. Poor use of grammar causes a lawyer to lose a case in court.
   f. Combustion causes an engine to run.
   g. Riding a bicycle causes good health.

11. State what is wrong with the following causal analyses:

   a. A runny nose causes the flu.
   b. I am fat because all the members of my family are fat.
   c. This morning my horoscope said that I should take risks, so I am going to invest my savings in speculative stock.
   d. The baby is crying; his diaper must be dirty.
   e. You had better stop driving; that scraping noise will certainly wreck your transmission.
   f. If you drink ten glasses of water a day, you will be the picture of rosy health.
   g. Skin color is the cause of racial strife.

12. Divide your life so far into segments that serve to illustrate major stages in your development. Base your division on a single principle, such as attitude toward parents, ability to be self-reliant, or physical growth.

13. Classify the following terms under headings that will indicate what they have in common:

a.	Swimming	g.	Sledding
b.	Gliding	h.	Flying
c.	Croquet	i.	Golf
d.	Tobogganing	j.	Water polo
e.	Skydiving	k.	Lacrosse
f.	Surfing	l.	Skiing

14. In the following passage, what subject is the author breaking up into two types? What is the principle on which he has based his division?

There is one sort of _____ which principally arises from that instinctive, disinterested, and undefinable feeling which connects the affections of man with his birthplace. This natural fondness is united with a taste for ancient customs and a reverence for traditions of the past; those who cherish it love their country as they love the mansion of their fathers. They love the tranquility that it affords them; they cling to the peaceful habits that they have contracted within its bosom; they are attached to the reminiscences that it awakens; and they are even pleased by living there in a state of obedience. This _____ is sometimes stimulated by religious enthusiasms, and then it is capable of making prodigious efforts. It is in itself a kind of religion: it does not reason, but it acts from the impulse of faith and sentiment. . . .

But there is another species of _____ which is more rational than the one I have been describing. It is perhaps less generous and less ardent, but it is more fruitful and more lasting: it springs from knowledge; it is nurtured by the laws; it grows by the exercise of civil rights; and, in the end, it is confounded with the personal interests of the citizen. A man comprehends the influence which the well-being of his country has upon his own; he is aware that the laws permit him to contribute to that prosperity, and he labors to promote it, first because it benefits him, and secondly because it is in part his own work.

—Alexis de Tocqueville, *Democracy in America*

15. Divide the subjects below, stating the principle on which you have based your division. (For example, if the subject were literature, the principle of division might be major genres, and the divisions would be short story, novel, drama, and poetry.)

a.	Movies	d.	Anger
b.	Dreams	e.	Virtue
c.	Food	f.	Scandal

7

What's the right word?

The power of words is nearly immeasurable but there is no doubt whatsoever that they can hurt at least as much as sticks and stones. We articulate our wishes, fears, dreams, and ambitions in words. Wars are begun, countries founded, marriages celebrated, and history commemorated with words. Possibly the entire concept of time, space, and identity is indissolubly bound up with the syntax and diction of language. Our discussion in this chapter on how words work and how you should use them centers around three main points:

1. Words are symbols.
2. Words have contexts.
3. Words have denotations and connotations.

WORDS ARE SYMBOLS

A symbol is something that stands for or represents another thing. Words are symbols since they stand for and represent either objects or concepts. *Hot dog* stands for an object—the peculiar sausage and bun combination we call by that name; *love* stands for a concept—attraction between people.

Symbols depend on and imply the existence of agreed-on meanings. A word communicates only because it means the same thing to people who speak the same language. Learning any language consists essentially of memorizing how words match up with the objects or concepts they represent. These "match-ups," in turn, are valid and consistent simply because the people who speak the language have implicitly agreed to them. You have learned the language when your response to its words begins to conform to the responses of others who speak it. When you know American English, *hot dog* will cause you to salivate if you are hungry; *halt* will cause you to stop, and *danger!* will cause you to stop and think. Your response in each case is evoked by the object or concept with which each word is matched up in your mind.

S. I. Hayakawa's "semantic triangle" explains how words derive their meanings from being matched up with an object or concept.

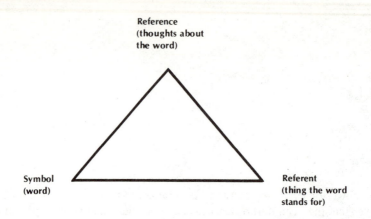

According to this theory, each word operates as a symbol with a referent (thing the word stands for) and a reference (thoughts about the word). In the case of *hot dog,* the triangle looks like this:

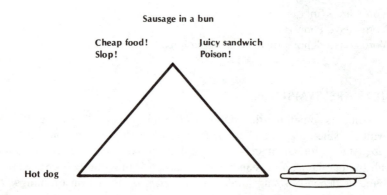

Some words are concrete, and some are abstract. A concrete word has an object as its referent; an abstract word has a concept as its referent. *Hot dog, chair, pencil* and *brick* are all concrete words since each has an object referent that can be produced in case of disagreement over meaning. With an abstract word, however, nothing tangible can be produced to settle disagreements, and the potential for misunderstanding is infinitely larger. For example, examine the semantic triangle for *liberalism* on the next page. Notice that other words that attempt to define the concept are now listed as the referent. An abstract word points to a concept that in turn is defined by more words. Political arguments owe much of their verbiage to this built-in

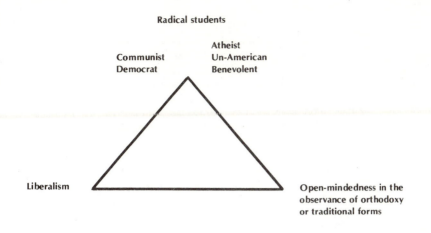

circularity of the abstract word; volumes can be, have been, and will be mouthed as contending factions search for a set of words that will define to everyone's satisfaction concepts like *liberalism*. Possibly no such set of words exists. But communication and life would be simpler if, like *hot dog,* an abstract word such as *liberalism* had an object referent that could be plopped down on the conference table to settle arguments over its meaning once and for all.

It is not only abstract words that hold different associations for different people. *Hot dog* will hold a markedly different reference (thoughts about the word) to the person who was almost poisoned by one from what it will to a person who has consumed hundreds with no side-effects. But in each case the referent will be the same object even though the emotional reaction to it might be vastly different. Abstract words, in contrast, are likely to have different referents for different people, as well as having different references.

There is a lesson in this that applies to your own writing. Many college students have a tendency to write in abstractions. Perhaps they feel that by presenting big general ideas in abstract words, they sound more intelligent. Nothing could be further from the truth. The best kind of writing is usually the most concrete because it is most likely to be clearly understood. Sometimes you do have to begin a piece of writing with a general statement, but as soon as you have done this, you should nail it down with concrete words. You might begin by saying, "For the past few months Harry has led a miserable existence." But as soon as possible, you had better add, "He suffers sharp pains from an ulcer." In this way you have moved from abstract *existence* to concrete *ulcer*.

Note, however, that some words can be more abstract or more concrete than others. Various words can be found to describe Harry's life that can be arranged in declining degrees of abstractness:

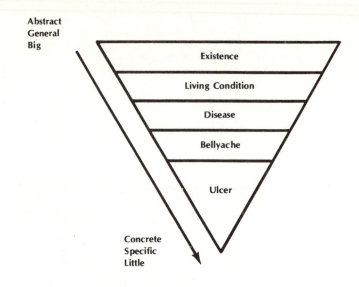

Abstract
General
Big

Existence

Living Condition

Disease

Bellyache

Ulcer

Concrete
Specific
Little

The vocabulary available for discussing any conceivable topic ranges from words that are most abstract to words that are most concrete, with intermediate level words between. In this case, you are being most abstract when you talk about Harry's existence and most concrete when you talk about his ulcer. When you talk about Harry's living condition you are being more abstract than when you talk about his disease, and when you talk about his bellyache you are being more concrete than both. As we said, a similar abstraction pyramid can be constructed for the range of words available in discussing any topic. It is best to keep your writing to the bottom half of the pyramid, to be as concrete as frequently as you can.

Pull your writing down to the concrete level as soon as you can!

WORDS HAVE CONTEXTS

No word ever has exactly the same meaning twice. The meaning of each word depends on its context, which includes both the physical and verbal setting or environment in which it is used. And because things are constantly changing in time and space, no word will ever have exactly the same meaning to the person hearing or seeing it repeated.

We understand words differently as their contexts change. The *physical* context of a word is the geographical and historical setting in which the word is *encoded* (spoken or written) or *decoded* (heard or read). Consider the name *Oswald*. Before the assassination of John F. Kennedy, this name could have appeared anywhere without causing a stir. But today, after Kennedy's assassination, *Oswald* evokes anger and disgust. It has acquired new meaning because the setting in which we decode it is different from what it was before Kennedy was killed. Similarly, our perception of the word *sex* is different if we encounter the word at age ten rather than at age thirty. Our reaction to the words *iced tea* will be different in 100-degree Texas heat than it will be in subzero arctic cold. And we will attach a totally different meaning to the word *marriage* depending on whether we are happily married, involved in a bitter divorce case, or happily settled as a single. In short, both geography and historical moment have a definite effect on the meaning of words. And since both geography and history change continually, the meanings of words also change continually.

Furthermore, words also depend on their verbal contexts for meaning. The *verbal context* of a word is determined by the words that precede and follow it. Verbal context often allows us to understand words we have never seen before. For example, take the sentence,

> He reached up to shave his *drundrearies*, which had grown thick on both cheeks.

From the context we guess that the little-used word *drundrearies* means whiskers. Again,

> The cows had to be herded back to their *byre* for milking.

Here the word *byre* means either barn or shed, as the context indicates.

The importance of verbal context is clear to foreigners learning English. What we take for granted, they must learn through hard experience—namely, that English is full of words whose meanings change with their verbal contexts. An example is the word *wing:*

> 1. Lady Macbeth stood in the *wings*, waiting for her cue.
> 2. My canary has white spots under his left *wing*.
> 3. She belongs to the left-*wing* faction of the party.
> 4. Hand me that *wing* nut so that I can screw it on.
> 5. I haven't studied; so I'll just have to *wing* it.
> 6. Don't wear your *wing* tips; wear your hush puppies.
> 7. Betty is a patient in the children's *wing* of the hospital.

> **Make perfectly clear the context in which you are using a word.**

WORDS HAVE DENOTATIONS AND CONNOTATIONS

Every word has a denotation and a connotation. *To denote* means "to point to"; *to connote* means "to imply." The denotation of a word is its bare dictionary definition; the connotation includes all of the emotional overtones suggested by the word. The word *home* denotes a place where one lives, but it connotes much more than that—warmth, shelter, coziness, and all the other qualities that have come to be attached to the total meaning of *home*. Words like *chair, typewriter, clothespin,* and *match* are usually used denotatively, pointing to specific, concrete things and nothing more. But words like *tempest, ghost, Christmas,* and *mother* are used connotatively for the emotional charge they seem to emit. To put this another way: the denotative meaning of a word comes directly from its referent; the connotative meaning is drawn from the ideas that cluster around the reference prong of the semantic triangle. Consider, for example, the semantic triangle on the word *winter:*

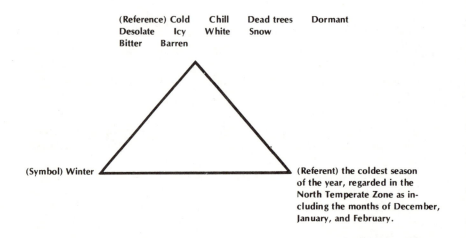

The referent shown was taken from *Webster's New World Dictionary.* The references will vary considerably among individuals but should cluster mainly around images of bleakness, desolation, and dormancy. Nevertheless, there is enough consensus on these various references to make the following connotative uses of *winter* intelligible to most people:

1. Laughter drives winter from the mind.
2. She is in the winter of her life.
3. This is the winter of his discontent.

Quibbles may legitimately be raised over faint shades of meaning, but most people would probably interpret these sentences in the same ways. Here are some possible interpretations:

1. Laughter drives bleakness from the mind.

   Skiing enthusiasts aside, winter is customarily associated in the minds of most people with dismal weather, storms, blizzards, and gloominess—the characteristics connotatively evoked in this use.

2. She is in the waning period of her life.

   Winter is the final season of the year, a time when bears hibernate, trees go dormant, and geese fly south. Rhymsters and versifiers therefore traditionally use *winter* to signify old age and death just as they customarily use *spring* to imply youth. Obviously, this poetic meaning is connoted here.

3. This is the bitterest period of his discontent.

   In this sentence, winter once again takes the rap as a season of bad weather and is used to connote discontent at its very worst.

The individual who takes the *winter* in the first sentence to mean "a joyful and cheerful time" obviously fails to share in the consensus of meanings existing in the reference on *winter* and the connotative value of the word is consequently lost on him. Perhaps he lives in the Antarctic, has heavily invested in a ski lift, or is yearning for the coming of the next ice age. No matter. The denotative meaning of a word is gained from the dictionary; the connotative meaning is ultimately deduced from one's experience. To accurately use a word connotatively, one must not only be aware of its referent meanings, but one must also share the consensus on its reference. If this consensus is not shared, the word cannot be used connotatively with any accuracy.

The connotations of some words are eminently clearer than the connotations of others simply because their references are more commonly known. Take the word *pig,* for instance, and the word *okapi. Pig* denotes a fat, four-legged animal with a curly tail, short ears, and squinting eyes. The referent of *okapi,* on the other hand, is an African animal related to the giraffe but with a considerably shorter neck. Yet most people would rather be called an okapi than a pig. It is a cliché that the pig is stupid, dirty, and greedy, and these connotations are intended when the term is applied to a person. If the same person is called a lion or a tiger the connotations are more positive, as the person's response is also likely to be, for the lion and the tiger are popularly thought of as hunters and masters in their dominions—a mystique that has transferred favorable connotations to both words. But the lowly okapi is more or less lost on the public consciousness. Its personal habits are unclear, its standards of hygiene or domination are known only to zoologists and zoo keepers. The dictionary, moreover, is of no help whatsoever in clarifying whether one should take insult or rejoice over being called an okapi. Says *Webster's New World Dictionary* of the okapi: "An African animal

137

(Okapia johnstoni) related to the giraffe, but with a much shorter neck.'' The moral of this discussion is that connotative meaning is more subtle and elusive than denotative meaning and requires familiarity with more than the dictionary referent. Or, to put it another way, you know the meaning of a word only when you understand its connotations.

It follows from this discussion that greater semantic skill is required for the connotative rather than the denotative use of words. People who learn another language begin by memorizing the hard and fast denotative meanings of words; only later, as they acquire familiarity with the particular culture, do the reverberations of words—their connotations—become clear. Similarly, when a native speaker first encounters a word and looks up its meaning in a dictionary, he gains primarily a denotative definition of it. Only later, after he has repeatedly heard and seen the word used in various spoken and written contexts, do its connotations sink in. Because of this lag between acquiring connotative and denotative meanings, the writer who habitually uses a barely familiar vocabulary runs the danger of sounding stilted and wooden—especially when he is trying hard to include big words lately culled from the dictionary. It is better to use only those words whose connotations and denotations you clearly understand.

Literature, especially poetry, uses words largely for their connotative meanings. On the other hand, technical and scientific writing primarily relies on the denotative use of words, with individual words functioning as concrete indicators of specific referents. Here, for example, is a passage taken from a pamphlet of technical instructions:

> Place the batteries over the band in the battery compartment for easy removal. When not using batteries for one month or more, be sure to remove them. If the batteries become weak, replace them with new ones as soon as possible.

On the other hand, in this stanza from a poem by John Keats, a haggard and heartbroken knight is described with words used chiefly for their connotations:

> I see a lily on thy brow,
> With anguish moist and fever dew;
> And on thy cheeks a fading rose
> Fast withereth too.

The stanza does not mean to literally suggest that a lily grows on the brow of the knight, or a rose on his cheeks. *Lily* connotatively suggests the paleness on the brow of the sorrowing knight; *rose*, likewise, connotatively refers to the pink fading from his cheeks. As might be expected, the language of literature is richer in connotations than the language of science and has contributed many new words to our everyday vocabulary. The following words, for instance, along with numerous others, all originated from literary sources: *Pecksniffian, robot, pandemonium, malapropism, braggadocio.* To find their literary origins, look them up in a dictionary.

Consider, as another example of connotation, any of the number of words that can be used to describe someone's way of walking. Here are a few choices, each connoting a different gait: *trot, sidle, shamble, slouch, amble, march, prance, swagger, saunter, trip, tramp, tiptoe, traipse, waddle, plod, clump.* A writer, depending on how she wishes to characterize a person's gait, would use one or another of these words in the following sentence:

> John _____ over to where Mary sat on the bench looking thoughtfully out at the river.

If John is an immensely fat old man, *waddle, clump,* or *plod* ought to do; if he is a surly adolescent in the middle of a row over his use of the family car, the choice is between *saunter, shamble, swagger,* or *slouch.* If John is an airy, light-footed ballet dancer, he might *prance* or *trip.* If he is a military man, ever conscious of his locomotion and posture, he might *march* or *amble.* If he is a horse, he would no doubt *trot,* and if a conspirator, he would probably *sidle* or *tiptoe.* In any event, the choice of one of these words to express John's gait would vary entirely with what sort of person or lifeform John is and how the writer wishes to characterize him for the reader.

Good writers will use words both for their denotative effects and for their subtle connotative overtones. As you write, try to be aware of the connotative meanings of words you use. *Tinkle* and *boom* both denote noises. But a sensitive writer will not say, "The silver bell *boomed*" nor "The huge cannons *tinkled.*" The writer might, however, quite appropriately say, "The silver bell tinkled," and, "The huge cannons boomed." Consider the following word choices in parentheses; the most appropriate words are italicized:

1. She knew that that black raven circling the sky was a bad (sign, *omen,* thing).
2. Suddenly Belinda's stomach (*twisted,* turned, did an about face).
3. Water (hit, bumped, *slapped*) the rickety pylons.
4. With (stuck-up, *haughty,* bragging) grandeur the old duchess arose from her chair.
5. We did not care for the ornate furnishings of the bedroom assigned to us and considered them quite (funny, ridiculous, *absurd*).

In each case the italicized word is the best choice within the context of the sentence, for it is the atmosphere of any given passage that dictates the choice of words. A dignified atmosphere requires dignified words (Tell the illustrious ambassador that his *dinner* awaits him below); a rough atmosphere requires rough words (O.K., you cursed lumberjack; you eat this *swill* because it's all you get). Choose words carefully for the atmosphere you wish to create.

Connotation in advertising

The men and women who write ads are masters of the connotative word. They know exactly which words play on our desire for the exotic, the daring, the durable, the latest. Without our awareness, they convince us that a person of our "exquisite tastes" and "good common sense" deserves the finest luxuries as well as the best quality. They suggest Sherwin Williams paint because we have a "queen's taste" and "it's fit for royalty." In line with our prudence, we should buy "Quaker State Motor Oil" at "no risk." Mazda, of course, is the car for us because it has "the engine of the future." Buy a certain brand of margarine and, poof, suddenly you have a crown.

A favorite advertising gimmick is the creation of moods, especially those far removed from the workaday world, through the use of connotative words. One ad, for instance, presents a woman in mod clothes wearing "Superior Optical" sunglasses. The advertising copy reads:

> I am. The finest all-by-itself house in Laurel Canyon. Yellow daisies if I'm buying, yellow daisies if he is. Tarot cards and murder mysteries and Kahlil Gibran. Saving for a whole summer in Paris. Champagne for breakfast or root beer popsicles. In love forever, every single time.

Clearly, the words of this ad suggest that a woman who wears "Superior Optical" sunglasses will lead a supposedly charmed life. This life is a blend of the arty (house in Laurel Canyon), the folksy (yellow daisies), the mysterious (Tarot cards and murder mysteries), the exotic (Kahlil Gibran), the sophisticated (champagne and Paris), the informal (root beer popsicles), and the passionate (in love forever, every single time). All this glamor and miscellaneous exotica are offered through the use of connotative words.

Connotation in politics

Verbal *brickbats* are words that arouse an unfavorable response among most people. Here are a few American brickbats:

communist	extremist
terrorist	dictatorship
fascist	subversive

Nothing is wrong with the words themselves, but when they are used as dirty names to condemn one person by playing on the prejudice or paranoia of another, then they are no longer neutral symbols with a specific referent; instead they become red flags that stir people's emotions rather than their minds.

Every political campaign offers abundant examples of brickbats, as candidates for office try to pull votes from the naive public. Democrats, Republicans, and Independents are all guilty. One candidate calls his opponent a *"self-serving hypocrite who panders to the interests of big business* while *ignoring the needs of little people."* His opponent counters with the accusation that the other candidate is *"spreading communist propaganda* and *campaigning over the enemy's borders."* He continues, "With his *reckless fiscal spending* he will *bind America with the chains of socialism* and send our country into the worst depression it has ever had."

The opposite of the verbal *brickbat* is the verbal *bouquet*—words that arouse a favorable response among most people. American examples include:

American	national safety
freedom	peace and prosperity
justice	patriotic

These words shed a healthy glow on any idea associated with them, regardless of evidence or logic to the contrary. Bouquets can be just as harmful in politics as brickbats. They can lull the gullible voter into a sense of false well-being or misplaced trust. Both sides in a political race may offer the voter an *issue-oriented campaign,* a country *where you can pursue happiness through self-government,* cities *made safe for the decent citizen,* a welfare program based *not on starry-eyed idealism, but on justice,* schools that *train our children to be good Americans,* and a new age of *spiritual enlightenment, moral commitment,* and *human rights.*

We have singled out these two political devices—the brickbat and the bouquet—because they are common and easily recognized. You should be wary of them when they are used in an argument; you should be convinced by the logic of the argument, not by the connotations of the words used. The phrase *labor leaders,* for instance, should connote neither a clique of racketeers nor a group of selfless individuals devoted to the welfare of the oppressed. Probably *labor leaders* is best understood as the leaders of an organized group claiming to represent the interests of the worker.

SLANG

Slang is not the same as profanity, bad grammar, or provincial language. In other words, *damn it, he don't know nothing,* or *I reckon* is not slang. Most slang simply consists of new words and phrases that people invent in their desire to give the language vigor and novelty. Often slang consists of coinages and figures of speech used by special subcultures, occupations, or social groups to communicate among themselves.

Slang is formed in many ways. It can develop by normal linguistic processes, such as compounding (*low-down, sob-stuff*), word shortening (*pro, gym, prof, mike, vet*), abbreviating (*VIP, OK, LSD*), generalizing proper names (*real McCoy, roger, guy, jerry*), or borrowing from other languages (*savvy, pronto, kaput*). Much slang develops through the wit of a single person whose catch phrase is so effective that others use it until it is widespread. Some slang is borrowed from the vocabulary of particular activities, as:

> *on the beam* (aviation)
> *behind the eight ball* (pool)
> *tune in, tune out* (radio)
> *cop out* (underworld)
> *cash in your chips* (poker)
> *lower the boom* (sailing)
> *wipe out* (surfing)

Some slang uses standard vocabulary, but twists its meaning, as:

> *bread* (money)
> *sweat* (trouble)
> *joint* (place, or marijuana)
> *drip, creep* (unattractive person)
> *sack* (bed)
> *lousy* (bad)

The good side of slang is that it is spontaneous and direct. The bad side is that it can be imprecise and is often understandable only to a particular group. For these two reasons, because of its imprecision and restricted use, slang should not be used in formal writing. A third and equally important reason is this: the use of slang in your writing will tend to give it a flippant and insincere tone. Unless this is the tone you are striving for (and it usually is not), you should keep slang out of your writing.

USING WORDS

The suggestions that follow should help you use words most effectively in your writing.

1. Use the correct word.
2. Choose concrete words.
3. Choose appropriate words.
4. Use words that sound right.

Use the correct word

Avoid words you do not understand. If you are in doubt about a word, look up its meaning in a dictionary. A paper filled with incorrectly used words sounds pitifully amateurish.

> *Wrong:* Everywhere we saw children who had been *depraved* of food.
> *Right:* Everywhere we saw children who had been *deprived* of food.
> *Wrong:* I will be happy to *appraise* you of what happened.
> *Right:* I will be happy to *apprise* you of what happened.

Choose concrete words

Students tend to use abstract words that cause vague and dull writing. Good writing deals in particulars. For instance, when you state, "My boss is conceited," you no doubt have details in mind—he brags about his money; he expects his help to grovel; he exaggerates his talents; and so on. Let your readers in on these particulars, or they may supply their own, perhaps inaccurately.

> *Vague:* *Everything* looked inviting.
> *Concrete:* The homemade potato salad and the apple pie looked inviting.
> *Vague:* He wore *unusual* clothes.
> *Concrete:* He wore a red gypsy shirt with blue denim overalls topped by a paisley turban.

Note that often you can make a vague sentence concrete by adding particulars:

> *Vague:* White people *deceived the Indians.*
> *Concrete:* White people deceived the Indians by breaking treaties, stealing pastureland, and herding them into sterile reservations.
> *Vague:* She stole the show with her *fine dancing.*
> *Concrete:* She stole the show with her fine dancing, a combination of well-executed pirouettes, bows, leaps, and half-twists.

Choose appropriate words

Your own good judgment and sensitivity to connotation and context must guide you here. Obvious lapses in tone and in style give your writing an awkward, erratic quality, as the following examples illustrate:

> *Awkward:* A student who hopes for a scholarship grant to continue his education will not *blow his chances* by rude attacks on the school board.
> *Better:* A student who hopes for a scholarship grant to continue his education will not *ruin his chances* by rude attacks on the school board.
> *Awkward:* Foolproof statistics about sex are difficult to compile, but one fact is apparent: girls *score* just as often as boys.
> *Better:* Foolproof statistics about sex are difficult to compile, but one fact is apparent: girls have as much sex as boys.

Use words that sound right

Words that rhyme in a single sentence and words that make up an alliterative cluster may make your writing comical or tongue-twisting when you do not wish it to be. Sentences that rhyme internally are easily corrected by rewriting:

> *Rhyme:* At dawn, from behind drawn drapes, we saw her mow the lawn.
> *Better:* At dawn we looked out the window and watched her mow the grass.
> *Rhyme:* Coaching is a demanding job that allows for no compromising in terms of excelling.
> *Better:* The job of coach tolerates no compromises in excellence.

Alliteration is a poetic device of grouping words together that begin with the same sound, like "*fine, frenzied fellow.*" Here the alliterative sound is the repeated initial *f* sound. Alliteration is well suited to poetry, but an obstruction to clear prose. Again, it is easy to correct an alliterative sentence:

> *Alliterative:* Perhaps his puny profits pose no persistently serious problem.
>
> *Better:* It is unlikely that his small profits will become a serious difficulty.
>
> *Alliterative:* Sloppy, slovenly, slatternly speech and inept, incoherent, inarticulate writing sometimes characterize students' work.
>
> *Better:* Students are occasionally careless and inept in their speech, while in their writing they often demonstrate a lack of coherence and articulation.

Both alliteration and rhyme draw attention to themselves and therefore away from your meaning. They should consequently be avoided.

EXERCISES

1. Create an abstraction pyramid (as on page 134) for the following words:

   a. Pencil
   b. Tooth
   c. Cat
   d. Rose

2. In each of the following samples of advertising copy, choose the more salable of the two terms listed.

   a. A (fleet, group) of jets is at your disposal.
   b. X is the restaurant for (fussy, discriminating) palates.
   c. The X slide projector has been especially (put together, engineered) to be run without noise.
   d. Do you want (definite, sure) traction? Get X tires.
   e. X pottery is made by (a craftsman's, talented) hands.
   f. Only X has the (seasoning, flavor) to match the good mood you're in.
   g. The (smell, fragrance) of this body lotion will last and last.
   h. X is made of soft vinyl that looks and feels like (real leather, genuine hide).
   i. (Smart buyers, penny pinchers) will love all the money they save when they buy X.
   j. The X Company hires only (certified personnel, experts) who know how best to meet your needs.
   k. X glue is (tough, strong) and ready.

3. In the following political address, circle the verbal brickbats and underline the verbal bouquets.

My fellow citizens, strange as the words may sound coming from one who has no greater pride than that which springs from his lifelong devotion to the ideals of the Democratic party, in a way it has been a blessing in disguise for us to be out of office. Now the country has had a bitter but eye-opening taste of what Republican rule means. The events of the past few years have exposed with the pitiless spotlight of truth the emptiness and hypocrisy of the promises foisted on the people by the New York advertisers who have been the GOP's propaganda hirelings.

Instead of the forward-looking, dynamic action—end quote—that the slick-penned sloganeers promised during the last campaign, we have witnessed reaction—reaction that has saddled us with the kind of government we once thought had ended forever in the Coolidge-Hoover era—government by and for the privileged few. The GOP still lives in the horse-and-buggy days, even though it rides around in Cadillacs.

The babble, bungle, and muddle in Washington is incredible. Faithful public servants, career people who had long experience in administering government affairs efficiently and economically, with favoritism toward none, have been shoved out to make room for high-paid executives from our giant corporations. As you and I know full well, you can't run a government the same way you run a big business. It takes special talents of the sort that thousands of loyal Democrats possess. But those talents aren't being used. No wonder we have government by confusion.

You are hard-working laboring people, the backbone and sinews of the nation. What have the Republicans done for the common people? Have they cut your taxes, while they slashed the tax rates for those who live in the lap of luxury from dividends, dividends made possible by the sweat of your brow?

Now is the time to redeem America from the money-changers. We must replace the people who swing the golf clubs with people who are ready and able to wield new brooms—brooms that will clean out the mess in Washington. This is our shining moment of opportunity.

—Richard D. Altick, adapted from "Exercise 17"

4. The words in the sets that follow have approximately the same denotations. Underline the word by which you would prefer to be called. Identify what connotation leads you to reject one member of the word pair.

   a. Fanatical/enthusiastic
   b. Politician/statesman
   c. Prying/curious
   d. Frigid/cold
   e. Compliant/servile
   f. Foolhardy/daring
   g. Gullible/trusting
   h. Modest/prudish
   i. Gabby/talkative
   j. Relaxed/loose

5. Explain the differences in connotation among the words in the groups below. Suggest contexts for the use of each word.

   a. Confess, grant, come clean
   b. Obese, plump, bulky
   c. Frighten, intimidate, startle

d. Apparel, outfit, costume
e. Grave, cemetery, final resting place
f. Earthy, terrestrial, mundane
g. Eager, anxious, yearning
h. Champion, back, advocate
i. Catching, infectious, communicable
j. Fragile, brittle, crisp

6. The italicized words in the following sentences tend to evoke negative feelings. Replace them with words that are more flattering.

   a. She is one of the most *bullheaded* people I know.
   b. Have you noticed that he always plays the role of *henchman?*
   c. Let us make sure that he is *blackballed* from our club.
   d. She has *hoarded* a great fortune.
   e. Please ask him to wait before *butting in* again.
   f. We would appreciate it if you would *procrastinate* no longer.
   g. His *dipsomania* should be curbed.
   h. If he were not quite so *bizarre,* he would make a good minister.
   i. We shall interview only people who have demonstrated that they are *pushy*.
   j. We have special jobs set aside for *crippled* people.

7. The following sentences contain words that are incorrect, abstract, inappropriate, or ill-sounding. Replace these words with better ones.

   a. I have no explanation for the fact that America has been a divided nation since its foundation.
   b. In the seventeenth century, John Locke demonstrated lots of guts when he summarized the attitudes that had prevailed time out of mind.
   c. A few minutes ago I had an unsuccessful experience.
   d. They decided to photograph the luxurious plants and flowers.
   e. As lovers they were doomed.
   f. Her vivid speech was indicative of her primitive background and her vivacious, expressive nature.
   g. Enrico Caruso was notorious for his operatic tenor.
   h. My soul is like an enchanted marine craft
      Which, like a sleeping swan, doth float
      Upon the silver waves of thy sweet singing.
   i. Now and then, when I am in a retrospective mood, I look deep into my soul and ask, Who are you?
   j. Dear Parent: I need your help in controlling Freddy's temper. Unfortunately, he tends to resort to physical means or muscular action as a way of winning his point or attracting attention.

k. As a motion picture, *The Godfather* turned me on. It was really out of sight.

l. We are sorry that you implied from our comments that she is angry with you.

m. The soldiers used modern weapons on the village.

n. He is a rocking-socking kind of man—tough in sports, blunt with words, and obdurate in his opinions.

o. Professor Ryan impressed us with quotations from Shakespeare, allusions to characters from the *Iliad,* and all sorts of other stuff scholars learn.

p. She worked on humanitarian projects.

q. Her mother builds things.

r. I get a kick from listening to Channel 28 because the programs are highly educational.

s. Harry hurried to help him lift the heavy steel handles.

8
*Why doesn't
that make sense?*

Logic is a public method of reasoning. It differs from other varieties of reasoning, such as intuition, or the hunch, because it requires that both the *process* and the *evidence* behind a conclusion be shown. The distinction between process and evidence is this: process asserts a relationship between ideas; evidence supports or denies the validity of the asserted relationship. For instance, the statement "Cigarette smoking can be harmful to your health" is asserting a causal relationship between smoking and poor health, in effect claiming that the one can cause the other. The validity of this relationship is supported by overwhelming evidence, such as the following mortality statistics listed in *Smoking and Health: Report of the Advisory Committee to the Surgeon General of the Public Health Service:* cigarette smokers have a 70% higher death rate from coronary artery disease; a 500% higher death rate from chronic bronchitis and emphysema; and a 1000% higher death rate from lung cancer, than nonsmokers. This evidence, along with numerous other facts, support the contention that cigarette smoking can be harmful to a smoker's health. The rules of logic demand that all statements linking ideas together in relationships must be similarly supported by evidence.

Your argument is logical when you can demonstrate that anyone using the same reasoning process and the same evidence must inevitably come to the same conclusion. It is illogical if it is based on a private process of reasoning, or if it fails to consider all the relevant evidence. Logic is simply the result of an attempt to create a method of reasoning that functions independently of any one person; it is essentially neutral and works for interchangeable minds so long as its rules are followed. The opposite of logic is mysticism, magic, or any other system whose claim to truth depends on the special talents of one person.

The reasoning process of a logical argument typically relates ideas by cause, consequence, category, or alternative. Usually, the ideas are connected by link words, such as *therefore, because, infer,* and *since.* Logic requires that the relationship asserted between the connected ideas be valid, be supported by evidence, and be made clear by the link word.

When ideas are related by *consequence,* if the first idea is true, then the second idea is also true as a consequence.

> The Constitution declares that all people are equal in the sight of the law. It is *therefore* illegal for any state to discriminate against any of its citizens.

An idea may be related to another by being its *cause*.

> I vote Democratic *because* that is the way I was brought up to vote.

When ideas are related by *category*, one idea is classified under another.

> From the pouch on this animal that it uses to nurse its young, we *infer* that it belongs to the marsupial order.

An idea may be related to another by being its *alternative*.

> *Either* we do something about pollution now on a gradual basis *or* we shall be faced later on with a massive clean-up bill.

PROCESS OF REASONING: DEDUCTION/INDUCTION

Process of reasoning involves two principal forms of logic—deductive and inductive logic. Deductive logic is reasoning that proceeds from the general to the specific, from something known to something unknown. Here is an example:

> All oranges have vitamin C.   *major premise*
> This fruit is an orange.   *minor premise*
> Therefore, this fruit has vitamin C. *conclusion*

The above formula is known as a categorical syllogism—a three-part logical statement that deduces a conclusion in the third part from information expressed in the preceding two parts. The syllogism is the mainstay of deductive logic and features commonly in our daily thinking. For instance, if you tell a friend, "Avoid buying a Speedmobile; Speedmobiles have bad ignitions," you are unconsciously using a shortened form of the categorical syllogism.

Inductive logic, on the other hand, proceeds not from a major premise to a specific conclusion, but from specific facts and evidence to a generalization. Here is an example. In 1750, James Lind, a surgeon's mate aboard the British ship H.M.S. *Salisbury,* decided to experiment with the effects of diet on scurvy—a disease that was then the terror of seamen all over the world. Lind isolated twelve scurvy victims, separating them into six groups of two. Each group was fed the daily rations of the Royal Navy along with different dietary supplements. Four groups were given cider, vinegar, and ordinary seawater to drink. The fifth group received a gruel recommended by a hospital surgeon, while the sixth group was given two oranges and a lemon each day. Of the twelve stricken men, only two recovered from the disease—the two given the oranges and lemon daily. Lind therefore generalized that the citrus fruit contained some substance beneficial to the cure of scurvy. Further tests confirmed this hypothesis.

Our daily operations in logic involve both deduction and induction. For instance, deductive logic persuades us that lightning, whether it flashes in Los Angeles or in Bangkok, is always electricity; that gravity will be found in Sydney, Australia, as well as in Reno, Nevada; and that the ostrich on the Serengeti Plain of Tanzania can no more fly than its counterpart in the Baltimore Zoo. In each case, deductive logic simply attributes to the individual occurrence or animal the characteristics known to apply to the category to which it belongs.

Inductive logic, on the other hand, provides us with new hypotheses to be used as major premises in deductions. For instance, before the Lind experiment, the policy of the British Admiralty, based on the premise that only malingerers contracted scurvy, was to flog any sailor complaining of its symptoms. After the Lind findings were published, the Admiralty abandoned its policy of flogging scurvy victims and, instead, fed them with daily doses of lemon juice. The shift in treatment represented the Admiralty's abandonment of its former major premise on the disease. Ideally, all reasonable people should react in a like manner to the introduction of any new hypothesis that is supported by substantial evidence.

No logical method is error free. Operations of deduction as well as induction are subject to common flaws. It is quite possible to deduce a patently false conclusion from a categorical syllogism, as in the following example:

All dogs have four legs.
This animal has four legs.
Therefore, this animal is a dog.

But the animal could also be a rabbit, a camel, or even a hippopotamus, to mention a few other possibilities. Here is a similar error, taken from a student paper:

I agree that the professor who refused to sign the loyalty oath of the university should be fired. If he was loyal, he would have signed the oath. Communists never want to sign loyalty oaths. And since the professor did not want to sign the oath, it is obvious to me that he is a communist.

The syllogism, once untangled, reads:

Communists don't sign loyalty oaths.
The professor didn't sign the loyalty oath.
Therefore, the professor is a communist.

This is a faulty conclusion, one that does not follow from the major premise. Every four-legged animal is not necessarily a dog, neither is everyone who refuses to sign a loyalty oath a communist. If the major premise of the syllogism had been, all who refuse to sign loyalty oaths are communists, then it would have followed that the professor, by refusing to sign, must also be a communist. But such a major premise would have been silly and patently untrue.

The presence of undefined, ambiguous terms in the major premise is another error of student syllogisms. For instance, consider the following:

Anyone who is against cleaning up the environment is obviously a right winger who only wants to make money. It has been shown that General Motors only wants to make big cars and is against cleaning up the environment. To me, this shows that General Motors is a right-wing company that is only interested in its profits.

"Right winger" is an ambiguous term. No amount of logical exertion will make this syllogism more than a mechanism for name-calling. The category of "right wingers" has to be more clearly defined before the reader can understand the characteristics being imputed to General Motors by the deduction.

Inductive logic, on the other hand, suffers from a common error known as the "hasty generalization." Consider, for instance, the following experience. A man goes to a movie one evening during which a slight, red-haired patron wearing a bowler hat goes berserk in the theatre. The following day at a baseball game, our man witnesses a fan in a bowler hat who runs onto the field and attacks the shortstop. Driving home from the game, our man pulls alongside a Cadillac at a stoplight and sees the driver, wearing a bowler hat, hitting a companion. That very evening, as our man watches the news on television, Walter Cronkite reports that a bowler-hatted sniper has occupied an apartment building, from where he is now taking pot-shots at pigeons in Central Park. Our man generalizes hastily from these four instances: All bowler-hatted men are dangerous. This become a major premise in his library of beliefs that he will use from now on to deductively implicate anyone he comes across who wears a bowler hat. Should a bowler-hatted person wish to move into his neighborhood, trouble will no doubt result.

The hasty generalization is an error caused by a misinterpretation of evidence. It cannot logically be deduced from four examples that all bowler-hatted men are dangerous. The evidence is simply not sufficient to support such a broad generalization. A generalization, to be reasonably accurate, must be based on what statisticians term an adequate sample—one large enough to be truly representative. The next time someone comes to you and admonishes, "Don't take a class from Professor X; he's a very tough grader," ask to see the evidence on which this generalization is founded. More likely than not, you'll find that the generalization is based on a cursory talk with two students, both of whom got D's from Professor X. A more reasonable interpretation of this evidence is that the two students deserved to get D's. Even if the evidence of Professor X's hardheartedness is based on the gloomy testimony of twenty students—all of whom got D's—this is still not sufficient evidence to convict Professor X of cruelty to students. Perhaps Professor X teaches a mammoth course that enrolls 1,000 students—in which case a mere 20 D's might be enough to charge him with excessive leniency. Or perhaps the course Professor X teaches is an intrinsically difficult course, such as calculus. Or the 20 D's given out by Professor X—compared to 100 D's for the same course given by Professor Y— make him by far the easier grader of the two. The point is that evidence is complicated and susceptible to being misread.

In student essays, hasty generalizations are often found masquerading as major premises in concealed syllogisms as, for instance, in the following student paragraph:

> When I was a sophomore in high school, I met a boy named Jamey. Jamey wore his hair long and dirty and hardly ever washed it. He also had a beard that the principal made him trim. When I first met Jamey, I could tell from his hair that he was a pot smoker. He asked me to go to the drive-in with him, but I said that I could not. I knew he was going to want to smoke.

Imbedded in this paragraph is the syllogism:

> All students with long hair and beards smoke pot.
> Jamey has long hair and a beard.
> Therefore, Jamey smokes pot.

The major premise proposes another "bowler hat" generalization and is consequently faulty. Common sense tells us that just because someone has long hair and a beard, it does not necessarily follow that he smokes marijuana. If the writer had investigated further, she would likely have discovered many long-haired, bearded students who do not smoke marijuana. Likewise, our man with the prejudice against bowler-hatted men would have found enough decent bowler-hatters to outfit an army.

The fairness and accuracy of any categorical syllogism rest on the accuracy of the information expressed in its major premise. An inaccurate major premise will unerringly lead to an inaccurate deduction. Carried to the extreme of inaccuracy, the categorical syllogism leads to stereotyping and prejudice. During the nineteen-sixties, for instance, it was commonly believed that people's political sentiments could be deduced from their appearance. Long hair on a man was thought to indicate a radical/liberal; short hair, a conservative. Studies have shown that this is a false notion; hair length does not indicate political leaning. The shallow evidence suggests that it does; deep evidence denies any connection. Deep evidence is not merely observational but is formally gathered and assembled by impartial research. All other evidence is shallow. Hasty generalizations are usually supported by shallow evidence but contradicted by deep evidence. Anyone who wishes to think logically must override any generalizations that are denied by valid, deep evidence.

Many arguments begin with an assumption that is based on an unproved generalization. This assumption is usually not stated, but implied:

Argument:	Capital punishment should be abolished *because* it has been proven to have no deterrent effect on crime.
Unstated assumption:	Capital punishment exists because people believe it to have a deterrent effect on crime.
Argument:	Violence on television should be censored before all our young people become criminals.
Unstated assumption:	Violence on television contributes to criminal acts among young people.
Argument:	I am a Democrat because I am a liberal.
Unstated assumption:	Democrats are liberal.

The assumption with which it begins is the jugular vein of any argument. The following arguments are doomed because they begin with an initial assumption that is questionable.

Argument:	We need more punishment, not less. All the statistics reveal that crime rates are up and are continuing to rise. What we need are more prisons, more guards, and most of all, severer punishment for criminals.
Questionable assumption:	Punishment deters crime.
Argument:	Pornography must be held in check unless we are willing to tolerate the rising incidence of rape.
Questionable assumption:	Pornography causes rape.
Argument:	The speaker, like all Republicans, was a conservative, and so it is to be expected that he will adopt a conservative position on this issue.
Questionable assumption:	All Republicans are conservative.

BREAKDOWNS IN THE PROCESS OF REASONING

A valid argument links ideas together in a valid relationship. Most errors in reasoning are caused by a breakdown in the linkage between ideas. Consequently, an argument is invalid if the relationship expressed by a link between ideas is false, if the link between ideas is blurred by poor wording, and if the argument fails to focus on the point of contention. The three most common errors in reasoning are, therefore,

1. Poor linkage caused by a faulty relationship
2. Poor linkage caused by poor wording
3. Poor linkage caused by the failure of an argument to focus

Faulty relationship

A breakdown in the reasoning process occurs when one idea is linked to another in a faulty cause, consequence, category, or alternative relationship. Here are some examples.

For many years baseball players have sported mustaches and long sideburns, and in my opinion they played better baseball. The batting averages were twice what they are today. I might add that with their mustaches and long sideburns the Oakland A's won the World Series. So, if long hair affects the players' performance, then all players should have long hair and mustaches.

157

In this example, the causal relationship is faulty. The link implies that long hair and a mustache causes a player to play better baseball. There is no evidence to substantiate such a relationship. A baseball player may simultaneously have long hair and a high batting average without the one causing the other.

> Women are by nature superior homemakers. Their natural talents lie in the realm of cooking and interior decorating. Therefore a woman's place to excel is in the home.

The consequence relationship in this argument is faulty. The fact that some of the greatest cooks and interior designers have been men is evidence to the contrary.

> The reason the Swiss are such good watchmakers is that they live in a small country; thus they become accustomed to working with diminutive machinery and tools.

This is an example of a faulty causal relationship. It is more likely the watchmaking ability of the Swiss is due to years of careful individual training.

> A man who has had only one homosexual experience must also be termed a homosexual.

The category relationship in this argument is faulty. According to the studies carried out by Alfred Kinsey and others, a majority of American men have had at least one exploratory homosexual experience before establishing a stable heterosexual relationship. Sociologists do not categorize such men as *homosexuals;* if they did, homosexuality would be the norm, rather than a minority form of sexual expression.

> What is a man? I say that a man is an animal who is strong, self-reliant, and willing to defend self and family against any danger.

The category linkage between ideas here is faulty. Based on the above, a bull also qualifies as a man.

> Either we stop the publication of *Hustler* magazine or we accept the fact that our children will be perverted.

This is an example of a faulty alternative relationship, also termed a faulty dilemma. The relationship suggests only two alternatives, when more are available.

A special kind of faulty relationship between ideas can occur when they are equated through the use of an analogy. Two ideas may be brought into relationship with each other despite the fact that they involve different values and principles. The result is likely to be an oversimplification of the argument.

> You wouldn't change surgeons in the middle of a difficult operation. Likewise, let us not change governors in these days of severe crisis.

The analogy here is simplistic and misleading. Governing a state has little in common with a surgical operation to justify the analogy. The following analogy is also simplistic:

> The Federal government and its budget are like a household and its budget. Either the spending is held to conform with the amount of money both have, or both will have to go bankrupt.

The Federal government is vaster and subjected to many more complex variables than a household.

Analogies serve a useful and explanatory purpose where they are used to illuminate minor points of an argument. It is, however, risky to frame a massive argument in the language of an analogy. Instead, deal directly with the issues of the argument, and use analogies to explain minor points.

Poor wording

Fuzzy wording blurs the relationship between the linked ideas.

> Should parents spend time openly discussing sex with their children? The advocates of this idea say that it is definitely part of *good parental training*.

The ambiguous wording of this argument implies that the parents are being trained by the children, rather than the other way around.

> *Rewrite:* Should parents spend time discussing sex with their children? The advocates of this idea say that it is definitely part of *the sound upbringing of any child*.

Here is another example.

> The theory of evolution is a complex idea wherein all living things are related to one another *since* they all come from the same common ancestor far back in geologic times. Through evolution new species arise from preceding species of plants and animals that were simpler. This has been happening since plants and animals first existed on earth, and it is still going on. *Therefore,* all living things bear a relationship to one another and this is called the theory of evolution.

This argument is hazy because the writer uses two link words when there are only two ideas to be linked: the theory of evolution and what it states.

> *Rewrite:* The theory of evolution states that all living things are related through a common ancestor. New species of plants and animals are believed to have evolved from simpler species. Evolutionists contend that the process has always occurred and is still occurring, and that *consequently* all living things bear a relationship to each other.

Now *consequently* is the only link word, and the relationship between the ideas is clearer.

> Studies show that *the murder rates* for policemen, guards, and private citizens are lower in states without the death penalty.

This statement implies that policemen, guards, and private citizens are doing the murdering. It also unnecessarily divides the population into three overlapping groups.

> *Rewrite:* Studies show that the murder rates are lower in states without the death penalty.

Failure of an argument to focus

If you attack an opponent instead of the opponent's logic, you are committing an error of process by failing to focus your argument on the point of contention. In a sense, you are linking ideas that really have no bearing on the issue. The commonest error of this type is called an *ad hominem* argument, meaning an argument against the man. Here is an example:

Ralph Nader's investigation of General Motors and his subsequent findings are probably best explained by his political leaning. His record reeks with what has been called "radical liberalism," which is an ingrained anti-Americanism.

Ad hominem arguments are frequently resorted to by debators and writers probably because they allow a vent of passions at little expense to the mind. However, from a logical point of view, they falsely link ideas that bear on personality, rather than on the issue.

Other evasions of process are cataloged by logicians under a variety of colorful names. An argument that "begs the question" is one that moves in circles. It neither says nor adds anything new to the proposition, as:

I am against prostitution because it causes women to sell themselves.

The "red-herring" is the introduction of a subsidiary, emotionally loaded issue that draws attention away from the real one. For instance, in an argument about whether or not schools should be allowed to lead children in group prayer, someone might stand up and say:

The question here is whether or not we intend to allow atheists to dictate school policy, whether or not we intend to allow the opinions of atheists to dominate our lives.

That, of course, is not the question. Nor does it follow that an opponent of public school prayer is necessarily an atheist. But the assertion is so emotionally loaded that it is apt to distract attention away from the real issue and, perhaps, to put the opponents of public prayer on the defensive.

The *ad populum* argument is an appeal to common feelings, passions, and prejudices through the selective use of unflattering phrases, such as "creeping red socialism," "robber baron businessmen," or "demagogue tendencies," to describe an issue to which one is opposed. Conversely, the favored issue is described with flattering phrases, such as "for our beloved country," "freedom to choose," and "good for the common man."

There are fascists who will encourage rampant slobbiness in our public parks. They will not stop the careless boobs who dump eggshells, beer cans, and waste paper in a spreading desecration of the purple mountains' majesty of our American landscape. I say the park should be fenced for the sake of loyal American patriots who love their land and want to keep it beautiful.

> A logical argument must meet the following demands of process:
>
> Its initial assumption must be true.
>
> It must focus on the subject and not on personalities or side issues.
>
> Ideas must be linked to express accurate, concise, and valid relationships between them.

EVIDENCE IN REASONING

Evidence is the bond between a reality and its representation by an idea. A student who writes, "I believe that capital punishment should be continued because it deters murders" is making an assertion about a reality. He is saying that a person on the verge of committing a murder could be deterred from doing it by the existence of a death penalty. If the evidence bears out his assertion, then he has accurately represented the reality; if it does not, then the reality is misrepresented in the assertion. The proof is to be found in evidence.

Evidence consists of the following:

1. Facts
2. Experience
3. Witnesses
4. Authority

Facts

A fact is information that accurately represents the reality. Facts are subjected to but unchanged by interpretation. For instance, the *Encyclopaedia Britannica* lists the following statistic on capital punishment as a fact:

> Between 1930 and 1965 . . . 50% of those executed for murder, 90% of those for rape, and 50% of the rest of those executed for some other crime were nonwhite.

One student may interpret this fact to mean that nonwhites were more harshly treated by the courts because of their lower status; another may conclude that nonwhites had a higher capital crime rate because of their poverty. But in either case, the statistic itself remains the same. To state that "American religion has been practical, pious, sentimental, childlike" cannot qualify as a fact because the statement is impossible to verify against reality. On the other hand, the statement that in 1976 the Hare Krishna religion numbered 2,500 core members can qualify as a fact because presumably this sect keeps records that can confirm or refute the accuracy of the number.

The following rules govern the use of facts:

1. Facts must be accompanied by a traceable source. It is not permissible to list an item as a fact without listing its source. The reader must have the opportunity to investigate a suspect source of facts.
2. Facts must be relevant to the argument. If you are writing a paper arguing for conservation of the bald eagle, you should list appropriate facts dealing with the decline of the eagle population. It is useless to include the metabolic rate of the bald eagle as a subsidiary fact unless this has some bearing on your argument.
3. Facts must either be current or still valid. If, for instance, you are quoting figures from a book, they should come from its latest edition unless they are unchanged from those in the previous edition. It is improper to quote an old study where a revised version with new data exists, unless you specify in a footnote what you are doing. An old study may be quoted so long as its information is still regarded as valid by experts in the discipline.
4. Facts must be used with integrity. While it is easy to distort, suppress, or misrepresent a fact, writers must resist all such temptations if they value their reputation.

Experience

Experience, where relevant to the issue being argued, is acceptable evidence. You can appeal to experience when a contention cannot be settled by facts and statistics but must be decided by common sense. Here, for example, an appeal to experience is made by an author who is arguing against the belief that punishment deters crime:

> This misplaced faith in punishment may rest on the unrealistic theory that people consciously decide whether to be criminal—that they consider a criminal career, rationally balance its dangers against its rewards, and arrive at a decision based on such pleasure-pain calculations. It supposedly follows that if the pain element is increased by severe punishments, people will turn from crime to righteousness. A little reflection reveals the absurdity of this notion. How many of the readers of this textbook can recall when they seriously considered a criminal career, not as a vague daydream but as a concrete possibility? How many weighed this possibility and, after balancing all the considerations, "decided" against it? For most law-abiding citizens this deci-

sion is not a conscious, rational choice, thoughtfully made at some crucial moment; it is an unconsciously developed way of life, a set of values, and a group of expectations, all emerging from the thousands of events and incidents forming their social experience. Nor is it likely that the professional criminal ever makes such a conscious choice.

An appeal to experience must involve a general and shared experience that is recognizable to typical readers. This kind of appeal is asking for common-sense reflection; if it is based on an esoteric experience few readers have had, it cannot evoke reflection. The appeal to experience cannot replace harder data; it can only supplement it.

A personal experience can strengthen an argument if the experience typically reflects a common condition. For example, the following Vietnamese student used her personal experience to support the thesis that war refugees face serious problems in their adopted countries:

My father was a pharmacist in Vietnam, but since he could not use his degree in the United States, he had to work as a janitor for a small printing shop. While he did this work gratefully, he felt that he was no longer achieving his career goals. My mother, because of the language handicap, could not find any job. She worried day and night about the financial state of the family. Moreover, because she could not speak the language and did not understand the customs of Americans, she had a very difficult time making any friends. Even though our entire family was better off materially in America, we all secretly admitted to ourselves that we had been happier in Vietnam.

Witnesses

Witness testimony is also acceptable evidence. A preamble to the testimony should identify the witness, place him at the scene, and list his claim to credibility. Here, for example, is witness evidence used in a paper arguing for the existence of UFO's:

Lonnie Zamora of Socoro, New Mexico, was a police officer for five years. His record indicated that he was a stable and honest person. He sighted a UFO on one of his patrols. He described the spaceship as "taking off straight up" with a deafening roar.

The fact that a witness is a police officer adds to his credibility and is therefore worth mentioning.

Some witness evidence will not require a direct quotation, but merely a paraphrase of what witnesses said they saw.

> In every major city in the world our air is full of smoke and smog. When the Apollo 10 astronauts flew over Los Angeles about twenty-five thousand miles away, they saw a yellow smudge.

Most of the witness testimony you use will come from other sources, which must be plainly listed in footnotes. In using witness testimony, you should bear these other points in mind:

1. Quoted testimony must not be edited to slant it in favor of your argument. If you use a partial quote from witness testimony, you should place three dots (called ellipsis) before or after your quotation to indicate its incompleteness.

> Alma Atkins, an off-duty nurse who witnessed the riot, was quoted in *Harper's* magazine as saying that, "The police seemed to come from nowhere. A brick was suddenly hurled by one of the demonstrators. . . ."

The dots indicate that further testimony following *demonstrators* has been omitted.

2. Quotations should be brief and relevant to your argument. Long quotations of witness testimony tend to clog the flow of your writing.
3. Discredited witnesses must not be quoted. If you use the original testimony of a witness who has since then been discredited, you should notify your reader either in a footnote or in your commentary.

Authority

Quoting an authority whose position coincides with your own can be an effective source of evidence. Its usefulness, however, will vary with the prestige of the authority. If he or she is prominently known in the field or on the subject under discussion, quoting can add substantially to your evidence; if he or she is relatively obscure, quoting may add nothing. The credentials of your authority should be mentioned as preamble to your quotation. Here are some sample statements introducing authorities about to be quoted from:

> As Professor Harold A. Thomas, Jr. of Harvard's Center for Population puts it . . .
>
> Another scientist, Colin M. MacLeod, formerly of the U.S. Office of Science and Technology, says . . .

U Thant, former Secretary General of the United Nations, has suggested . . .

Research by Margaret Mead on this subject indicated that . . .

An authority may also be anonymous. The opinions stated in reputable dictionaries and encyclopedias are also accepted as a kind of authority evidence.

It may take some detective work on your part to verify the credentials of your chosen authority. Just because someone has published and has a degree, it does not follow that this person is necessarily an authority in that field. The final criterion is whether or not the person is recognized as an authority by peers. Some common-sense research may therefore be necessary into the credentials and accomplishments of your chosen authority. An excellent reference source for this sort of information is the *Who's Who* series, which lists noted specialists in a variety of subject areas.

If the individual is not listed in *Who's Who,* you should check such items as the school at which he or she was trained, membership in recognized professional organizations, publications, and academic honors. While it is easy enough to check on the publications of a chosen authority, it is more difficult to assess the quality and reputation of the journals in which these publications may have appeared. The simplest thing to do in that case is to ask someone in the field. For instance, if you want to know whether a certain history journal is regarded highly, ask a history instructor. Bear in mind also that a person may be trained in one field and considered an authority in another. Ralph Nader, for instance, is trained as a lawyer, but is widely regarded as an authority in consumer affairs. Conversely, a person may be highly qualified in one area, but definitely no authority in another. It would be a waste of time, for instance, to quote Nader as an authority on theology. His standing in the field of consumer affairs gives him no particular authority in theological matters.

Authority evidence, like witness testimony, should be used to supplement data uncovered by your own research. It cannot replace factual evidence. Argumentative papers call for original probing of your own; a student who simply catalogs a variety of opinions from authorities and then quotes them in good reportorial fashion is evading the assignment and is likely to be rebuffed by the instructor. The ideal is to intersperse your own findings with those of authorities.

A good argumentative paper will draw on various kinds of evidence. It will amass facts of its own, support interpretations of them with quotations from authorities, appeal to experience where common sense can add to an understanding of the issue, and quote witnesses where appropriate.

BREAKDOWNS IN EVIDENCE

Various breakdowns of evidence can occur. We will deal with the commoner failings:

1. Congested and unnecessary evidence
2. Uninterpreted evidence
3. Dogmatic generalizing from evidence
4. Vague evidence
5. Distorted evidence

Congested and unnecessary evidence

Congestion occurs when too much evidence is incoherently marshaled behind the line of an argument. Bear in mind that evidence is merely backing for a contention; it should support the thesis of your argument, not usurp it. This example is drawn from a paper arguing for the legalization of prostitution:

> In Paris there are an estimated 10,000 prostitutes. In London, estimates have placed the prostitute population at 6,500. In Hamburg, Germany, there are an estimated 5,000 prostitutes. In New York City, the "hooker" population has been put at 8,000 by police. The prostitute population of Plato's Athens has been estimated in the hundreds. In Egypt, during the reign of the Pharaohs . . .

And on to China, Hong Kong, and Babylon. The point? A frail, "There have always been prostitutes." The evidence overproves the point; moreover it bogs down the line of argument.

> *Better:* Evidence indicates that prostitution flourished in Plato's Athens, in ancient Egypt, dynastic China, and even in the Babylon of Biblical times. Today, the prostitute population ranges from an estimated 10,000 in Paris, 8,000 in New York City, to 6,500 in London. Prostitution is likewise found in every major urban area of the world.

Sometimes evidence is simply unnecessary. One student accumulated an impressive battery of statistics to prove that obesity is due to a high caloric food intake—a contention readily accepted today by most people. An argument will sink with too much evidence, just as it will float away with too little.

Any evidence used must have a direct bearing on the thesis of an argu-

167

ment. Here, for instance, in a paper arguing that the 1972 United States sale of grain to Russia caused a marked price inflation in our country, a student becomes fascinated with Soviet agriculture after the Second World War. The reader is deluged with subsidiary information about it:

> After the Second World War the idea of collectivization was obnoxious to the Russian, Ukrainian, and Turkic peasants of the U.S.S.R. and was opposed by them. For instance, instead of working the land in large brigades, collective farm workers preferred smaller work units, consisting of members of one household, which in essence meant operating an individual farm within the collective system. Some peasants went so far as to illegally increase their private plots to the detriment of the collective property. This eventually led the government to transform the collective farms into amalgamated collective farms called *sovkhozy.*

These facts, while providing the reader with interesting information about agrarian Russia, have no direct bearing on the argument that the grain sale caused inflation in the United States. The student's side excursion merely dulls the force of the thesis.

Use evidence to prove, not to impress!

Students sometimes believe that a wealth of evidence showing diligent research will make a better paper. This is not necessarily so. You should deploy only the evidence required to reinforce your major contention. Most likely, you will not be able to use all the evidence your research turned up. Some of it will have to be left out.

Uninterpreted evidence

Uninterpreted evidence is meaningless. You should immediately blend all evidence into the thrust of your argument by interpreting it. Furthermore, evidence stockpiled in one paragraph and then interpreted two paragraphs later loses its impact on the reader. All evidence should be interpreted as soon as it is given. The interpretation should answer the question, So what? immediately after the evidence is given. Here is an example:

> *Evidence:* In 1830 there were 1 billion people on earth. By 1930 there were 2 billion, and by 1960 there were 3 billion. Today the population is 3½ billion persons. By the end of the century or within the next thirty years the population will be approximately 7 billion persons.

So what? Many experts believe that a population of 7 billion persons would exert such a drain on our resources that the species itself may be imperiled.

Dogmatic generalizing from evidence

Nevertheless, it pays to be cautious in interpreting the meaning of evidence. Too often, students base dogmatic and rash assertions on frail and inconclusive evidence. Most of the time, an assertion almost as strong could be made from the evidence if it were properly worded to allow a cautious edge. Here are some examples:

Dogmatic: The evidence means, finally and flatly, that UFO's do exist, and that they are surveying the earth and its lifeforms.
Cautious: Indications are firm and strong from the evidence, that UFO's do exist, and are possibly involved in surveying the earth and its lifeforms.
Dogmatic: And so, from the evidence, evolution is shown to be dead wrong, and the Bible's account of how life began on earth is shown to be the correct version.
Cautious: The evidence indicates that, once the premise of the Bible is accepted, a strong case can be made for the accuracy and consistency of its version of how life began on this earth.

Few things are flatly one way or the other. Most of us have to pick our way cautiously through complex and often conflicting evidence. Dogmatism in a conclusion is therefore most often seen as an indication not of foolproof evidence but of a closed mind.

Word your conclusions cautiously!

Vague evidence

The best evidence is the most specific; the worst is the most vague. Here is an example of vague evidence:

Every year, tons and tons of pollution caused by human beings enter the air in the United States.

The assertion is undoubtedly true, but vague.

> *Better:* It is estimated that some 200 million tons of pollution caused by human beings enter the air in the United States each year.

Numbers have a finite, visible, and persuasive effect. Use specific evidence wherever possible.

Distorted evidence

Evidence, properly orchestrated, highlighted, or suppressed, can be manipulated as proof for almost any assertion. Statistics are especially vulnerable to distortion. A bank may advertise that the amount of money it will lend is high but will not mention that its interest rates on saving accounts are low. A law school may proudly proclaim that more of its students have passed the bar this year than in any previous year but will neglect to add that this year's enrollment is also larger. Political candidates occasionally brag about the revenue they have brought to their states, conveniently overlooking any outrageous expenditures. Statistical evidence is especially easy to distort because of its inaccessibility to most readers, who will simply accept an author's statistics as accurate. The more specific the statistic looks, the more believable it seems. To illustrate how facts can be distorted, we offer the following piece of nonsense:

> Pickles are associated with all the major diseases of the body. Eating pickles breeds war and communism. They can be related to most airline tragedies. Auto accidents are caused by pickles. There exists a positive relationship between crimes and consumption of this fruit of the cucumber family. For example:
>
> 1. Nearly all sick people have eaten pickles. The effects are obviously cumulative.
> 2. 99.9% of all people who die from cancer have eaten pickles.
> 3. 100% of all soldiers have eaten pickles.
> 4. 96.8% of all communist sympathizers have eaten pickles.
> 5. 99.9% of the people involved in air and auto accidents ate pickles within 14 days preceding the accident.
> 6. 93.1% of juvenile delinquents come from homes where pickles are served frequently.
>
> Evidence points to the long-term effects of pickle eating.
>
> 1. Of all the people born in 1839 who later dined on pickles, there has been a 100% mortality rate.
> 2. All pickle eaters born between 1849 and 1859 have wrinkled skin, have most of their teeth missing, have brittle bones and failing

eyesight, if the ills of pickle eating have not already caused their death.

Even more convincing is the report of a noted team of medical experts:

3. Rats fed 20 pounds of pickles per day for 30 days developed bulging abdomens and their appetite for wholesome food was destroyed.

In spite of all the evidence, pickle growers and packers continue to spread their evil. More than 120,000 acres of fertile soil are devoted to growing pickles. Our per capita consumption is nearly four pounds. Eat orchid petal soup. Practically no one has as many problems from eating orchid petal soup as they do from eating pickles.

Ignoring the context of an assertion is another way to distort evidence. A word or sentence meaning one thing when quoted alone can easily mean something quite different when surrounded by other words or sentences. Advertisements for movies frequently use out-of-context quotes from reviews. For example, the review might say: "For about five minutes *Fruits of Desire* is a topnotch movie, brilliantly acted and magnificently photographed. After that it degenerates into a dismal spectacle of Hollywood hokum." But the advertisement quotes: "topnotch movie, brilliantly acted and magnificently photographed." The point is that you must not take other people's words out of context to make them support your point of view.

THE USE OF EVIDENCE

Evidence should not only be used to support a thesis; it should also play a part in the selection of a thesis. An initial assumption should always be tested for deep evidence before it is used as the premise of an argument. The evidence will indicate whether or not the assumption is defensible as a premise. For instance, if you were writing a paper arguing in favor of capital punishment, you could adopt various premises. Your argument is immediately indefensible, however, it it opens with the premise that capital punishment is worth saving because it deters crime. The evidence shows clearly that capital punishment does not prevent crime. For your argument to be convincing, a new premise must be adopted. Ideally, if you were in favor of capital punishment because you mistakenly believed that it did deter crime, you should be prepared to abandon your support after reviewing the evidence. However, if you continue to be in favor of capital punishment, you must find a new premise for your argument. The new assumption, in turn, will influence the kind of evidence you must gather. Your new defense of capital punishment could be based on a calculation of the cost of executing an incorrigible criminal versus the cost of locking him or her up for life. The argument now rests on the assumption that some lives have no value and should not be maintained at the taxpayer's expense. And evidence can be gathered to show the greater cost to taxpayers if a criminal is given life imprisonment over the death penalty.

Some ideas cannot be supported with evidence. Cosmic generalizations cannot be proven either true or false by evidence; neither can value judgments. Here are some examples of insupportable ideas:

> The bathtub is the most dangerous place in the world.

This is insupportable because the assertion calls for an absurd comparison. What is a "place"? Can the bathtub be compared with the pinnacle of Mt. Everest as a place of potential danger?

> *Better:* Accidents are more likely to occur in a bathtub than anywhere else in the home.

This assertion is supportable with evidence. It may or may not be true, but statistics can be tracked down that show where most home accidents occur.

> Americans are the most God-fearing people in the world.

This statement is insupportable because there is no agreed-on measure of "God-fearingness."

> *Better:* Church attendance in America is among the highest of any nation.

Now the statement can be supported with evidence. Presumably such statistics are kept by someone and can be researched.

Bear in mind that an issue cannot be argued unless it is so worded that it is finite, measurable, and arguable.

> **Word your thesis so that it is supportable with evidence!**

PERSUASIVE ARGUMENTS

The primary function of logic is to persuade. If you observe the demands of logic to show process and evidence, your argument will be logical, but it may not be persuasive. Being persuasive involves more than being logical; it takes in the whole range of writing skills—conciseness, clarity, and the ability to infuse a prose style with personality. We will end this chapter by listing some characteristics of a persuasive argument.

1. A persuasive argument begins at the point of contention. Here are two sample beginnings from student papers arguing against the construction of the trans-Alaska pipeline:

   > *Bad:* I oppose the construction of a trans-Alaska pipeline. But before I give my reasons why I oppose this project, I would like to review the various present sources of crude oil in our country.
   >
   > *Better:* I oppose the construction of a trans-Alaska pipeline because such a project would, in the name of oil, destroy thousands of miles of our northern wilderness, adding to the already staggering amount of pollution on earth.

   Your opening sentence should concisely state the thesis of your argument and your position.

2. A persuasive argument draws its evidence from multiple sources. This is self-evident, yet it is frequently ignored. Sometimes a student will draw on a single authority for the bulk of evidence to support a thesis. Ideally, the direction and force of your research should lead you to different kinds of evidence. Many students, however, in a nonideal manner, confine their research to the minimal number of sources demanded by the instructor. The cure for this is to select a topic that you are really interested in.

3. A persuasive argument is concise and focused. It does not drift off into side issues. If your thesis is, *The polarization of sex roles in American society contributes to the high incidence of divorce,* your essay should marshal facts and evidence to substantiate that contention, ignoring such secondary issues as sex discrimination in employment or why many housewives are pursuing employment outside the home. A concentrated and focused argument is generally more persuasive than an argument that strays and wanders.

4. A persuasive argument has discernable movement. It does not become clogged with evidence nor bogged down with hair-splitting. We suggest that you bear in mind the typical reader's reactions to any argumentative essay or speech:

a. Ho-hum!	(Wake up your reader with a provocative introduction.)
b. Why bring that up?	(State your argument in clear, forceful language.)
c. For instance?	(Supply evidence and facts.)
d. So what?	(Restate the thesis; say what you expect the reader to do.)

5. A persuasive argument begins with an assumption that is either grounded in evidence or defensible. It confines itself to issues that can be supported with evidence, does not attempt to argue the unarguable, nor try to prove the unprovable. While the realm of the unarguable is constantly shrinking before an onslaught of mysticism and fantasy, many instructors would nevertheless find the following theses entirely unacceptable in an argumentative essay.

   a. Hell exists as a place of punishment for sinners to atone for wrongdoing committed on earth.

   b. The Great Depression of the 1930s was caused by a destructive astrological conjunction between the planets Venus and Mars.

   c. Cats and all manner of feline creatures are despicable, nauseating beasts.

   d. Arthur Conan Doyle, creator of Sherlock Holmes, was the greatest detective story writer of all times.

All four propositions are based on personal belief and therefore unprovable in a strictly logical sense.

6. A persuasive argument anticipates the opposition. For instance, if you were arguing that a controversial cancer drug should be legalized, you must not only marshal evidence to show the effectiveness of the drug, you must also answer the arguments of those opposed to its legalization. You might, for instance, introduce these arguments this way: "Opponents to the legalization of this drug claim that its use will prevent the cancer patient from using other remedies proven effective against cancer. This claim, however, misses the point." And then you get down to the point that has been missed.

7. A persuasive argument will sometimes supplement facts, statistics, and evidence with emotional appeal, which must, however, be used with discretion and caution. Emotional appeal is no substitute for reasoned argument or solid evidence. But used in supplementary doses, emotional appeal can starkly dramatize an outcome or condition in a way that evidence and facts alone cannot. For instance, in his argument against capi-

tal punishment, the French philosopher, Albert Camus, after citing impressive statistics to show its lack of usefulness as a deterrent, relates the experience of his father, who had witnessed the guillotining of a murderer in Paris. Camus described in detail what his father had seen, how he had been made physically sick by the experience, and how his father thereafter became a vocal opponent to the death penalty. By narrating the experience of his father, Camus dramatized the brutalizing effect of capital punishment on the lives and values of ordinary people in a way that a detached recounting of the evidence alone could not.

8. A persuasive argument ends with a bang, not a whimper. The conclusion forcefully sums up what the evidence was intended to prove.

> *Weak:* And so, those are the reasons why I favor government subsidy of all campaigns for political office.
>
> *Better:* Clearly, then, a government subsidy of all campaigns for political office would make sure that our elected officials represent people and not money.

EXERCISES

1. Critically analyze the logic of the following generalizations. What objections could you raise? What are the assumptions underlying the statements? Why might a person make such a statement? With what biases?

   a. Culture is dead in our time. There are no Bachs, Mozarts, or Leonardo da Vincis; art now is just manufactured for cheap mass consumption; there are no values or discrimination left in the arts.

   b. I do not know what the world is coming to: nothing but crime and violence in daily newspaper headlines and television news programs; the old values are disregarded shamefully; no one these days has any moral sense, and the world is filled with swindlers.

   c. What the world needs now is love.

   d. If there were not so many foreigners in this country, there would not be so much crime.

   e. Considering the money involved, it is obvious that the only sort of person who goes into the teaching profession is the kind who cannot make a success out of anything else.

   f. Prisoners have an easy life—three meals a day, air-conditioned cells, television, and nothing to worry about.

   g. If only we could live forever! Then we would be *really* happy.

   h. New Yorkers are more sophisticated than Californians, as is a well-known fact.

    i. Wine is better than beer.

    j. Social protestors make America appear to have a lot more problems than it really does. They threaten our way of life.

2. The following arguments do not center on the real issue. How do they get diverted?

    a. The issue in the gasoline rationing threat is whether or not we want to ruin our free enterprise system by encouraging black market activities.

    b. I will never understand what movie critics see in Marlon Brando. He is rude, conceited, and immoral. His first marriage was a scandal.

    c. The Pure Food and Drug Act has prevented the sale of food and drugs that are harmful to the body. In the same way, Congress should investigate ways to eliminate unscrupulous publishers.

    d. No body can be healthful without exercise. And certainly to a nation, a just and honorable war is the true exercise. A civil war, indeed, is like the heat of a fever; but a foreign war is like the heat of exercise and serves to keep the nation healthful.

3. The following arguments are weak due to flimsy evidence. Explain what is wrong with the evidence in each case.

    a. Naturally she is delinquent. She reads ten comic books a week.

    b. Obviously, a marriage works out better if the couple lives together first on a trial basis.

    c. I usually vote the way my banker tells me, since bankers are conservative.

    d. Once criminals get out of jail, in a few months they kill again and get thrown back into jail. This does not make sense to me.

    e. Los Angeles has more alcoholics than any city in the world, as anyone who walks through MacArthur Park on a Sunday afternoon can plainly see.

4. In the following arguments the relationship between the connected ideas is invalid. Identify the problem in each case.

    a. Judging from the trouble in America during the past few years, it is obvious to anybody with a mind that education creates nothing but social unrest, turmoil, and anarchy. Students are a bunch of dirty-minded hippies, led astray by harebrained so-called professors who are bored and so make trouble for decent people.

    b. If big business cannot have tax loopholes, then the consumer will eventually pay the cost of the big business tax loopholes.

    c. If people were virtuous, there would be no need for government. But people are not virtuous; therefore government is necessary.

d. A rise in juvenile delinquency became noticeable after the Second World War. It is clear that war causes juvenile delinquency.

e. Industrialism was not established until after the Protestant Reformation; therefore, Protestantism was one of the causes of industrialism.

f. My parents were like yours: plain, simple, hardworking folks. And if you vote for me, you can be sure that the rights of the common people will be safeguarded.

g. Ivan Ivanovitch has to be a communist. You can tell by his name.

h. She could not have killed her husband because she is the mother of two darling children.

i. Car dealers are dishonest. They are dishonest because they never give you a fair deal.

j. *Valley of the Dolls* must be a good book; it sold over a million copies the first year of its publication.

5. Below is an eleventh-century proof of the existence of God. Analyze its logic.

God is, by definition, an infinitely perfect being. Such a being must have all the essential properties, since it is infinitely perfect. Existence is an essential property. Therefore, God must have existence.

6. Below are three student arguments written on the following assignment: "Would you vote for a female candidate for President? Explain why you would or why you would not." Analyze the logic of each argument. Give reasons for your view.

a. I would vote for a female candidate for President. In fact, I think a woman would make a great President. Women are fairer than men, more patient and less aggressive. These are exactly the qualities our country desperately needs: fairness, patience, and peacefulness.

b. I would vote against a female candidate for President, not because I have anything against women, but because I think that a President needs to put forward an image of strength, and men project more strength than women.

c. I would not vote for a woman because she is a woman; and I would not vote for a man because he is a man. Being a woman or a man has nothing to do with being a good President. The job demands character, strength, and moral leadership. These are sexless qualities which are as likely to be found in a woman as in a man. If given the choice to vote between two candidates, one a woman and the other a man, I would vote for the more qualified.

7. Analyze the logic of the following argument:

In the dawn of human civilization, asserts the Biblical record, a man named Cain rose up and murdered his brother, Abel, in a fit of rage

(Genesis 4:1–8). What was the punishment which God imposed on Cain for this first recorded homicide? Interestingly, it was not the death penalty.

Rather, as you read the account, you will discover that Cain was banished from society—exiled into the wilderness of Nod (verses 9–16). In this case, God allowed Cain to live; the world's first murderer was not put to death.

After those days, according to the Biblical account, men began to multiply on the earth. And soon there followed the second recorded murder in history, when Lamech, a descendant of Cain, slew a young man who apparently had fought with him (Genesis 4:23). No mention is made of Lamech being put to death for his homicide (verse 24).

But as men began to multiply, the earth became filled with increasing violence (Genesis 6:1, 11–12). A cursory study of the Biblical account shows that, in the absence of a death penalty for crimes, the earth became filled with violence! One might conclude that since criminals were not speedily executed or dealt with appropriately, the world experienced a spiraling crime epidemic!

8. The following are poorly worded assertions. Rewrite them to make them more effective.

   a. The criminals chose to murder and, in most cases, have no desire for rehabilitation, or would benefit from psychiatric help.
   b. The editor raises the question, Do parents have the right to defend their children against harm? In defense of this idea he states that the Supreme Court has determined that states have the right to protect the moral development of children.
   c. If we allowed radical students to run rampant, society will be embroiled in chaos.
   d. It has been determined that most murders are passion murders, and therefore they should not be executed.
   e. The problem with the P.O.W. issue is that North Vietnam holds all the trump cards. If we are to get them back, we must meet their terms.
   f. The great majority of crimes have absolutely no relation to drugs. I am not saying none do, for there is a great deal of drug traffic involving crime.
   g. As for the parents, I feel that they have no authority to decide that the embryos will never have the opportunity to experience life, just as they had.
   h. The senator has consistently pursued an evenhanded policy between Israel and the Arab states.
   i. The state university has no business using the taxpayers' money to buy books for the library, which they have not read a lot of that are already in the library.

9. Label and explain the fallacies in each of the following arguments:

    a. The Bible is divinely inspired because God spoke to the prophets of old, who wrote down His Word.

    b. Since our nation is a big business, it should be run by qualified business executives.

    c. Let me tell you what is wrong with the concept of compulsory medical insurance. It is a half-baked plan cooked up by people who are more interested in giving in to the pressures of creeping red socialism than they are in providing better medical care. These people will sacrifice everything to their bigoted faith in a system of fascist regimentation that is abhorrent to the American people.

    d. I shall never vote for Bixel's proposed tax reforms because he was a personal friend of Petro Giardelli, a man suspected of Mafia ties.

10. Analyze the logic of the following syllogistic statements:

    a. No well-educated person would ever pass up an opportunity to travel to Paris. Since Mr. Smedley traveled to Paris, he must be well educated.

    b. Wise men hate violence and crime. Robert Collins hates both of these, which just proves to me that he must be very wise.

    c. Chess is a game played by many brilliant people. When I found out that the Democratic candidate plays chess, I immediately decided to vote for him because he is obviously brilliant.

    d. Tomboys love football. Marjorie loves football. Therefore Marjorie is a tomboy.

    e. My test of whether or not a person is an intellectual is to ask the person about football. If the person likes the game, I know that he or she is not an intellectual. If the person hates football, then I know that he or she is obviously an intellectual.

9

How do I
polish the finish?

MAKE YOUR TITLE DESCRIPTIVE

BEGIN WITH A SIMPLE SENTENCE

PRUNE DEADWOOD

DO NOT OVEREXPLAIN

BE SPECIFIC

AVOID TRITE EXPRESSIONS

USE THE ACTIVE VOICE

MAKE YOUR STATEMENTS POSITIVE

KEEP TO ONE TENSE

PLACE KEY WORDS AT THE BEGINNING OR END OF A SENTENCE

PRUNE MULTIPLE OF'S

BREAK UP NOUN CLUSTERS

USE EXCLAMATION MARKS SPARINGLY

VARY YOUR SENTENCES

KEEP YOUR POINT OF VIEW CONSISTENT

USE STANDARD WORDS

YOUR ESSAY SHOULD END RATHER THAN STOP

REVISING THE ESSAY

Most writers do not produce flawless copy on first try. Instead, they patiently prune their first drafts of deadwood, smooth the rhythm of their sentences, and check their paragraphs for coherence and effect. Revision is this act of cleaning prose of all its linguistic litter. You should revise as often as you think necessary, until you are satisfied with the smoothness of your writing. However, before revising it is best to let the paper sit a day or two to allow yourself to recover from the numbness that comes from overexposure to your own writing.

This chapter is a checklist focusing on the fundamentals of style and usage. You should have your paper in front of you and be going over it as you read. If your writing suffers from such severe mechanical problems as fragments, comma splices, dangling modifiers, and the like, you should consult with your instructor on how to deal with these problems. He or she will probably recommend time in the remedial laboratory or work with one of the practical handbooks in print.

1. MAKE YOUR TITLE DESCRIPTIVE

The title of a paper should describe its content. Avoid puffy, exotic titles like this one on a paper dealing with the use of fantasy in Keats's poetry:

> *Keats: The High Priest of Poetry*
>
> *Rewrite: The Use of Fantasy in Keats's Poetry*

2. BEGIN WITH A SIMPLE SENTENCE

It is stylistically good sense to open your paper with a short and simple sentence. A long and involved opening will repel, rather than attract, a reader.

> The problem that has come up again and again before various workers in the social sciences, and especially before sociologists and anthropologists, and one that has been debated at length in the journals of both disciplines as well as in the classrooms of various universities and colleges across the country, and one to which various answers, none satisfactory, have been proposed, is this: Are social scientists politically neutral, or are they *ipso facto* committed by their research?

If the reader is to be drowned in words, it is more useful to drown him later, after he has committed himself by reading part of the paper. Otherwise, he will simply turn away bored.

> *Rewrite:* The question is this: Are social scientists politically neutral, or are they committed by their research?

3. PRUNE DEADWOOD

Deadwood refers to any word, phrase, or sentence that adds bulk to writing without adding meaning. It accumulates wherever the writing is roundabout and indistinct. Some styles of writing are so vested in wordiness that it is impossible to assign blame to any single word or phrase.

> There are many factors contributing to the deficiencies of my writing, the most outstanding being my unwillingness to work.
>
> *Rewrite:* I write badly mainly because I am lazy.
>
> Anthropologists carrying their studies of primate behavior deep into the tropical forests of Malaysia contribute, through the pursuit of their specialized interest, to the one field that in fact gives us our broadest perspective of human beings.
>
> *Rewrite:* Anthropologists add to our knowledge of human beings by studying primate behavior in the forests of Malaysia.

The solution to wordiness is to be plain and direct—to state your ideas without fluff or pretension.

Aside from wordiness there are other, more specific kinds of deadwood.

a. Many *there are*'s and *there is*'s can be cut, thereby tightening a sentence.

> There are many reasons why businesses fail.
>
> *Rewrite:* Businesses fail for many reasons.

> There is a cause for every effect.
>
> *Rewrite:* Every effect has a cause.

b. Cut all *I think*'s, *I believe*'s and *in my opinion*'s. Such phrases make the writer sound insecure.

> I think that Freud's approach to psychology is too dominated by sex.
>
> *Rewrite:* Freud's approach to psychology is too dominated by sex.
>
> I believe that women should be paid as much as men for the same work.
>
> *Rewrite:* Women should be paid as much as men for the same work.
>
> In my opinion, marriage is a dying institution.
>
> *Rewrite:* Marriage is a dying institution.

c. Cut all euphemistic expressions.

> He went to Vietnam and paid the supreme sacrifice.
>
> *Rewrite:* He was killed in Vietnam.
>
> Last year for the first time I exercised the right of citizens on election day.
>
> *Rewrite:* Last year I voted for the first time.

d. Cut *-wise, -ly,* and *-type* word endings. Such words, easily concocted from adverbs and adjectives, have become popular in college writing.

> *Poor:* Moneywise, she just didn't know how to be careful.
> *Better:* She didn't know how to be careful with her money.
> *Poor:* Firstly, let me point out some economic problems.
> *Better:* First, let me point out some economic problems.
> *Poor:* A jealous-type man annoys me.
> *Better:* A jealous man annoys me.

e. Eliminated all redundant phrases or expressions that can be rewritten more concisely. Here are some typical examples followed by suggested substitutes:

Redundant	Rewrite
in a hurried manner	hurriedly
the fact that she was not happy	her unhappiness
This is a matter that	This matter
She is a woman who	She
owing to the fact that	because
plus the fact that	and

f. Cut all preamble phrases such as *the reason why . . . is because.*

> The reason why wars are fought is because nations are not equally rich.
>
> *Rewrite:* Wars are fought because nations are not equally rich.
>
> The thing I wanted to say is that history has shown the human being to be a social predator.
>
> *Rewrite:* History has shown the human being to be a social predator.
>
> The point I was trying to make is that reality is sometimes confused with fantasy in Keats's poetry.
>
> *Rewrite:* Reality is sometimes confused with fantasy in Keats's poetry.

In all such cases the rewrite principle is the same: lift out the heart of the idea and state it plainly.

g. Cut all rhetorical questions.

> That illusion though deceptive is more consoling and less hostile to human needs than reality, appears to be a central theme in Keats's poetry. Why would anyone feel this way? Why did Keats himself feel this way? Possibly because he had tuberculosis and knew he was going to waste away and die.
>
> *Rewrite:* That illusion though deceptive is more consoling and less hostile to human needs than reality, appears to be a central theme in Keats's poetry. Keats possibly felt this way because he had tuberculosis and knew he was going to waste away and die.

4. DO NOT OVEREXPLAIN

> Some critics sneered at Keats for being an apothecary-surgeon, which is what he was trained for.

> *Rewrite:* Some critics sneered at Keats for being an apothecary-surgeon.

If Keats was an apothecary-surgeon, then that is obviously what he was trained to be.

> As president of the company, which is an executive-type position, he never scheduled work for himself during April.
>
> *Rewrite:* As president of the company, he never scheduled work for himself during April.

The term *president* already lets the reader know that the position is an executive one.

> The watch is gold in color and costs $30.00 in price.
>
> *Rewrite:* The watch is gold and costs $30.00.

That gold is a color and that $30.00 is the price are self-evident.

5. BE SPECIFIC

Lack of specific detail will infect your prose with a pallid vagueness.

> The effect of the scenery was lovely and added a charming touch to the play.
>
> *Rewrite:* The scenery, which consisted of an autumn country landscape painted on four flats extended to cover the entire background of the stage, added a charming touch to the play.

Wherever possible, be specific in description and detail.

6. AVOID TRITE EXPRESSIONS

Some words, phrases, or expressions through overuse have become unbearably hackneyed and should be avoided. Following are some of the most glaring offenders:

187

> in conclusion, I wish to say
> last, but by no means least
> in terms of
> at this time
> each and every
> in this day and age
> slowly but surely
> to the bitter end
> it goes without saying
> by leaps and bounds
> few and far between
> first and foremost
> in the final analysis

Some figurative expressions—most coined centuries ago—have become trite enough to numb. Listed below are a few of these that ought to be carefully scrubbed from every paper:

> busy as a bee
> white as a sheet
> cold as ice
> green with envy
> slow as molasses
> by the sweat of his brow
> over my dead body

7. USE THE ACTIVE VOICE

The active voice is more vigorous than the passive because it allows a subject to stand in its familiar position in front of its verb.

> I took a walk.

The subject *I* occupies the position immediately in front of its verb, *took*. With the passive voice, immediacy between subject and verb is denied. Moreover, the familiar positions are reversed. The verb stands at one end of the sentence; the subject is shunted to the other end. A *by* intervenes between them.

> A walk was taken by me.
>
> During the Depression, fruits and vegetables were hawked on the pavements by unemployed executives.

In some passive constructions, the subject is dropped and the verb orphaned.

> My last trip to Jamaica will always be remembered.

Converting to the active voice reunites subject and verb in their familiar and immediate constructions. The prose is consequently more vigorous.

> *Rewrite:* During the Depression, unemployed executives hawked fruits and vegetables on the pavements.
>
> I will always remember my last trip to Jamaica.

The use of the passive voice is stylistically justified only when an action is more important than its actor.

> There, before our eyes, two human beings were burned alive by gasoline flames.

In this case, human beings are more important than gasoline flames. The passive voice is therefore effective.

8. MAKE YOUR STATEMENTS POSITIVE

Statements that hedge, hesitate, or falter in the way they are worded tend to infuse your style with indecision. Whenever possible, word your statements positively.

> *Poor:* He was not at all a rich man.
> *Better:* He was a poor man.
> *Poor:* "The Cherry Orchard" is not a strong play; it does not usually sweep the audience along.
> *Better:* "The Cherry Orchard" is a weak play that usually bores its audience.
> *Poor:* A not uncommon occurrence is for rain to fall this time of the year.
> *Better:* It commonly rains this time of the year.

9. KEEP TO ONE TENSE

Once you have decided to summarize an action or event in one tense, you must thereafter stick to that tense. Don't start in the past and shift to the present; nor start in the present and shift to the past. Notice the corrections in the following passage:

> Here is what I saw: For two acts the ballerina pirouetted, lept, and
> **fell**
> floated like a silver swallow; then suddenly, she ~~falls~~ to the ground
> **was**
> like a heavy boulder. Her leg ~~is~~ fractured. For years before I ob-
> **had**
> served this spectacular drama, I_∧often heard of this artist's brilliant
> **had watched**
> career. Now I ~~am watching~~ her final performance.

10. PLACE KEY WORDS AT THE BEGINNING OR END OF A SENTENCE

> Workers today have forgotten the meaning of the word
> *quality,* so most craftsmen tell us.
>
> *Rewrite:* Workers today, so most craftsmen tell us, have forgotten
> the meaning of the word *quality.*
>
> Generally speaking, wars cause civilized nations to change
> into barbaric tribes.
>
> *Rewrite:* Wars, generally speaking, cause civilized nations to change
> into barbaric tribes.

11. PRUNE MULTIPLE *OF'S*

A double *of* construction is tolerable; a triple *of* construction is not.

> The opinions *of* the members *of* this panel *of* students are
> their own.
>
> *Rewrite:* The opinions expressed by this panel of students are their
> own.

A good way to break up an *of* construction is to add another verb. In the above example the verb *expressed* is inserted in the sentence.

12. BREAK UP NOUN CLUSTERS

A noun cluster is any string of noun + adjective combinations occurring at length without a verb. The cluster is usually preceded by either *the* or *a*. Noun clusters contribute a tone of unarguable objectivity to writing and have consequently found favor in the writing styles of textbooks, the government, and the social sciences. Note the italicized noun clusters in the following:

> We therefore recommend *the utilization of local authorities for the collection of information on this issue.*
>
> *The increased specialization and complexity of multicellular organisms* resulted from *evolution according to the principles of random variation and natural selection.*
>
> *The general lessening of the work role in our society* does not mean that we have abandoned *the work basis for many of our values.*
>
> One cannot doubt *the existence of polarized groups in America.*

The test for a noun cluster is whether or not it can be replaced by a single pronoun. Each of the above can be.

To rewrite noun clusters, convert one of the nouns to an equivalent verb form.

> *Rewrite:* We therefore recommend the use of local authorities to collect information on this issue.
>
> Multicellular organisms specialized and evolved in complexity by the principles of random variation and natural selection.
>
> Because people today work less than they used to is no reason to believe that we have abandoned work as a basis for many of our values.
>
> One cannot doubt that polarized political groups exist in America.

Noun clusters clot the flow of a sentence. Avoid them by being generous in your use of verbs.

13. USE EXCLAMATION MARKS SPARINGLY

The exclamation mark should be used rarely, and only when a strong emotion is being expressed, as in the following.

> Get out of here, you brute!
> This is what we fought our wars for!

Otherwise, it adds a forced breeziness to your prose.

> We must have urban renewal; and we must have it now!

14. VARY YOUR SENTENCES

Do not begin two sentences in a row with the same word or phrase unless you are deliberately aiming for an effect.

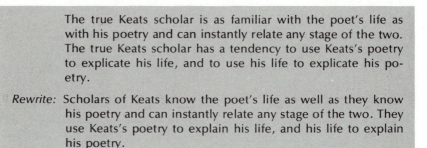

> The true Keats scholar is as familiar with the poet's life as with his poetry and can instantly relate any stage of the two. The true Keats scholar has a tendency to use Keats's poetry to explicate his life, and to use his life to explicate his poetry.
>
> *Rewrite:* Scholars of Keats know the poet's life as well as they know his poetry and can instantly relate any stage of the two. They use Keats's poetry to explain his life, and his life to explain his poetry.

Vary the length of your sentences.

> The man was angry and wanted his money back. But the officer would not give it back and told him to leave. That made the man angrier, and he threatened to call the police.
>
> *Rewrite:* The man was angry; he wanted his money back. But the officer would not give it back to him, and told him to leave, which made the man angrier. He threatened to call the police.

The rewrite is more effective because the sentences have a greater variety in length and style.

15. KEEP YOUR POINT OF VIEW CONSISTENT

When you begin a sentence by referring to *I*, but end it by referring to *one*, you have made the error known as shift in point of view. Such shifts can occur because there are several ways in which you can refer to yourself, your audience, and people in general. You can refer to yourself as *the writer*, *I*, or *we*. You can refer to your audience as *you*, *we*, or *all of us*. You can refer to people in general as *people*, *one*, or *they*. The rule is that once you have chosen your point of view, it must remain consistent.

> *Wrong:* Do not buy Oriental rugs at an auction because if we do, we may get cheated.
>
> *Better:* Do not buy Oriental rugs at an auction because if you do, you may get cheated.
>
> *Wrong:* I try to take good care of my car, for when one does not, they usually pay a big price.
>
> *Better:* I try to take good care of my car, for when I do not, I usually pay a big price.
>
> *Wrong:* Everyone stood aghast when I told them about the accident.
>
> *Better:* They all stood aghast when I told them about the accident.

16. USE STANDARD WORDS

College students can be unrelenting in their invention of newfangled vocabulary and often fall prey to the excesses of neologisms—new or coined words. Voguish words fade as quickly as they appear. By the time this book sees print, such words as *cool, groovy, vibes, stoned, hangups, gyve,* and *fox* will have evaporated from the language. You should use neologisms sparingly—if at all—in your writing. Instead, draw your primary thrust from the vocabulary established over the centuries.

Remember, too, standard words must be written in standard spelling. Double-check any doubtful spelling in a dictionary.

17. YOUR ESSAY SHOULD END RATHER THAN STOP

The ending of your essay should add an air of finality to your thoughts without skidding to a sudden halt. It should cinch your argument, summarize your main point, reassert your thesis, urge some kind of action, or suggest a solution. Regardless of the method, the goal is to leave the reader with the feeling that you have said all that needs to be said. It would be useless to supply you with isolated examples of good endings because each ending must be judged by what was written before. Several kinds of endings, however, should be *avoided*.

a. Endings that are trite

> In conclusion I wish to say . . .
>
> And now to summarize . . .

Such endings are too obvious. If your essay has been properly developed, no special announcement of the conclusion is necessary.

b. Endings that introduce a new idea

If an idea has not been covered earlier, do not be tempted to introduce it as a novelty item in the final paragraph.

c. Endings that are superfluous

> And so these are my thoughts on the subject.
>
> As you can see, my essay proves that carbohydrates are bad for our health.
>
> From these thoughts you will clearly see that Diaghilev is a dominant figure in modern ballet.

These endings to not reflect thoughtfulness on the part of the writer; they are useless in an essay.

REVISING THE ESSAY

Beyond the points that we have listed, polishing an essay involves smoothing out rough spots, shifting ideas, enlarging on a point, or substituting more precise wording. Once you become adept at this kind of doctoring, you will find it enjoyable because it allows you to see your product blossom into excellence. Following is the first draft of a student paper, with revisions marked in boldface. In the left margin we have noted the rule broken.

The Loss of Horror in Horror Movies

SEE RULE 1

~~Goosepimples, Where Are You?~~

SEE RULE 6

~~For various and sundry reasons~~ Audiences are no longer scared as they once were by the old-fashioned horror movies. Over the years people

vampires, werewolves, zombies, and mummies

SEE RULE 5

have been exposed to so many ~~monsters~~ that such creatures have lost their effectiveness as ob-

SEE RULE 3g

jects of terror. ~~Why do you think this happened?~~

Lack of novelty has produced indifference. Originally, a movie monster, such as Frankenstein, terrified audiences simply because the con-

was

SEE RULE 9/3e

cept of a man creating human life ~~is~~ new. ~~Plus the fact that~~ Frankenstein had a sinister plausibility that people of the 1930s had not experienced. But then the public was inundated by a deluge of Frankensteins and other film monsters as studios tried to capitalize on the success of the original. Gradually audiences grew bored as these creations became trite and shopworn. Fearing loss of business, ambitious movie producers tried to in-

lure

SEE RULE 3d/5

vent fresh ~~type,~~ grisly shapes that would ~~bring~~ moviegoers back into the theaters. But their attempts had no effect on a public surfeited with horror, so Frankenstein, Wolfman, and Dracula eventually became comic creatures in Abbott and Costello films.

SEE RULE 12

to produce
Most modern horror films fail ~~in the produc-~~ ~~tion of~~ genuine, goosepimply terror in their audiences. Of course, it may be argued that films like "The Exorcist" and "Jaws" scared many

SEE RULE 5

hysterical screams.
people—even to the point of ~~great fear~~. But these films relied heavily on shock rather than on fear.

SEE RULE 8

differs from fear.
Shock ~~and fear are not the same.~~ Genuine fear involves the unknown or the unseen.

It
~~Genuine~~ ~~fear~~ seduces the imagination into fantastic

SEE RULE 14

and appeals
realms. ~~Genuine fear appeals~~ to our innate store of nightmares. But shock is merely synonymous with repulsion. People are shocked when they see something they don't want to see. For example, the scene of a man being devoured by a shark will shock. The flaw here is that the shock value of such a scene serves more to ~~give the~~

SEE RULE 16

repulse or offend
~~creeps or the heebie jeebies~~ than to frighten.

Today shock devices are used far too frequently in motion pictures; yet, the sad truth is that these graphic displays of blood and gore lack imagination. In older horror movies, the audience was not privy to the horrible details of mur-

der. Scenes ~~which~~ merely suggested evil ~~were~~

SEE RULE 7

audience's imagination supplied the details.
~~used~~ instead, and the ~~details were supplied by~~

~~the audience's imagination.~~ This approach is

SEE RULE 4

more effective ~~in its results~~ than shock because it

spurs the viewers to conjure up their own images

of the unseen. The old movie formulas did not

have to use shock devices, such as bloody mur-

ders, to achieve a pinnacle of horror. Unfortu-

nately, today's audiences have become

bigger and more bizarre
"shock-proof" in the sense that it takes ~~more and~~
doses of horror   One wonders what the ultimate

SEE RULE 5

~~more~~ to scare them. ~~In conclusion, horror movies~~
horror movie will be.

SEE RULE 17a

~~have truly lost their effect.~~

Here is the polished version of the paper, ready to be submitted to the instructor.

The Loss of Horror in Horror Movies

Audiences are no longer scared as they once were by the old-fashioned horror movies. Over the years people have been exposed to so many vampires, werewolves, zombies, and mummies that such creatures have lost their effectiveness as objects of terror.

Lack of novelty has produced indifference. Originally, a movie monster, such as Franken-stein, terrified audiences simply because the concept of a man creating human life was new. Frankenstein had a sinister plausibility that people of the 1930s had not experienced. But then the public was inundated by a deluge of Frankensteins and other film monsters as studios tried to capitalize on the success of the original. Gradually audiences grew bored as these creations became trite and shopworn. Fearing loss of business, ambitious movie producers tried to invent fresh, grisly shapes that would lure moviegoers back into the theaters. But their attempts had no effect on a public surfeited with horror, so Frankenstein, Wolfman, and Dracula eventually became comic creatures in Abbott and Costello films.

Most modern horror films fail to produce genuine, goosepimply terror in their audiences. Of course, it may be argued that films like "The Exorcist" and "Jaws" scared many people—even to the point of hysterical screams. But these films relied heavily on shock rather than on fear. Shock differs from fear. Genuine fear involves the unknown or the unseen. It seduces the imagination into fantastic realms and appeals to our innate store of nightmares. But shock is merely synonymous with repulsion. People are shocked when they see something they don't want to see. For example, the scene of a man being devoured by a shark will shock. The flaw here is that the shock value of such a scene serves more to repulse or offend than to frighten.

Today shock devices are used far too frequently in motion pictures; yet, the sad truth is that these graphic displays of blood and gore lack imagination. In older horror movies, the audience was not privy to the horrible details of murder. Scenes merely suggested evil, and the audience's imagination supplied the details. This approach is more effective than shock because it spurs the viewers to conjure up their own images of the unseen. The old movie formulas did not have to use shock devices, such as bloody murders, to achieve a pinnacle of horror. Unfortunately, today's audiences have become "shock-proof" in the sense that it takes bigger and more bizarre doses of horror to scare them. One wonders what the ultimate horror movie will be.

III

SPECIAL
ASSIGNMENTS

10
The research paper

A research paper assignment is customarily greeted by bestial groans and growls, but if properly executed it can be an exhilarating and creative experience. Writing the research paper will give you the opportunity to become expert in a topic few of your friends, relatives, or instructors may know anything about. Discipline and research know-how, moreover, are added benefits gained from the effort—skills that will be valuable for the rest of your life.

WHY RESEARCH PAPERS ARE ASSIGNED

The research paper is a demonstration of your ability to gather, interpret, organize, and report ideas with objectivity, honesty, and clarity. The exercise will sharpen four special skills:

1. The ability to locate information
2. The ability to sift out pertinent material from a mass of information
3. The ability to acquire a thorough grasp of a limited subject area
4. The ability to write effectively

WHAT THE RESEARCH PAPER IS AND WHAT IT IS NOT

In its finished form your research paper should be the unbiased development of a thesis, carefully documented with pertinent information. As the word suggests, reSEARCH means tracking down information from various sources—perhaps the most intriguing part of preparing the paper since you become a veritable detective of ideas. Your research paper is not a novel or a doctoral dissertation; that is, you are not expected to cover a wide-ranging subject or to aim primarily for a dramatic or poetic impact. You are simply to present in cogent, lucid form the results of a focused investigation. Your final product must be the presentation of an idea, relying on other sources for explanation and persuasiveness.

In developing your paper through research, five common errors should be avoided:

1. A mass of quotations following one another to produce choppy, undigested material
2. A summary of ideas from only one source rather than researching several sources that give varied opinions and facts
3. Mechanical and rhetorical sloppiness, which makes the paper difficult to read
4. Plagiarizing passages from your research sources
5. Use of irrelevant material to comply with an assigned length

KINDS OF RESEARCH PAPERS

College research papers consist of two kinds: 1. the argumentative paper, which evaluates research and takes a stand on it; 2. the report paper, which simply lists the results of research. Your instructor will specify which of these two papers you are expected to write. Because it attempts to prove a point, the following thesis will result in an *argumentative* research paper:

> Far from being the worthless tramps that some people describe, Mexican illegal aliens contribute money and labor to the American economy.

Because it simply requires a survey of eyewitness testimony, the following thesis will result in a *report* research paper:

> American prisons recently have been undergoing reforms in order to improve the environment of prisoners.

Both kinds of research papers are valid college assignments. Many instructors, however, believe that a student's ability to demonstrate judgment and logic are better measured by the argumentative paper than by the report paper, since the latter tends to measure only accuracy, organization, and thoroughness.

Your paper, whether argumentative or report, will consist of three parts:

1. The introductory statement of the purpose or thesis of your paper
2. The body of the paper, made up of supporting evidence for the thesis, presented convincingly and with proper documentation
3. The conclusion, which summarizes the main points of your findings or restates your thesis

What follows is a step-by-step guide to writing the research paper.

STEP 1: FINDING A RESTRICTED TOPIC

The first and most important step in writing a research paper is to choose a subject narrow enough to be handled in five to ten double-spaced and typed pages—generally the length assigned. Do not tackle the job haphazardly. Listen to your instructor's explanation of the kind of work he or she expects. If your instructor assigns a specific topic, your job is considerably simplified. But suppose your instructor has given you the freedom to choose a topic. The job of choosing a topic will require discretion. Here are some suggestions for choosing a usable topic:

1. Choose a subject you enjoy. Subjects chosen for ease alone may bore you and make the assignment intolerable. Browse among the library stacks; pick books that look interesting; leaf through them to discover their contents. Check the magazine racks and reference department for subjects that arouse your curiosity. If you are interested in its topic, your research paper will seem more invigorating than horrendous. Your chances for producing a respectable piece of work are also increased if you have some expertise in the chosen subject. For instance, if you spent last summer visiting the Navajo wildlands, the trip could be the basis for a paper on the Navajo Indians.

2. Choose a narrow topic. The choice of too broad a topic can cause student, paper, and instructor to founder in a bog of unassimilated facts, misunderstood notions, and irreconcilable theories. Avoid such Gargantuan topics as: The History of the Feminist Movement; Great Opera Singers of the World; The Career of Napoleon Bonaparte; Reasons for Wars; The History of the Renaissance. If you have a general subject in mind but not a narrow enough application of it to fit into a paper, you should begin to browse in the subject area. Eventually, some suitably narrow aspect of the subject will catch your interest and lead you to a topic for the paper.

The narrowing of a topic is illustrated in the following example:

Broad Topic	*Narrow Topic*	*Narrower Topic*
The Russian Revolution	The Tsar's family during the Russian Revolution of 1917	The fate of the Grand Duchess Anastasia during the 1918 Ekaterinburg massacre
Whales	The extinction of whales	The ecological extinction of the blue whale

American poets	Edgar Allan Poe	The beauty-death theme in Edgar Allan Poe's poetry
The Dark Ages	The advancement of learning during the Dark Ages	The influence of scholasticism on the advancement of learning in the Dark Ages
The Great Depression of 1929	Financial aspects of the Great Depression of 1929	The results of "Black Thursday" on the 1929 job market

3. Choose a topic for which information is available. If the topic is obscure, new, or specifically related to a foreign country, most of your time will be spent tracking down information instead of assimilating it. It is better to choose a subject about which plenty of information can be located in your school or local public library. If you have doubts about the availability of material, consult your instructor or college librarian.

4. Choose an appropriate topic. The topic should be both intellectually respectable and within your ability to comprehend.

   The following topics are generally unsuitable for college research papers:

   A. A paper that is merely a collection of trivial information is a waste of your time as well as your instructor's. The subject of your paper should be substantial enough for you and the instructor to learn something new from it. The following topics are not important enough to warrant the effort of a research paper:

      The manufacturing of lollypops
      Categorizing the plots in True Romance Magazine
      The political opinions of students at Swanee High School
      How dogs react to various brands of dog food

   B. A paper that depends on a personal opinion for its conclusion will be a waste of your research. For instance:

      What I've observed at rock concerts
      Jesus as my best friend
      Why redheads make the best lovers
      Richard Nixon's cold personality

   C. A paper on a highly controversial issue is dangerous because the issue is usually so obscured by emotion and bias that it is difficult to separate truth from falsehood. Controversial topics such as the following are best avoided:

Abortion—boon or curse
Premarital intercourse—right or wrong
Busing—good or bad
Hollywood—den of iniquity or haven for honest emotions

D. A paper that is too technical and lies outside your instructor's field of knowledge may not get a fair evaluation. For example, if you have a deep-rooted interest in the use of photovoltaic cells in solar energy programs, but your teacher has little or no background in the technical aspects of solar energy, then a paper on that topic would not be a good choice and is not likely to receive a fair evaluation. Likewise, without a solid background in biology and medicine, you would be ill advised to attempt a paper on the use of penicillinase by gonococci in the resistance to penicillin. As a general rule, avoid topics that involve technical terms and concepts and that require esoteric and specialized knowledge.

FOLLOWING THE PROCESS OF AN ACTUAL STUDENT PAPER

A diligent freshman college student by the name of Cory Stewart has been assigned a research paper, which must be completed within six weeks. Observing his work from start to finish, we shall see how the student accomplished the job of writing a research paper.

Cory had no trouble picking a general topic because for some time he has been greatly interested in snakes. From his knowledge of the serpentine legend in the Bible and in Greek mythology, he became convinced that most people harbor an archetypal fear-fascination with snakes. But was this fear based on an inherent, formidable power in snakes or was it simply the result of legend transmitted from one generation to another until snakes had become a culturally embedded phobia? Because he wanted to see what snakes were like in the pure light of science, Cory quickly narrowed down the general topic of snakes to the specific subject of the biological nature of snakes.

Once he had narrowed his topic, he was ready to move to step two.

STEP 2: DISCOVERING THE LIBRARY

Familiarity with the library system is essential to good research because it helps cut down on aimless, unproductive searching for information. Most libraries provide specific written instructions on how to use their facilities.

Some instructors invite the librarian to give an annual orientation lecture. An adequate library should have these materials:

1. Books cataloged according to subject matter
2. Reference works, such as encyclopedias, indexes, atlases, yearbooks, and dictionaries
3. Magazines, newspapers, and periodicals

Generally, the best sources to begin reading on a subject are general works—articles in encyclopedias, chapters in textbooks, histories, biographical references, and dictionaries.

Most American college libraries arrange their materials according to the Dewey Decimal Classification System or the Library of Congress System. Descriptions of the major divisions of these systems should be found at the main desk of the library. Each row of bookshelves will be labeled with the proper catalog numbers. The main divisions of the Dewey system of classification are:

000–099	General works
100–199	Philosophy and psychology
200–299	Religion
300–399	Social sciences
400–499	Languages
500–599	Pure sciences
600–699	Applied sciences
700–799	Fine arts and recreation
800–899	Literature
F	Fiction in English (listed alphabetically by the author's last name)
900–999	History, travel, collected biography
B	Individual biography (listed alphabetically by subject)

The above numbers are expanded by adding decimal places, each with a specific meaning. (For instance *811.52* is the code for *The Complete Poems of Carl Sandburg,* revised and expanded edition.)

The main divisions of the Library of Congress classification are:

A	General works
B	Philosophy, psychology, religion
C–D	History and topography (except America)
E–F	America
G	Geography, anthropology, sports and games
H	Social sciences
J	Political sciences
K	Law

L	Education
M	Music
N	Fine arts
P	Language and literature
Q	Science
R	Medicine
S	Agriculture, forestry
T	Engineering and technology
U	Military science
V	Naval science
Z	Bibliography

This system is expanded by adding letters and arabic numerals. (For instance, *PS 3537.A618 1970* is the code for *The Complete Poems of Carl Sandburg,* revised and expanded edition).

We do not suggest memorizing the cataloging system of the library you intend to use, but you should become familiar with the general number of the subject you have chosen. In many books published in 1972 and later you will find Cataloging in Publication (CIP) data printed on the copyright page. This entry includes all the information on the Library of Congress card except the number of pages in the book and the year of publication, which appear on the same page in the copyright notice. CIP data can be used in making full and accurate records about the materials you have used without having to go back to the card catalog. Since it includes all the classification numbers and tracings (*see below*), you can determine in which categories you will find other useful materials.

Most materials in a library are registered in the card catalog, which consists of an alphabetical file of 3 x 5 cards describing the books the library contains. In addition, some large libraries provide users with printed book catalogs to use in deciding which materials they want to read. You will find three main kinds of cards in a card catalog: 1. author, 2. title, 3. subject.

Attention to the following traditions in library filing will save you time:

1. *Periodicals*. Alphabetically arranged according to titles, current periodicals, such as *Time, Newsweek, The New Yorker, Sports Illustrated, National Geographic,* and the like, are not listed in the card catalog but are usually shelved in a special place in the library.
2. *Clippings*. Many libraries maintain a file of clippings from magazines or newspapers. These are listed not in the card catalog but in special files according to subject.
3. *Microform*. Many libraries have *microfilm* or *microfiche* copies of books, magazines, and newspapers. Microfilm is kept on a spool; microfiche is framed in a card. Both reproductive methods require a mechanical viewer through which a magnified version of the film can be read. Since

AUTHOR CARD

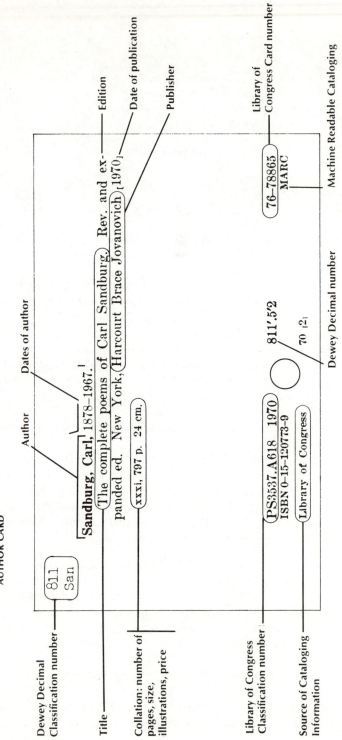

Dewey Decimal
Classification number

Author   Dates of author

Edition

Date of publication

Publisher

Title

Collation: number of
pages, size,
illustrations, price

811
San

Sandburg, Carl, 1878–1967.
    The complete poems of Carl Sandburg. Rev. and ex-
panded ed. New York, [Harcourt Brace Jovanovich] [1970]

xxxi, 797 p. 24 cm.

PS3537.A618 1970
ISBN 0-15-120773-9

Library of Congress

811'.5'2

70 [2]

76–78865
MARC

Library of Congress
Classification number

Source of Cataloging
Information

Dewey Decimal number

Library of
Congress Card number

Machine Readable Cataloging

TITLE CARD

811
San

The complete poems of Carl Sandburg

Sandburg, Carl, 1878–1967.
The complete poems of Carl Sandburg. Rev. and expanded ed. New York, Harcourt Brace Jovanovich [1970]

xxxi, 797 p. 24 cm.

PS3537.A618 1970   811'.5'2   76–78865
ISBN 0-15-120773-9   MARC

Library of Congress   70 [2]

SUBJECT CARD

811
San

Poetry -- Collections

Sandburg, Carl, 1878–1967.
The complete poems of Carl Sandburg. Rev. and expanded ed. New York, Harcourt Brace Jovanovich [1970]

xxxi, 797 p. 24 cm.

PS3537.A618 1970   811'.5'2   76–78865
ISBN 0-15-120773-9   MARC

Library of Congress   70 [2]

microform takes up only 6 percent of the space previously required by regularly bound volumes, it is becoming increasingly popular. Microform is sometimes listed in the card catalog. When in doubt, consult your librarian.

4. *Library Co-ops*. Libraries in the same vicinity generally cooperate with each other in lending material. If a document you need is not available in your library, ask if it can be acquired through a library co-op.

5. *The Readers' Guide to Periodical Literature*. This is perhaps a researcher's most valuable tool. It is an index to most magazine articles published since 1923. Articles in this index are alphabetically arranged by subject and author. The following facsimile of a page from the 1976 volume will help you to interpret its listings:

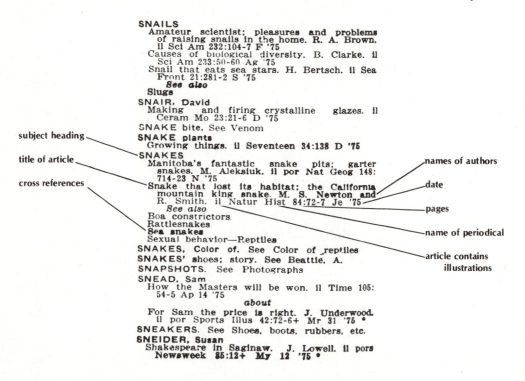

Step 2 cannot possibly convey everything you should know about libraries. Each student must master the intricacies of his or her own school library. After spending approximately thirty hours in his college library, Cory Stewart reported that by the time his research on snakes was finished, he had become familiar enough with all of the major operations of his college library to simplify any future research.

Below are some problems Cory confronted during his research, followed by the solutions he devised. We present them for your scrutiny since these or similar problems are commonly faced by most students engaged in research.

Problem: The back issues of a magazine were not among the bound volumes.
Solution: Past issues were available on microfilm.

Problem: Cory wanted to take home a magazine article or book chapter that had been placed on reserve.
Solution: He photocopied the article or chapter in question.

Problem: An important source was not available at the school library.
Solution: The source was obtained from a library co-op.

Problem: Cory wanted to know if a certain book was available for purchase.
Solution: The information was found in *Books in Print,* a publication available in all libraries.

Problem: Cory wanted to know if a certain author was considered an expert in his field.
Solution: He checked the various *Who's Who* volumes, which are arranged according to subject matter and geographical area.

STEP 3: BUILDING A BIBLIOGRAPHY

After selecting a narrowed topic and becoming familiar with the library, the next task is to assemble a *working bibliography*—a list of sources you think you will use. (The *final bibliography* is a list of references actually used.) Your efforts to work up a useful bibliography may yield nothing or may yield too much. If no information is available, shift to a new subject; if too much information is on hand, narrow the topic further. Assemble the working bibliography with care. Don't clutter it with entries that have only a faint chance of helping you. Resist the temptation to overwhelm your instructor with a vast number of sources; reject all vaguely related material or repetitious material.

Learn to make an intelligent guess as to whether or not a source might be useful by scanning the table of contents and indexes of books and the bibliography at the end of the chapter or at the end of the book.

Record each usable reference in ink on a separate 3 x 5 card. Each card should contain the following information:

1. Name of author
2. Title of work

3. Facts of publication
4. The library the work is from (public or personal)
5. The library's call number for the work
6. A notation of why the work is likely to be useful and which part (article, chapter, pages) especially so

Following is a sample bibliography card from Cory Stewart's stack:

library call number — 598.1 Sha

College Library — libra

Shaw — ident name

all information necessary for footnotes — Shaw, Charles E., and Sheldon Campbell. *Snakes of the American West.* New York: Alfred A. Knopf, 1974.

personal note about why the book may be useful — Chapter 1 contains some useful information about the internal organs of snakes.

Most research sources will be books or articles. However, a personal interview, a public lecture, or a recording that sheds light on your subject may also be part of your bibliography.

You will delete or add cards as you sharpen the focus of your paper in preparation for formulating a thesis. Never throw away a bibliography card; set it aside in an inactive pack. Later, you may wish to include it. A bibliography properly recorded and kept up to date needs only alphabetizing to be typed up in final form from the cards.

Bibliography form for books*

The information in a bibliographical entry for a book should always appear in the following order: Author. <u>Title.</u> Editor or translator. Edition. Series. Volumes. Publication facts. If any of these items are not pertinent to a given entry, they are simply skipped over.

*All bibliography forms in this chapter conform to the 1977 edition of the *MLA Handbook.*

AUTHOR

Author's surname, followed by given name or initials, followed by a period.

Book with one author

> Highet, Gilbert. The Art of Teach-
>
> ing. New York: Vintage Books,
>
> 1958.

Book with more than one author

If the book has more than one author, invert the name of the first author only:

> Barzun, Jacques, and Henry F. Graff.
>
> The Modern Researcher. 3rd ed.
>
> New York: Harcourt Brace
>
> Jovanovich, Inc., 1977.

For three authors, separate the authors by commas. If there are more than three authors, use the first author, followed by et al.:

> Baugh, Albert C., et al. A Literary
>
> History of England. New York:
>
> Appleton-Century-Crofts, Inc.,
>
> 1948.

TITLE

Title of the book, underlined, followed by a period.

Due to the modern electric typewriter, continuous underscoring is now acceptable.

> Seton, Anya. Devil Water. New York:
>
> Avon, 1962.

Internal titles

When a book contains separate articles or chapters by different authors, the article or chapter referred

to appears in quotation marks, followed by a period.
The word *In* precedes the title of the collection.

```
Bettelheim, Bruno.  "Violence: A
    Neglected Mode of Behavior."  In
    Violence: A Reader in the Ethics
    of Action.  Ed. George Estey
    and Doris Hunter.  Waltham, Mass.:
    Xerox College Publishing, 1971.
```

EDITOR OR TRANSLATOR

Name of the editor or translator, preceded by Ed.
or Trans., followed by a period.

```
Yerby, Frank.  "Health Card."  In Black
    Literature in America.  Ed.
    Raman K. Singh and Peter Fellowes.
    New York: Thomas Y. Crowell
    Company, 1970.


Defoe, Daniel.  Moll Flanders.  Ed. J.
    Paul Hunter.  New York: Thomas
    Y. Crowell Company, 1970.


Dante, Alighieri.  The Purgatorio.
    Trans. John Ciardi.  New York:
    New American Library, 1961.
```

If you wish to cite a complete edited collection, the
editor's name appears in the position of the author's
name, followed by ed. (See Hardin Craig entry
below.)

EDITION

Edition used, whenever it is not the first, followed
by a period.

```
Van Doren, Carl C.  The American
     Novel: 1789-1939.  2nd ed.  New
     York: The Macmillan Company,
     1940.

Craig, Hardin, ed.  The Complete
     Works of Shakespeare.  Rev. ed.
     Glenview, Ill.: Scott, Foresman
     and Company, 1964.

Dixon, Raymond J., ed.  Granger's
     Index to Poetry.  4th ed., rev.
     and enl.  New York: Columbia
     Univ. Press, 1953.
```

SERIES

Name and number of the series followed by a period.

```
Unger, Leonard.  T. S. Eliot.  Uni-
     versity of Minnesota Pamphlets
     on American Writers, 8.  Minne-
     apolis: Univ. of Minnesota
     Press, 1961.
```

VOLUMES

Number of volumes under this title, in Arabic numerals, if all the volumes have been used.

```
Harrison, G. B., et al., eds.  Major
     British Writers.  2 vols.
     New York: Harcourt Brace Jovano-
     vich, Inc., 1959.
```

If all the volumes have not been used, indicate the ones that have been used after the publication information.

> Baker, Ernest A. The History of the
> English Novel. London: H. F. and
> G. Witherly, 1924-39. Vols. II
> and III.

For volumes with separate titles, use the following format:

> Seton-Watson, Hugh. The Russian
> Empire 1808-1917. Vol. III of
> Oxford History of Modern Europe.
> Oxford: Clarendon Press, 1967.

PUBLICATION FACTS

Place, publisher, and date of publication, followed by a period. Use a colon to separate the place from the publisher, and a comma to separate the publisher from the date. If more than one place of publication appears, choose the major city (usually New York). If more than one copyright date is mentioned, cite the most recent one, unless your study is specifically concerned with an earlier edition.

> James, Henry. The Portrait of a Lady.
> New York: Washington Square
> Press, Inc., 1963.

If necessary for clarity, include the name of the state or country.

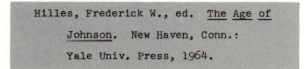

> Hilles, Frederick W., ed. The Age of
> Johnson. New Haven, Conn.:
> Yale Univ. Press, 1964.

If the place or date of publication is not provided, inset n.p. or n.d. for "no place" or "no date." If only a publisher's name is provided, look up the location of the publisher's office (the place of publication) in the publisher's catalog, available in any library or bookstore.

Bibliography form for periodicals

The information in an entry for a periodical should appear in the following order, leaving out items for which no information is available and going on to the next item: Author. "Article Title." Periodical Title, date, pages.

AUTHOR
: Author's surname, followed by given name or initials, followed by a period.

```
Reid, Ron.  "Black and Gold Soul
     with Italian Legs."  Sports
     Illustrated, 11 Dec. 1972, pp.
     36-37.
```

If there is more than one author, follow the same rules suggested for books with more than one author (see page 215).

ARTICLE TITLE
: Complete title of article, enclosed in quotation marks and followed by a period.

```
Spender, Stephen.  "Is a New Litera-
     ture Possible?"  Saturday Review,
     22 Sept. 1962, pp. 16-19.
```

PERIODICAL TITLE
: Name of periodical, underlined and followed by a comma.

```
"The War: A Shattering Disappointment."
     Editorial.  Time, 25 Dec. 1972,
     p. 9.
```

DATE
: Date of monthly or weekly periodicals, followed by a comma.

> Yee, Min. "Chinatown in Crisis."
>   *Newsweek*, 23 Feb. 1970, pp. 57-
>   58.

If the periodical does not appear regularly on a specified date, then supply the month and year.

> Riesman, David. "Where Is the Col-
>   lege Generation Headed?" *The*
>   *Atlantic*, April 1961, pp. 39-45.

If the periodical is paged anew for each issue and the exact date of publication is not given, then supply the volume and number of the issue in order to simplify the reader's search for the journal.

> Elkins, William R. "Thoreau's Cape
>   Cod: The Violent Pond." *Okla-*
>   *homa* *English* *Bulletin*, 2, No. 2
>   (1965), 57-59.

If a periodical uses continual pagination throughout the annual volume, supply volume number and page reference.

> Ramsey, Jarold W. "The Wife Who
>   Goes Out Like a Man, Comes Back
>   as a Hero: The Art of Two Oregon
>   Indian Narratives." *PMLA*, 92
>   (1977), 9-18.

PAGES   Page numbers for the entire article, not just for the specific pages cited, followed by a period.

```
Fetterman, John.   "The People of
     Cumberland Gap."  National
     Geographic, Nov. 1971, pp.
     591-621.
```

When a volume or issue number is given, the pp. in front of the page numbers is omitted.

```
"The Stature of a Genius."  Editorial.
     House Beautiful, 101 (Oct. 1959),
     208, 275-77.
```

Bibliography form for newspapers

The bibliographical listing for a newspaper item is the same as for a periodical, except that in addition to giving the date and page on which the newspaper article appeared, you will also give the special section and column number:

```
Getze, John.   "Alaskan Oil to Over-
     flow West."  Los Angeles Times,
     28 August 1977, Part VIII, p. 1,
     col. 5.
```

If the article is an editorial, use the following format:

```
"A Card, a Simple Card."  Editorial.
     Los Angeles Times, 28 August
     1977, Part IV, p. 2, cols. 1-2.
```

Bibliography form for special items

Since the nature of published as well as unpublished documents is infinitely varied, we cannot provide standardized forms of citation for all types.

221

Use common sense in giving sufficient information so that your reader can locate the reference or at least understand it. The following are examples of types of references you may wish to cite.

Mimeographed item

> Witt, Charles B. "The Common Cold."
> Los Angeles, 1976. (Mimeo-
> graphed.)

Letter

> Wood, Miriam. Letter to author.
> 19 Feb. 1976.

Interview

> Bietz, Arthur L. Telephone inter-
> view. 4 Nov. 1975.

Recording

> Eagle, Swift. The Pueblo Indians.
> Caedmon, TC 1327, n.d.

Television or radio program

> World of Survival. Narr. John
> Forsythe. CBS Special. 29
> Oct. 1972.
>
> "Chapter 2." Writ. Wolf Mankowitz.
> Dickens of London. Dir. and prod.
> Marc Miller. Masterpiece Theater.
> Introd. Alistair Cooke. PBS, 28
> August 1977.

Pamphlet

> Registrar-Recorder for County of Los
>
> Angeles. County Counsel's Analysis,
>
> Arguments for, and Proposed Charter
>
> Amendments. Pamphlet enclosed in
>
> official Sample Ballot, Los Angeles,
>
> California, 1972.

Public document

> Cong. Rec. 7 Feb. 1977, pp. 3830-35.
>
> U.S. Const. Art. 1, sec. 2.

Encyclopedia article

> Swinburne, Algernon Charles.
>
> "Marlowe, Christopher." En-
>
> cyclopaedia Britannica, 1963 ed.

Cassette

> Beckhofer, Robert. Death of History.
>
> University of Michigan. n.d.

More and more libraries are treating and cataloging
cassette tapes as books.

When copying your cards for the final bibliography, follow the format used in the sample paper, page 271.

STEP 4: TAKING NOTES

Note-taking—the groundwork of research—should be done accurately,
intelligently, and economically. The best way to keep notes is on 4 × 6

cards. The experience of numerous researchers and scholars has verified the superiority of note cards over sheets of paper. Cards can be easily shuffled, discarded, and added while sheets of paper must be cut into strips and pasted in order.

Every note card should contain a headnote and an abbreviated source from which the note is taken. (For the full source, you will refer to your bibliography cards.) Following are two sample note cards from Cory Stewart's stack:

Headnote

Source —— *Ditmars, p. 121.*   *Origin of snakes*

"*looked at from a concise standpoint, snakes may be described as the most specialized among all living reptiles, having originated from the lizards.*"

Quotation

Bellairs & Carrington, p. 100.   *Methods of devouring prey*

Many snakes devour their prey alive. They usually grab the prey by the head, which suffocates it. The powerful digestive juices may also contribute to the death of the prey.

Paraphrase

Learn to take notes sparingly. Include in your notes only information crucial to the paper and directly related to the narrowed subject. (See sample note cards accompanying Cory Stewart's paper at the end of this chapter.) If, after prudent scrutiny, you remain doubtful, include the note; you can always discard it but trying to find it again later may be time-consuming. As with bibliography cards, never throw away a note card; simply place it in a separate inactive pack, in case you need it later. Each note card should be limited to one idea. If you cannot squeeze the idea onto one card, then continue on a second card labeled B. The information contained on your note cards will be of four kinds:

1. Quotation
2. Paraphrase
3. Summary
4. Personal comment

The first three kinds of information must be documented—you must give credit in footnotes or parentheses for ideas not your own. Passing off as your own the ideas of another is called plagiarism. No self-respecting scholar wants to plagiarize. He or she knows that to do so is self-defeating since the purpose of writing is the improvement of one's own powers of thinking and communication. Some students, pressured by time or a lack of confidence, plagiarize deliberately; others plagiarize unintentionally because they are confused about the proper use of other people's ideas. In the following discussion we will attempt to clear up any possible confusion about what information must be documented.

Direct quotations

When you use the exact words of other writers or speakers, you are quoting them, and you must name them as the source. Short quotations must be placed in quotation marks and must fit into your text coherently. If you take care of this during the note-taking stage, you will save yourself considerable editing later.

Incoherent   The novel arose at a time when "culture which, in the last few centuries, has set an unprecedented value on originality, on the novel; and it is therefore well named."[1]

Better

> According to Ian Watt, the novel is well named
> because it is "the logical literary vehicle of a
> culture which, in the last few centuries, has set
> an unprecedented value on originality, on the
> novel."[1]
>
> [1]Ian Watt, *The Rise of the Novel* (Berkeley,
> Calif.: University of California Press, 1964),
> p. 13.

Long quotations (exceeding three lines) are not placed in quotation marks but are double-spaced and indented ten spaces. They should always be introduced, as in the following example:

> In his section on "Poetic Language," Anthony Winkler draws
> attention to the relationship between a poem and its social
> and language environment:
>
> > A poem is a system. Like every other system it is
> > made up of components which function in unison.
> > And like any other system it is subject to wear
> > and tear. This does not mean that a poem is
> > likely to throw a valve as a car might. But it
> > does mean that at the moment of its inception the
> > good poem relies heavily on the subtleties of
> > language which, though perfectly obvious to a
> > reader of its time, may cease to function for a
> > reader one hundred years later.[2]
>
> [2]Anthony C. Winkler, *Poetry as System* (Glenview, Ill.:
> Scott, Foresman, 1971), p. 1.

If you wish to omit irrelevant words or lines from a quoted passage, do so by using ellipses. Use three spaced dots when the omission is at the beginning or in the middle of a sentence.

"All of the functions of language . . . in some ways

affect the most basic need of any living organism,

survival."[3]

[3]John C. Condon, Jr., <u>Semantics and Communication</u> (New York: Macmillan, 1966), p. 6.

According to John C. Condon, language is personal; it

is ". . . determined by the training, whims, and his-

torical accidents of our culture, community, and fam-

ily."[4]

[4]Condon, p. 31.

Use four spaced dots (with no space before the first dot) when the omission occurs at the end of a sentence.

"By the age of five the child knows the sound and

structure of its language better than most foreign

students with years of training. . . ."[5]

[5]Condon, p. 25.

Use a full line of spaced dots to indicate the omission of an entire paragraph or more.

Do not overuse quotations. A paper riddled with quotations does not read well because each quotation reflects a different style, causing a choppy effect. The overuse of quotations also makes you look unsure, as if you lacked the ability to say anything on your own. In fact, you should use quotations only when an author has stated an important idea in a brilliant way or when the statement is controversial or obscure. Facts that are common knowledge need not be documented or quoted. As a rule of thumb, if you have read five sources making the same point, that point may be considered general knowledge. For instance, "American jails contain many males arrested for the crime of homosexuality" is a commonly known fact and does not need to be quoted. So is the statement, "Neil Armstrong was the first man to set foot on the moon." In contrast, the statement, "Children in America are often subjected to unnecessary surgeries because Medicaid is there to pay the bill," is controversial since critics disagree in their views on the subject. We need to know who made the statement and where. Again, a little-known fact such as, "Ten thousand people in the United States are equipped with artificial heart valves made of dacron mesh" needs to be quoted accurately and its author identified.

1. **Copy quotations exactly.**
2. **Place short quotations in quotation marks; indent and double space long quotations.**
3. **Introduce the quotation or make it fit grammatically into your text.**
4. **Quote sparingly.**

Paraphrase

To paraphrase is to say in your own words what someone else has said. You read an author's material, you digest the idea, and then you restate the thought, using approximately the same number of words as the original, but using your own vocabulary and your own way of expressing yourself. Paraphrasing does *not* mean using an author's words in a different order so they will not be recognized and then passing them off as your own. Proper paraphrasing is a vital and legitimate part of research. In fact, most of your research papers will consist of paraphrasing—thoroughly digested information presented in your personal style. Paraphrasing achieves two purposes: first, it indicates that you are on top of your information, having assimilated it thoroughly. Second, it gives your paper a smooth, consistent style. In the example below the original passage is on the left, and the paraphrase is on the right.

Original	*Paraphrase*
It is no longer sufficient for Johnny to understand the past. It is not even enough for him to understand the present, for the here-and-now environment will soon vanish. Johnny must learn to anticipate the directions and rate of change. He must, to put it techni-	In a world where present customs and values quickly give way to new customs and values that have no recognizable connection with what went on before, it is no longer sufficient for a student or teacher to know history and current events. Both student and teacher

Original	Paraphrase
cally, learn to make repeat-	must become future-oriented
ed, probabilistic, increas-	by learning to anticipate
ingly long-range assumptions	and project advancing trends
about the future. And so	and to guess the rate at
must Johnny's teacher.[6]	which change will occur.[6]

[6]Alvin Toffler, Future Shock (New York: Bantam Books, 1971), p. 403.

In the event that you want to preserve key words or phrases from the original text, a combination of paraphrase and quotation may be used. Below we have changed the paraphrase from Alvin Toffler to a combination paraphrase and quotation:

As Alvin Toffler points out, in a world where "the here-and-now environment" quickly vanishes, giving way to new customs and new values, it is no longer enough for a student or a teacher to know history and current events. Both student and teacher must become future-oriented by learning to make "repeated, probabilistic, increasingly long-range assumptions" about advancing trends and the rate at which change will occur."[6]

[6]Alvin Toffler, Future Shock (New York: Bantam Books, 1971), p. 403.

Whether you paraphrase completely or use a combination of paraphrase and quotation, you must list in a footnote the exact source of the material you are presenting.

Finally, limit your paraphrases to significant ideas that support your thesis. Material of lesser importance should be summarized.

1. **Paraphrase by digesting and rewriting the original material; do not merely rearrange words.**
2. **Paraphrase only important material.**

Summary

A summary is a condensation of a piece of writing. The extent of the condensation varies. You may want to condense an entire book into one paragraph, as in this summary of Arnold Toynbee's *Study of History,* Volume IV:

Arnold Toynbee argues that nothing is more conducive to the decay of a civilization than worldly success. As soon as a nation has reached a peak and begins to settle back on its laurels, it is on the downward grade, because it is then no longer willing to respond to new challenges as they present themselves. It begins to mark time instead of to go forward. Inertia sets in as the leaders dream about the glory of their past achievements instead of blazing new trails. Toynbee refers to this tendency for the very success of a civilization to make it unfit for further growth as "the intoxication of victory." (IV, 505) Examples of it can be seen in the self-adulation of Persia, of Greece, and of Rome. The creative energies of these three civilizations hardened into self-stultifying idolatry, which then was followed by a decay of the civilization.[7]

[7] Arnold Toynbee, A Study of History, IV (New York: Oxford University Press, 1934-54).

The purpose of such a tight summary is to set in relief the main ideas of a work, usually in order to give weight to your own thesis by citing an important source, or to present in uncluttered and direct form an otherwise complicated or verbose argument. Note that you must tell the reader, either in the text or in a footnote, exactly what work you are summarizing.

Most often you will want to summarize one or several pages into a single paragraph, maintaining the essential nature of the original work, its context, connotation, and purpose, but using your own language. If the original passage was ironic or satirical, this tone should be reflected in your version. A good way to do this is to quote key words or phrases typical of the author's attitude. The following is a summary of Willie Morris's "Miss Abbott":

Willie Morris's reminiscence of a terrifying grade school
teacher leaves the reader frightened and amused. "Miss
Abbott" emerges as a red-eared religious fanatic who talks
through her pink nose, makes fawning slaves out of her girl
students, and teaches all of her classes to learn by rote.
When she is "knocked out cold" by a student's stray softball,
we hardly blame the little boy who wrote: "I wich the old
bich had been hit by a hard ball," nor do we condemn the
author when he confesses, "I prayed that she would die."
But, of course, Miss Abbott revives to continue her academic
harassment, which all of us who have ever hated a grade
school teacher, view with remembered terror.[8]

[8]Willie Morris, North Toward Home (Boston: Houghton
Mifflin Company, 1967), pp. 10-12.

Summaries are particularly useful when you are trying to capture concisely a factual report. In such a case, you must be meticulous about the accuracy of your facts and be extremely careful about what you leave out when you condense. The following paragraph summary of the bulky Walker Report concerning the riots in Chicago during the 1968 Democratic National Convention is a good example of careful condensation.

According to the Walker Report three factors were mainly
responsible for the violent confrontations between the Chicago police and the demonstrators during the 1968 National
Democratic Convention:

1. Various real and imagined threats to the city were inferred from inflammatory statements and from informants.
2. The city responded to the threats by refusing the permits
   for marches and meetings and by deploying armed troops.
3. The city had officially ignored police violence in earlier
   demonstrations and riots.

Next, the report stresses eyewitness accounts that accused the Chicago police of using unnecessary force in dealing with media representatives as well as demonstrators, especially at the Hilton Hotel, in Lincoln Park, and in Old Town.

Finally, the report recommends that disciplinary action be taken against policemen who lost control, since the problem is a matter of worldwide concern.[9]

[9]Daniel Walker, *Right in Conflict* (New York: E. P. Dutton, 1968), p. 29.

In summarizing you should:
Abridge the original accurately
Extract the most significant ideas
Retain the tone and mood of the original

Personal comments

Personal comments on the research you have done are an indispensable part of your paper. They will consist of introductions to the ideas of others, reactions to problems, insights into situations, clarification of issues, transitions from one thought to the next, or conclusions drawn from the evidence presented. You also may point up inconsistencies and unanswered questions, or you may suggest solutions. Whatever your comments are, as they present themselves to your mind, write them down on your note cards. Any work of this sort accomplished during the note-taking stage will save time later. The following are three sample personal comments.

Reaction to the reviews by critics of Erich Segal's *Love Story:* In their attacks on Segal's slick plot, stereotyped characters, and excessive sentimentality, critics seem to ignore two aspects of Segal's work: 1. the lucid style, and 2. the uncluttered purpose. Both of these qualities, after all, are important ingredients of good art.

Reasons why, according to one study, the number of academic underachievers in grade school is higher among bright boys than bright girls: It seems reasonable to assume that one cause for the difference in achievement patterns between girls and boys is family expectation. Since the male in our society is still the one who "must" achieve and "get ahead," more parental pressure may be placed on the male than on the female. This difference in motivation might well result in achievement differences. In other words, the pressure produces a paralytic effect.

> **Transitional paragraph for moving from one stage to the next in the development of Joan Miró's art:** The third and last stage in Miró's art is a shift away from the representational element characterizing his second stage, to a new surrealistic approach reflected in strong primary colors and curved lines. A layman looking at Miro's paintings from this period might well compare them to drawings of multicolored amoebas, except that on close scrutiny, the forms approach real-life subjects.

Unless your personal comments contain quoted words, they need no documentation.

STEP 5: FORMULATING THE THESIS AND SHAPING THE OUTLINE

You are now ready to formulate a thesis—the controlling idea that holds the entire paper together. The thesis will probably begin to take shape as soon as you have done some extensive reading on your narrowed topic. It will not be found ready-made somewhere in the reading material; rather, it will emerge as an answer to some question, as an opinion you have formulated, or as a summary of the ideas you have digested. Through reading and note-taking it was clear to Cory that the "biological nature of snakes" was not precisely the topic on which he wanted to focus his paper. He posed this question to himself: "Is the snake a fearsome monster or is it a harmless reptile?" The answer emerged with clarity as he read and took notes. In the end, he chose the following thesis: "Far from being the overwhelming monster of the Bible and mythology, the snake is simply a cleverly evolved reptile that has adapted to its environment in order to survive."

Once you have developed a thesis, you are ready to outline your paper. The outline is a method of focusing the paper so that you do not stray from your thesis. Major ideas are placed in their proper place and sequence.

To prepare the outline, spread out your note cards where you can see them and assemble them in a logical sequence, according to the most important ideas. Cory grouped his cards under the following major headings:

I. How snakes overcome the problem of being limbless
II. How, despite deafness, snakes can stalk their prey
III. How snakes devour their prey
IV. How snakes survive enemies and harsh environments
V. How snakes are helpful to human beings

The outline will reveal areas in the subject that have been under-researched and require more information, or areas that have been over-researched and need thinning. In the end, Cory decided to omit Section V, "How snakes are helpful to human beings," because he did not have enough

233

information on this topic and also because he felt its inclusion would ruin the unity of his paper.

Before going on to Step 6, go back to Chapter 4, page 52, for guidelines on how to outline logically and with the proper visual form.

STEP 6: WRITING THE ROUGH DRAFT

When you are ready to begin the rough draft, you are further along than you think. But do not delay your writing until the night before your paper is due. As we said earlier, for most people writing is a demanding task. Paragraphs that express exactly what you want them to say, in a smooth style, will not miraculously flow from your pen, but will require reworking and editing. Be prepared to write at least two drafts—one rough and one final. Everything you have learned so far about good writing must be brought to bear at this stage, from effective words, sentences, and paragraphs to unity, coherence, and logic. Deliberate *care* is your watchword. Do not muddle through fast just to get the job over with. Slow down, think, and construct with exactness.

Most of the time you will have to reword your notes to fit into the context of the paper. Occasionally, a note can be used as originally set down. When this is the case, do not waste time by copying, but staple the entire note card to your typing sheet. When additional transitions, observations, or personal comments are needed, work these in with a view toward purposeful progression, constantly asking yourself, Is my thesis being supported? Am I expressing myself clearly? Am I placing the emphasis where it belongs? When you confront a particularly complex idea, work it out on scratch paper first; this will keep your rough draft from being illegibly messy. Keep a dictionary and a thesaurus handy to look up the meaning and spelling of words and to make your vocabulary more varied.

Since your first draft will suffer considerable handling, shuffling, penciling, and erasing, use a heavy bond paper rather than flimsy scratch paper. Also, leave wide margins and spaces between lines so that you have plenty of room for revisions. Type or write on one side of your paper only.

Endnotes versus footnotes

Instructors are divided on the question of whether students should supply endnotes or footnotes. Endnotes appear collected at the conclusion of the text, numbered consecutively, and listed under the title ''Notes,'' centered at the top of the first endnote page. Footnotes, on the other hand, appear separately at the bottom of each page where the note is indicated. Our sample student paper uses footnotes, but we have also supplied alternate endnotes so that either method can be followed.

Special attention must be paid if you use footnotes. At the bottom of each page you will need to leave enough room for the required number of footnotes. Use three spaces (double-space twice) to separate the body of your paper from the first footnote. Use a separate line for each footnote. Single-space each footnote, but double-space between the notes. Following is a sample of the last line on a page, followed by two footnotes.

Thus the novel catered to the same kind of taste that also

[5]Ian Watt, The Rise of the Novel (Los Angeles: University of California Press, 1964), p. 54.

[6]Helen Sard Hughes, "The Middle Class Reader and the English Novel," Journal of English and Germanic Philology, 25 (1926), 362-78.

If the length of a footnote requires that it be continued on the following page, type a solid line across the new page one full line below the last line of the text, double-space twice, and continue the note. Footnotes pertaining to this new page should immediately follow the completion of the note continued from the previous page. The following technique will help you save enough space for footnotes at the bottom of a page:

1. Count the number of lines needed for each footnote.
2. Add five lines for the bottom margin of the page.
3. Add three lines to separate the first footnote from the body of the paper.
4. Add two lines for each space between footnotes.

According to this formula, the above example of two footnotes would require that you stop typing when you have fifteen lines left on the page. You should have no trouble ending at the proper spot on the page if you make a light pencil mark where you should end the text.

Footnoting is simple when you keep a model in front of you. It is easier, and more accurate, to check your style sheet each time you write a footnote than to try to memorize the proper format. Footnote entries are different from bibliography entries, as the following list of forms will show.

Footnote/endnote forms for books*

Information provided in a footnote citation of a book should always appear in the following order: Author, Title, Editor or translator, Edition, Series (Publication facts), Volume, page. If no information is available for one item, skip it and go on to the next.

* All footnote/endnote forms in this chapter conform to the 1977 edition of the *MLA Handbook*.

AUTHOR

Name of author or authors, in normal order, followed by a comma.

Book with one author

> [1]J. Hillis Miller, The Disappearance of God: Five 19th-Century Writers (New York: Schocken Books, 1965), p. 8.

Book with more than one author

> [2]Harold Barlow and Sam Morgenstern, A Dictionary of Musical Themes (New York: Crown Press, 1948), p. 84.

For three authors, separate the authors by commas. If there are more than three authors, use the first author, followed by et al.

> [3]Evan J. Crane et al., A Guide to the Literature of Chemistry, 2nd ed. (New York: John Wiley & Sons, Inc., 1957), p. 10.

TITLE

Title of the book, underlined and followed by a comma unless the next item is enclosed in parentheses.

> [4]Edith Hamilton, Mythology: Timeless Tales of Gods and Heroes (New York: Mentor Books, 1942), pp. 30-33.

Internal titles

In a collection of essays or a book with chapters or sections by different authors, the title of the essay or chapter is enclosed in quotation marks, followed by a comma and the title of the larger work preceded by in.

> ⁵R. W. Short, "Melville as Sym-
> bolist," in Interpretations of American
> Literature, ed. Charles Feidelson, Jr.
> and Paul Brodtkorb, Jr. (New York:
> Oxford Univ. Press, 1959), pp. 106-07.

EDITOR OR TRANSLATOR

Name of editor or translator, in normal order, preceded by ed. or trans., followed by a comma unless the next item is enclosed in parentheses.

> ⁶William Hamilton, "The Death of
> God," in Contemporary Religious Issues,
> ed. Donald E. Hartsock (Belmont,
> Calif.: Wadsworth Publishing Company,
> Inc., 1968), pp. 14-15.
>
> ⁷Nathaniel Hawthorne, The Scar-
> let Letter, ed. Kenneth S. Lynn (New
> York: Harcourt, Brace & World, Inc.,
> 1961), p. 31.
>
> ⁸Homer, The Iliad, trans. Rich-
> mond Lattimore (Chicago: Univ. of
> Chicago Press, 1962), p. 10.

If you wish to cite a complete edition collection, use the following format.

> ⁹Gerald W. Haslam, ed., For-
> gotten Pages of American Literature
> (Boston: Houghton Mifflin Company,
> 1970), p. 43.

EDITION

Edition used, whenever it is not the first, followed by a comma unless the next item is enclosed in parentheses.

> [10]Laurence Perrine, <u>Sound and Sense</u>, 5th ed. (New York: Harcourt Brace Jovanovich, Inc., 1969), pp. 134-35.
>
> [11]Everard M. Upjohn, Paul S. Wingert, and James G. Mahler, <u>History of World Art</u>, 2nd ed., rev. and enl. (New York: Oxford Univ. Press, 1958), p. 58.

SERIES

Name and number of series, followed by a comma unless the next item is enclosed in parentheses.

> [12]William van O'Connor, William Faulkner, rev. ed., <u>University of Minnesota Pamphlets on American Writers</u>, 3 (Minneapolis: Univ. of Minnesota Press, 1964), p. 36 ff.

PUBLICATION FACTS

Place, publisher, and date of publication within parentheses. A colon separates the place of publication and the publisher's name, and a comma separates the publisher's name and the date. Another comma follows the end parenthesis.

> [13]Alvin Toffler, <u>Future Shock</u> (New York: Bantam Books, 1970), pp. 219-21.

If necessary for clarity, include the name of the state or country.

> [14]Andrew Wright, *A Reader's Guide to English and American Literature* (Glenview, Ill.: Scott, Foresman and Company, 1970), p. 15.

If more than one place of publication appears, choose the major city (usually New York). Also, if more than one copyright date is mentioned, use the most recent, unless your study is specifically concerned with an earlier edition. If the place or date of publication is not provided, insert n.p. or n.d. If only a publisher's name is provided, look up the location of the publisher's office (the place of publication) in the publisher's catalog available in any library or bookstore.

VOLUME

Number of the volume from which you are citing if the work contains more than one volume with the same title, in Roman numerals, followed by a comma.

> [15]Charles W. Dunn, "Geoffrey Chaucer," in *Major British Writers*, ed. G. B. Harrison, enl. ed. (New York: Harcourt, Brace & World, Inc., 1959), I, 3.

PAGE

Page number(s) in Arabic numerals, followed by a period.

> [16]Horatio Alger, Jr., *Adrift in New York and The World Before Him*, ed. William Coyle (New York: The Odyssey Press, Inc., 1966), p. 69.

If you are citing one volume of a multivolume work, leave out the p. or pp.:

> [17]Northrop Frye, "George Gordon, Lord Byron," in <u>Major British Writers</u>, ed. G. B. Harrison, enl. ed. (New York: Harcourt, Brace & World, Inc., 1959), II, 159.

Small Roman numerals are often used in books for numering the pages of prefaces or introductions.

> [18]Milton Hindus, <u>F. Scott Fitzgerald: An Introduction and Interpretation</u>, American Authors and Critics Series (New York: Holt, Rinehart and Winston, Inc., 1968), p. vii.

Notice the following common usage when giving page numbers: pp. 92–93, *not* pp. 92–3; but pp. 215–18, *not* pp. 215–8 or pp. 215–218.

Footnote/endnote forms for periodicals

In footnotes citing a periodical, information is arranged in the following order: Author, "Article Title," <u>Periodical Title</u>, Volume, date, page.

AUTHOR   Name of author, in normal order, followed by a comma.

> [1]Stephen Spender, "Is a New Literature Possible?" <u>Saturday Review</u>, 22 Sept. 1962, pp. 16-19.

If there is more than one author, follow the same rules suggested for books with more than one author (see page 236).

ARTICLE   Title of article, followed by a comma and enTITLE   closed within quotation marks.

> [2]Stanley Kunitz, "Frost, Williams and Company," Harper's, Oct. 1962, p. 23.

PERIODICAL TITLE

Name of the periodical, underlined, followed by a comma.

> [3]Paul Engle, "Paean for a Poet by a Poet," Life, 15 June 1959, pp. 65-66.

VOLUME AND DATE

Omit the volume number for weekly or monthly periodicals that are paged anew in each issue. Give instead the complete date, set off by commas.

> [4]Leon Edel, "Spirals of Reason and Fancy," Saturday Review, 5 Sept. 1964, p. 23.

If pagination of the issue is separate and the month is not given, supply volume and issue number in Arabic numerals, or volume and year of publication.

> [5]William R. Elkins, "Thoreau's Cape Cod: The Violent Pond," Oklahoma English Bulletin, 2, No. 2 (1965), 15.
>
> [6]Robert Frances et al., "On Robert Frost," Massachusetts Review, 4 (1963), 238.

PAGE

Page number(s), in Arabic numerals, followed by a period.

> 7"The Election that Nobody
> Won," Editorial, <u>Time</u>, 13 Nov. 1972,
> pp. 32-35.

When the volume number is included, omit p. or pp.

> 8Dorothy Dudley, "The Acid Test,"
> <u>Poetry</u>, 23 (March 1924), 328-35.

Footnote/endnote form for newspapers

The footnote/endnote form for a newspaper item is the same as that for a periodical, except that in addition to giving the date and page on which the newspaper article appeared, you will also provide the column number and special section.

> 9John Peterson, "Assault on Heart Disease," <u>National
> Observer</u>, 20 July 1970, Sec. 1, p. 1, cols. 4-5; <u>p. 17,
> cols. 1-6</u>.
>
> 10Jim Murray, "Please Pass the Iguana," <u>Los Angeles
> Times</u>, 9 Nov. 1972, Sec. 3, p. 1, col. 1.

Footnote/endnote forms for special items

As with bibliographical forms, we cannot provide examples for all the eventualities that may occur, but where no examples are given, use your common sense or ask your instructor how to handle specific footnote problems. In all cases, be consistent.

Classical works

For long classical works that appear in several editions, you must give the reader more than just the page number. Include in parentheses the number of the book, part, act, scene, and line, whenever appropriate. In such instances, the use of Arabic numerals is becoming more common.

> 1Homer, <u>The Iliad</u>, trans. Richmond Lattimore (Chicago:
> Univ. of Chicago Press, 1951), p. 101 (III. 38-45).
>
> 2Plato, <u>The Republic</u>, trans. Paul Shorey (Cambridge,
> Mass.: Harvard Univ. Press, 1937), p. 225 (III. vi).

When one underlined title is followed by another, separate the titles with the word *in*.

> ³Sophocles, Oedipus the King, in The Complete Greek Tragedies, ed. David Grene and Richmond Lattimore (Chicago: Univ. of Chicago Press, 1959), II, 52 (II. 977-83).
>
> ⁴William Shakespeare, Antony and Cleopatra, in The Comedies and Tragedies of Shakespeare, ed. Warren Chappell (New York: Random House, 1944), II, 934 (II. vi. 13-19).

If you are making numerous subsequent citations to a work, you may place an abbreviated version of the reference in parentheses in your text.

> Even near death, Antony has no thought but for Cleopatra:
>
> I am dying Egypt, dying; only
> I here importune death awhile, until
> Of many thousand kisses the poor last
> I lay upon thy lips. (Antony IV. xv. 18-21)

Encyclopedias

> ⁵E. F. Kook, "Stage Design," Encyclopaedia Britannica, 1963 ed.

Authors of encyclopedia articles are usually identified by initials that are interpreted in the encyclopedia index. Footnotes to unsigned articles begin with the title of the article.

> ⁶"Sitting Bull," Encyclopedia Americana, 1962 ed.

References to sections that are alphabetically arranged need not be identified by volume and page. It is not necessary to give the names of the editors of an encyclopedia or the name and location of the publisher.

Critical reviews

> ⁷Charles Rolo, rev. of The Status Seekers, by Vance Packard, The Atlantic (May 1959), p. 91.

Poems

> [8]T. S. Eliot, "The Love Song of J. Alfred Prufrock," in
> <u>Modern</u> <u>American</u> <u>Poetry</u> <u>and</u> <u>Modern</u> <u>British</u> <u>Poetry</u>, ed. Louis
> Untermeyer (New York: Harcourt, Brace, and Company, 1950),
> pp. 398-401.

In the case of long classical poems, follow the form for classical works given above.

The Bible

The names of sacred scriptures, both Christian and non-Christian, are not underlined, nor are the names of the individual books. Chapter and verses are indicated by small Roman numerals and Arabic numerals, separated by a period.

> [9]Psalms xiv.5.
>
> *Alternate style :* [9]Psalms 14:5.

The King James version of the Bible is assumed to have been used unless otherwise indicated.

> [10]Acts xiii.42 (J. B. Phillips).
>
> *Alternate style :* [10]Acts 13:42 (J. B. Phillips).

Subsequent references

Once you have provided full information for a reference, your subsequent footnotes for that same source will be brief. The use of Latin abbreviations, such as *op. cit., loc. cit.,* and *ibid.,* is out of style. In most cases, the last name of the author and the page number will suffice. The *MLA Handbook,* 1977 edition, allows subsequent brief references to appear in parentheses within the text.

> [2]Miller, p. 76.
>
> (Miller, p. 76) <u>within the text</u>

However, if you are citing more than one title by the same author, use the author's last name, followed by a key word from the title, followed by the page number. (The whole title is *The Raven and the Whale.*)

```
²Miller, Raven, p. 26.
```

If you are citing authors with identical surnames, you must add the given name to each reference:

```
²Perry Miller, p. 20.
```

If two or more authors are involved, use the last names of both, or et al.:

```
Barlow and Morgenstern, p. 20.

Crane et al., p. 15.
```

Content footnotes/endnotes

Occasionally you may wish to use a footnote not for documentation, but for special comment. Such a comment may consist of a definition, explanation, judgment, or cross-reference. The purpose is to avoid distracting your reader from the main thrust of your paper. Here are some examples of content footnotes:

```
     ¹Briefly, archetype is a term brought into literary
criticism as a result of the work of psychologist Carl
Jung, who held that behind each "unconscious" lies the
"collective unconscious," that is, the blocked-off memory
of our racial past.  This racial memory, according to
Jung, is expressed in repeated images, which are found in
early myths, religions, and dreams.

     ²Unfortunately, this comment was not made until after
the author's death.

     ³For an explanation of this seeming contradiction, see
p. 3 of this paper.

     ⁴Cf. the following lines from Wordsworth's "Lines
Written in Early Spring":

     To her fair works did Nature link
     The soul that through me ran;
     And much it grieved my heart to think
     What man has made of man.

     ⁵This veiled reference is probably to Sir Joshua
Reynolds.
```

Abbreviations

Use abbreviations often and consistently in your footnotes and bibliography, but avoid them in your text. In footnotes you should abbreviate dates (Jan., Feb.) and institutions (Univ., Assn.). The following are abbreviations commonly encountered or used.

A.D. *Anno Domini.* Refers to years after Christ's birth, as "A.D. 200."

anon. Anonymous.

art., arts. Article(s).

B.C. Before Christ. Refers to years before Christ's birth, as "50 B.C."

bk., bks. Book(s).

ca. *Circa. About,* used to indicate an approximate date, as "ca. 1730."

cf. *Confer. Compare* one source with another.

ch., chs. Chapter(s).

col., cols. Column(s).

comp. Compiled by or compiler.

diss. Dissertation.

ed., eds. Editor(s), edition, or edited by.

e.g. *Exampli gratia. For example,* preceded and followed by a comma.

enl. Enlarged, as in "enl. ed."

et al. *Et alii. And others,* as in "John Smith et al."

f., ff. Page(s) following, as "pp. 8 f." meaning page 8 and the following page.

i.e. *Id est. That is,* preceded and followed by a comma.

l., ll. Line(s).

MS, MSS Manuscript(s).

n.d. No date.

no., nos. Number(s).

n.p. No place.

p., pp. Page(s).

passim *Here and there throughout the work,* as "pp. 67, 72, et passim."

pseud. Pseudonym.

pt., pts. Part(s).

rev. Revised, revision, reviewed, review.

rpt. Reprint, reprinted.

sec., secs. Section(s).

sic *Thus,* placed in brackets to indicate that an error exists in the passage being quoted, as "sevral [sic]."

st., sts.   Stanza(s).
trans.   Translator, translated, translation.
vol., vols.   Volume(s).

STEP 7: WRITING THE FINAL COPY

When your rough draft has been completed, set it aside for a day or two to give your mind some rest from the subject. Then pick it up again with fresh objectivity and give it one final, ruthless criticism. Do not be soft on yourself. It is better to catch errors and clumsy passages yourself rather than have your instructor unearth them for you. After careful review and editing, type the final copy according to the format used in our sample paper on pages 250–67. Unless your instructor wishes you to follow a specific format, the rules that follow should prove helpful.

The outline

Your outline precedes the text of your paper and should look uncluttered and balanced. You need not number the pages of your outline. See sample student paper outline on pages 250–51.

The body of the paper

1. Hire a typist if your typing is sloppy. Too many erasures or typographical errors prejudice the reader.
2. Use heavy 8½ x 11 white bond paper, observing 1-inch margins at the top, bottom, and both sides of the paper. Avoid erasable bond as it smudges and will not take corrections in ink.
3. Double-space throughout your paper, including quotations and endnotes. Footnotes require double-spacing between notes but single-spacing within. See sample student paper.
4. A research paper does not need a title page; instead, the author's name, instructor's name, course number, and date should appear on the first page of the text in the upper right-hand corner. The title should be centered and double-spaced below the date. See sample student paper.
5. Number pages consecutively throughout the paper in the upper right-hand corner. Do not follow page numbers by hyphens, parentheses, periods, or other characters. Do not number the first page of the paper, but begin with 2. Do not number the first page of endnotes or bibliography but include it in the total page count.

6. If your paper contains subdivisions, use subtitles aligned with the left margin and underlined but not capitalized.
7. Place footnote/endnote numerals within the text of your paper one half space above the line. Each numeral immediately follows the material to which it refers.
8. Each footnote at the bottom of the page must appear on the same page as the numeral referring to it, unless otherwise indicated by your teacher. The first line of each footnote is indented five spaces, but the second and subsequent lines are aligned with the left margin. Single-space each footnote, and double-space between footnotes.
9. In a typed manuscript, italics are indicated by underlining. Generally, any title on the outside cover of a work is italicized. Titles appearing inside the cover are placed inside quotation marks. (Exceptions are plays, long poems, movies, and operas, which are always underlined.)
10. If possible, use pica type, since it is easier to read than elite.
11. Proofread your paper again and again. Regardless of who types your paper, you alone are responsible for the final copy. Failure to proofread may result in careless errors that will lower your grade. If you cannot retype pages that contain errors, make corrections neatly in black ink.

The bibliography

Bibliography entries are arranged alphabetically according to surname of the author (or first word in entry where no author appears). Double-space between and within entries. If an entry has more than one line, indent the second and subsequent lines five spaces. Start the bibliography on a new page and type "Bibliography" or "Selected Bibliography," centered at the top of the page. See student sample.

CHECKLIST

_____ 1. My introduction is strong and includes my thesis.
_____ 2. My paper follows my outline.
_____ 3. My paragraphs are coherent.
_____ 4. The language sounds like me.
_____ 5. I have not quoted excessively.
_____ 6. I have not plagiarized.
_____ 7. My thesis is supported by evidence in the paper.
_____ 8. My paper looks neat.
_____ 9. I have proofread for mechanical errors.
_____10. My footnotes and bibliography are accurate in content and in form.

SAMPLE PAPER

Following is a facsimile of Cory Stewart's finished paper, complete with sentence outline, body, and bibliography. For your convenience in studying the development of the paper, we have supplied the appropriate note cards from which each page was developed. And in the right-hand margin, we have noted where each Roman numeral of the outline begins.

1

THE ADAPTABILITY OF SNAKES

Thesis: Far from being the overwhelming monster of the
Bible and mythology, the snake is simply a
cleverly evolved biological animal that has
adapted to its environment in order to survive.

I. The Bible and mythology have portrayed the snake
as a monster imbued with evil supernatural powers.
   A. The Bible tells of a serpent who seduced humans
      to disobey God.
   B. Such mythological creatures as the lamia and
      Medusa were fearsome monsters.
   C. Today snakes are still universally feared.

II. Despite the disadvantage of being limbless, snakes
have developed an efficient means of locomotion.
   A. The snake's backbone is composed of numerous
      vertebrae.
      1. Each vertebra has a pair of ribs.
      2. The entire spine is very flexible.
   B. The snake propels its body forward in a series
      of ripples from the head to the tail.
   C. The ventral scales keep the snake from slipping
      backwards.

III. Because snakes have no external ears, other senses
are used in stalking prey.
   A. Snakes have no external ear.
      1. Snakes do have a well-developed inner ear.
      2. The snake hears by picking up vibrations as
         its body contacts the ground.
   B. The forked tongue is used by the snake for
      smelling.
      1. The tongue is rich in nerve endings.
      2. It picks up odorous particles in the air.
      3. The particles are transferred to an ol-
         factory organ.

IV. Snakes have very effective methods that help them
swallow their prey.
   A. The jaws can be unhinged to accommodate prey
      larger than the snake's head.
   B. The teeth are sharp and curved toward the rear
      of the mouth to hold the prey in.
   C. The windpipe may be pushed aside to make room
      for the prey in the snake's mouth.
   D. The salivary glands secrete large amounts of
      saliva to aid the snake in swallowing.
   E. The skin of the snake will stretch to accom-

modate large animals in the snake's mouth.

V. As an organism, the snake can survive enemies and harsh environments in spite of its disadvantages.
   A. Snakes are cold-blooded.
       1. The body temperature is regulated by the surrounding environmental conditions.
       2. To avoid freezing, snakes must hibernate in the winter.
   B. Because snakes have little defense against enemies, they often bluff their way through.
   C. A snake is able to survive for a year or more without food.

Introduction

In the Bible and mythology the snake is revealed as an evil monster with supernatural powers. After the serpent has seduced Eve and Adam in the garden of Eden, God curses him:

"Because you have done this you are accursed more than all wild creatures. On your belly you shall crawl and dust you shall eat all the days of your life." Genesis 11.14.

Monsters like the lamia and Medusa contribute to the evil image.

Cory Stewart

Professor McCuen

Eng. 101

May 15, 1977

The Adaptability of Snakes

The Bible and mythology have combined to portray the   (I)
snake as a monster imbued with evil supernatural powers.
The Bible tells of how in the garden of Eden a serpent
seduced human beings from a state of happy innocence to
tragic guilt by telling them to disobey God. As a result,
God cursed the snake in these awesome words:

> Because you have done this you are accursed
> more than all cattle and all wild creatures.
> On your belly you shall crawl, and dust you
> shall eat all the days of your life.[1]

In Greek mythology the snake appears in such images as that
of the serpent-woman lamia, who was reputedly so horrible
that she preyed upon humans and sucked the blood out of
children. There is also the gorgon Medusa, whose hair
consisted of snakes writhing all over her head, and who
was so terrifying that a human being staring at her would
instantly be frozen into a statue. Nor has time improved

---

[1]Genesis ii.14 (Cambridge University).

253

Carr, p. 19.   Image of a snake

"Besides the waning of their food supply as rodents and frogs grow fewer and besides the growing toll that cars take on multiplying highways, snakes face the indifference and active antipathy of most of the human race."

Possible thesis

Unlike the overwhelming monster of the Bible and mythology, the snake is simply a well-adjusted biological creature.

Bellairs & Carrington, pp. 98-100.   Loss of Limbs

One of the snake's disadvantages is being limbless. This may be the result of specialization through evolution. The large lizards of prehistoric times had large, heavy, cumbersome legs. Today's lizard's limbs are modified, so the lizard gets around much more quickly. The snake is not hampered at all by the loss of limbs. We know snakes once had legs. Some boas and pythons still have vestigial limbs — two tiny spurs at the base of the tail.

2

the serpent's image. Still today, the sight of a snake causes shrieks of fear and cries of hysteria. But this deeply rooted view of snakes is ironic. According to Archie Carr, in fact, the snake is more sinned against than sinning: "Besides the waning of their food supply as rodents and frogs grow fewer, and besides the growing toll that cars take on multiplying highways, snakes face the indifference or active antipathy of most of the human race."[2] Far from being the overwhelming monster of the Bible and mythology, the snake is simply a cleverly evolved biological animal that has adapted surprisingly well in order to survive.

To begin with, snakes have many disadvantages not (II) experienced by other animals. As a matter of fact, snakes are physically handicapped in comparison to other reptiles, but evolution and specialization have made up for these deficiencies, so that from the point of view of adaptability, they are most remarkable.

For example, the snake has no limbs. This loss of limbs may be due to the evolutionary process. The great lizards of long ago had huge, cumbersome legs. Gradually, these legs probably became smaller and more modified to allow for greater mobility. The snakes, having evolved from the lizards, developed a method of locomotion that did not require the use of limbs.

[2]Archie Carr, "In Praise of Snakes," Audubon Magazine, 73 (July 1971), 19.

Bellairs & Carrington, p. 98.   Locomotion A

"The backbone has, of course, become enormously elongated, and contains up to 400 separate
vertebrae, all of which, except for the
first one or two behind the head and those
of the tail, carry long movable ribs."

Bellairs & Carrington, pp. 98-100.   Locomotion B

The snake throws its body into a series
of waves or ripples that go from the head
to the tail. The sides of the body push
against objects on the ground, propelling
the snake forward. The snake's belly is
covered by a single row of ventral scales,
which prevent the snake from slipping
backwards.

Pope, p. 437.   Stalking Prey

The snake does not have to hunt
very often, which is clearly to its advantage.
In fact, any healthy snake can go an entire
year without eating if necessary.

3

Instead, the backbone of the snake extends throughout most of its body and may be constructed of up to four hundred vertebrae, each with a pair of ribs. It is unusually flexible and allows for much freedom of movement. The snake propels itself forward by throwing its body into a succession of ripples. The sides of the body push against the contours of the ground and the broad ventral scales of the belly keep the snake from going backward.[3]

The snake has no trouble moving about, but a lack of appendages necessarily creates certain problems in the search for food. However, here again nature has provided a number of compensations to prevent snakes from going hungry. First of all, a snake does not have to feed very often. A healthy snake can fast for a year or more if necessary.[4] Snakes are also equipped with the means to swallow large prey, so a single meal often lasts a week or more.

Second, while snakes have no external ear with which (III) to pick up sounds in the normal sense, they do have an

[3]Angus Bellairs and Richard Carrington, The World of Reptiles (New York: American Elsevier Publishing Company, Inc., 1966), pp. 98-100.

[4]Clifford H. Pope, "Snake," World Book Encyclopedia, 1969, p. 437.

Zim & Smith, p. 71.   Stalking Prey

Snakes have no external ear, therefore they cannot hear in the normal sense. The snake does have a developed inner ear, so it hears by picking up vibrations when contacting the ground.

Goin, p. 52.   Stalking Prey

The snake has a forked tongue with many nerve endings. The tongue is really a type of smeller. It picks up particles in the air and transfers them to Jacobson's organ. This organ has two small cavities located internally on each side of the snout. Ducts lead to an opening in the roof of the mouth.

Ditmars, p. 119.   Swallowing

The snake can swallow an object bigger around than its head, mostly because of its jaws. The jaws of a snake are attached by a ligament and become "unhinged" when the snake swallows. The jaws will move separately as the snake "crawls" over its food. The jaws are extremely mobile since they are not securely connected to the skull.

4

inner ear that picks up vibrations by touching the ground.[5]
By this method a snake "hears" what is going on around it
and can locate prey to eat.

More than anything else, the snake's tongue is an
aid in hunting. The tongue is forked and contains many
nerve endings. As the snake travels, it flicks out its
tongue, which picks up odorous particles in the air.
These particles are then transferred to Jacobson's organ,
an olfactory center consisting of two small cavities located on each side of the snout.[6] The snake frequently
locates its prey by this method.

Contrary to popular opinion, most snakes do not   (IV)
have a specialized method of striking. If possible, the
snake will seize the prey by the head in an attempt to
suffocate the victim. Then the prey is usually swallowed
head first. Due to the construction of its jaws, a snake
can swallow prey larger around than its own head. This
ability is due to the fact that, unlike human jaws,
serpentine jaws are not securely attached to the skull,
but instead are connected by a ligament that becomes
unhinged in the process of swallowing, allowing each jaw

[5]Herbert S. Zim and Hobart M. Smith, Reptiles and
Amphibians (New York: Golden Press, 1953), p. 71.

[6]Coleman J. Goin and Olive B. Goin, Introduction to
Herpetology (San Francisco: W. H. Freeman and Company,
1962), p. 52.

Pope, p. 437.   _Swallowing_

A snake has as many as four rows of teeth in the upper jaw and two rows in the lower jaw. The teeth are small, sharp, and curved toward the roof of the mouth. The curvature of the teeth helps keep the prey in the mouth. The harder the prey struggles, the worse it gets caught by the teeth.

Bellairs & Carrington, p. 101.   _Swallowing_

The salivary glands of snakes are very well developed. They produce large amounts of saliva which help to force the prey downward. Venomous snakes have been able to convert some salivary glands into venom-manu-facturing organs.

Bellairs & Carrington, p. 101.   _Swallowing_

The snake is a very effective eating machine when swallowing: the front of the windpipe can be pushed aside to make room for the prey. This also helps the snake to breathe. In some snakes the windpipe may even function as a lung, when its real lung can't function when the air supply is cut off due to large prey in the gullet.

5

to become extremely mobile and to move independently of the other. Thus, the snake "crawls" over the prey as the mouth stretches.[7] Humans might well envy this biological serpentine phenomenon.

Serpentine teeth can be considered as substitutes for hands and function to keep the prey in the mouth. A snake may have as many as four rows of teeth in the upper jaw. They are small, sharp, and curved toward the rear of the mouth. When the prey struggles to get out, it gets caught by the teeth and is held in, unable to free itself.[8]

The salivary glands of the snake are well developed. They secrete large amounts of saliva that help in the passage of food whenever the snake is feeding.[9]

A snake may have difficulty breathing when swallowing a large animal. Its windpipe can be pushed aside to alleviate this problem. This action also helps the snake to accommodate the large prey. If by chance the air supply is cut off in the process of swallowing a big prey that lodges in the gullet, the windpipe may function as another lung.[10] This fact can be very advantageous to the snake, since the swallowing process can be strenuous.

[7]Raymond L. Ditmars, Reptiles of the World (New York: The Macmillan Company, 1910), p. 119.

[8]Pope, p. 437.

[9]Bellairs and Carrington, p. 101.

[10]Bellairs and Carrington, p. 101.

Bellairs & Carrington, pp 100-101.   <u>Swallowing</u>

When swallowing large prey the skin of the snake stretches to make room for the object. The scales may move apart so that the skin underneath the scales may be visible. The underlying skin is frequently a different color than on the surface. Because of its potent digestive juices, the snake can digest even such things as fur, feathers, and bones.

Shaw & Campbell, p. 14.   <u>Snakes as organisms</u>

The internal organs of snakes are elongated in order to fit into the body. The snake has only one lung, which may extend halfway through the body. Paired organs, such as the kidneys, exist one behind the other. Also, one is usually more developed than the other.

Personal observations   <u>Snakes as organisms</u>

Snakes are coldblooded. This means that their body temperature is regulated by the temperature of the environment. In the winter snakes cannot tolerate the cold and must hibernate for several weeks up to several months.

Even the snake's skin plays a role in the act of swallowing. The skin actually stretches as the food goes down, revealing itself underneath the scales.[11] The underlying skin may be a different color from the scales on the surface, causing an artistic display of motley patterns. Snakes can devour their prey whole because their stomach's strong digestive juices can break down everything, including fur, feathers, and bones.[12] Ulcers, gallstones, or other human digestive diseases are unknown to snakes. They have the proverbial cast iron stomach.

As an organism, the snake must overcome many dis-   (V)
advantages in order to survive. Most significantly the internal organs of the snake have evolved into bizarre shaped so as to fit inside its body. For example, the snake has room for only one lung, which extends more than halfway through the body. Furthermore, paired organs, such as the kidneys, do not exist side by side but one behind the other.[13] Still, the snake adjusts to these oddities.

Snakes, like all reptiles, are cold-blooded. Their body temperatures are regulated by the temperature of the surrounding environment. To avoid freezing in the winter,

[11]Bellairs and Carrington, p. 101.

[12]Bellairs and Carrington, p. 100.

[13]Charles E. Shaw and Sheldon Campbell, Snakes of the American West (New York: Alfred A. Knopf, 1974), p. 14.

Shaw & Campbell, pp. 64-65, 69-70.   <u>Snakes as organisms</u>

Nonvenemous snakes have little defense when provoked. Most snakes are very good bluffers when confronted with potential danger. A snake will try to imitate its attacker. This can be done, depending on the species, by hissing, playing dead, puffing up, or some other means. Most snakes will try to flee or camoflage themselves by blending in with the background.

Zim & Smith, p. 9.   <u>Snakes as organisms</u>

"As a group they [reptiles] are neither 'good' nor 'bad' but are interesting and unusual although of minor importance. If they should all disappear, it would not make much difference one way or the other."

7

snakes must hibernate under the ground, where the temperature is relatively stable.

The elements are not the snake's only enemy. Most
snakes are poorly equipped to defend themselves from other
animals. When provoked, some snakes will try to intimidate
their adversary by bluffing. Methods of bluffing include
hissing furiously, puffing up so as to appear bigger, or
even playing dead. Usually though, snakes will attempt to
flee instead of fight. If cornered, of course, a snake
will bite.[14]

Perhaps the worst enemy of snakes is the human species.
Many people hate or fear them without realizing what
amazing creatures snakes are. Unfortunately, the status
of snakes is not very high, according to Herbert Zim and
Hobart Smith:

> As a group they /reptiles7 are neither
> "good" nor "bad" but are interesting and un-
> usual, although of minor importance. If they
> should all disappear, it would not make much
> difference one way or the other.[15]

[14] Shaw and Campbell, pp. 64-65, 69-70.
[15] Zim and Smith, p. 9.

265

8

Even if snakes would not be missed, they will probably be
around for a long time to come. They have adapted surprisingly well to a harsh environment. If people were to
study this aspect of their nature, they might find snakes
more fascinating than repulsive.

(Alternate endnote method)

Notes

[1]Genesis ii.14 (Cambridge University).

[2]Archie Carr, "In Praise of Snakes," Audubon Magazine, 73 (July 1971), 19.

[3]Angus Bellairs and Richard Carrington, The World of Reptiles (New York: American Elsevier Publishing Company, Inc., 1966), pp. 98-100.

[4]Clifford H. Pope, "Snake," World Book Encyclopedia, 1969, p. 437.

[5]Herbert S. Zim and Hobart M. Smith, Reptiles and Amphibians (New York: Golden Press, 1953), p. 71.

[6]Coleman J. Goin and Olive B. Goin, Introduction to Herpetology (San Francisco: W. H. Freeman and Company, 1962), p. 52.

[7]Raymond L. Ditmars, Reptiles of the World (New York: The Macmillan Company, 1910), p. 119.

[8]Pope, p. 437.

[9]Bellairs and Carrington, p. 101.

[10]Bellairs and Carrington, p. 101.

[11]Bellairs and Carrington, p. 101.

[12]Bellairs and Carrington, p. 100.

[13]Charles E. Shaw and Sheldon Campbell, Snakes of the American West (New York: Alfred A. Knopf, 1974), p. 14.

[14]Shaw and Campbell, pp. 64-65, 69-70.

[15]Zim and Smith, p. 9.

Bibliography

Bellairs, Angus, and Richard Carrington. The World of
    Reptiles. New York: American Elsevier Publishing
    Company, Inc., 1966.

Carr, Archie. "In Praise of Snakes." Audubon Magazine,
    73 (July 1971) 19-25.

Ditmars, Raymond L. Reptiles of the World. New York: The
    Macmillan Company, 1910.

Goin, Coleman J., and Olive B. Goin. Introduction to
    Herpetology. San Francisco: W. H. Freeman and
    Company, 1962.

The New English Bible. New York: Cambridge University
    Press, 1971.

Pope, Clifford H. "Snake." World Book Encyclopedia, 1969.

Shaw, Charles E., and Sheldon Campbell. Snakes of the
    American West. New York: Alfred A. Knopf, 1974.

Zim, Herbert S., and Hobart M. Smith. Reptiles and
    Amphibians. New York: Golden Press, 1953.

SELECT LIST OF REFERENCE WORKS

This list has been compiled to help you find general background material for your research paper. The list is in two main parts: general reference works and reference works in subject fields.

GENERAL REFERENCE WORKS

Unabridged English-Language Dictionaries

Craigie, Sir William A., and James R. Hulbert, eds. *A Dictionary of American English on Historical Principles*. 4 vols. 2nd ed. Chicago: Univ. of Chicago Press, 1960.

Funk & Wagnalls New Standard Dictionary of the English Language. New York: Funk & Wagnalls, 1959.

Murray, Sir James A. H., et al., eds. *A New English Dictionary on Historical Principles*. 13 vols. New York: Oxford Univ. Press, 1888–1933.

The Oxford English Dictionary. 12 vols. London: Oxford Univ. Press, 1961.

Random House Dictionary of the English Language. New York: Random House, 1966.

Webster's New International Dictionary of the English Language. 2nd ed. Springfield, Mass.: G. & C. Merriam, 1959. The third edition (1961) contains many thousands of new expressions, but for all-round use the second edition is preferred by many teachers.

Abridged English-Language Dictionaries

The American College Dictionary. rev. ed. New York: Random House, 1957.

The American Heritage Dictionary. Boston: Houghton Mifflin, 1969.

Funk & Wagnalls Standard College Dictionary. rev. ed. New York: Funk & Wagnalls, 1969.

Random House Dictionary. New York: Random House, 1966.

The Shorter Oxford English Dictionary. 3rd ed., rev. Oxford, Eng.: The Clarendon Press, 1959. Also known as *The Oxford Universal Dictionary,* this one-volume work is based on the "historical principles" that distinguish the larger work in thirteen volumes.

Webster's Seventh New Collegiate Dictionary. 7th ed. Springfield, Mass.: G. & C. Merriam, 1963.

General Encyclopedias

The Encyclopaedia Britannica. 24 vols. Chicago: Encyclopaedia Britannica, 1961.

The Encyclopedia Americana. 30 vols. New York: Grolier, 1961.

General Indexes

Annual Magazine Subject Index: A Subject Index to American and English Periodicals. Comp. F. W. Faxon. Boston: Boston Book, 1908.

Book Review Digest. New York: H. W. Wilson, 1946– . Monthly, except February and July.

International Index. New York: H. W. Wilson, 1913– . Quarterly, with annual and two-year cumulations. First published (1907) as a supplement to the *Readers' Guide* in order to index more scholarly and technical periodicals. Since 1955 it has carried the subtitle, "A Guide to Periodicals in the Social Sciences and the Humanities."

New York Times Index. New York: The New York Times, 1913– . Semimonthly, with annual cumulations.

Nineteenth-Century Readers' Guide to Periodical Literature, 1890–1899. 2 vols. New York: H. W. Wilson, 1944. Author and subject index to some fifty periodicals published in the 1890's.

Readers' Guide to Periodical Literature. New York: H. W. Wilson, 1900– . Semimonthly from September to June, monthly in July and August, with annual and five-year cumulations. Indexes about 125 periodicals of a general nature, by author, title, and subject. Scientific periodicals have been included since 1953.

Biographical Aids—Living Persons

Biography Index: A Cumulative Index to Biographical Material in Books and Magazines. New York: H. W. Wilson, 1947– . Quarterly, with annual and three-year cumulations.

Current Biography: Who's News and Why. New York: H. W. Wilson, 1940– . Monthly, except in August, with annual cumulation.

Who's Who in America. Chicago: A. N. Marquis, 1899– . Biennial. Includes noteworthy persons in all fields.

World Biography. 5th ed. Bethpage, N.Y.: Institute for Research in Biography, 1954.

In addition to the foregoing, there are "who's who" publications by country, by region, by race, and by profession.

Biographical Aids—Persons No Longer Living

Dictionary of American Biography. Published under the auspices of the American Council of Learned Societies. 21 vols. New York: Scribner's, 1928–37. Supplement One (to December 1, 1935), 1944. Supplement Two (1936–1940), 1958.

Dictionary of National Biography. Ed. Leslie Stephen and Sidney Lee. 63 vols. London: Smith, Elder, 1885–1900. Supplements at ten-year intervals; the latest, covering 1941–50, published in 1959. Includes notable persons of Great Britain and the colonies from the earliest historical period.

Atlases and Gazetteers

Collocott, T. C. and J. O. Thorne, eds. *Macmillan World Gazetteer and Geographical Dictionary*. rev. ed. New York: Macmillan, 1957.

Encyclopaedia Britannica World Atlas. Chicago: Encyclopaedia Britannica, 1960.

Rand McNally Standard World Atlas. Chicago: Rand McNally, 1958.

Miscellaneous Handbooks and Yearbooks

Bartlett, John, ed. *Familiar Quotations*. 13th ed., completely rev. Boston: Little, Brown, 1955.

Chambers, Robert. *The Book of Days: A Miscellany of Popular Antiquities in Connection with the Calendar, Including Anecdote, Biography, and History, Curiosities of Literature and Oddities of Human Life and Character . . .* 2 vols. Edinburgh: W. & R. Chambers, 1899.

Collier's Year Book. New York: Collier, 1938– .

Kane, Joseph N. *Famous First Facts*. rev. and enl. ed. New York: H. W. Wilson, 1950.

New Century Cyclopedia of Names. Ed. Clarence L. Barnhart, with the assistance of William D. Halsey et al. 3 vols. New York: Appleton-Century-Crofts, 1954.

The Oxford Dictionary of Quotations. 2nd ed. New York: Oxford Univ. Press, 1953. Popularity, not necessarily merit, has determined the quotations contained.

Peterson, Houston, ed. *A Treasury of the World's Great Speeches*. New York: Simon & Schuster, 1954.

Statesman's Yearbook. New York: Macmillan, 1864– . Gives statistical and historical information about the countries of the world and about international organizations such as NATO and the United Nations.

Stevenson, Burton Egbert, ed. *Home Book of Quotations*. 9th ed. New York: Dodd, Mead, 1959.

Taylor, Archer, and Bartless J. Whiting, comps. *A Dictionary of American Proverbs and Proverbial Phrases, 1820–1880*. Cambridge, Mass.: The Belknap Press of Harvard Univ., 1958.

World Almanac and Book of Facts. New York: World Telegram and Sun, 1868– .

Bibliographies

American Book Publishing Record. New York: R. R. Bowker, 1960– . Monthly. Provides a complete record of American books published.

American Book Publishing Record Annual Cumulatives. New York: R. R. Bowker. Annual volumes.

Books in Print 1972: An Index to the Publishers' Trade List Annual, 2 vols. (Authors Index; Titles Index). New York: R. R. Bowker, 1972.

N. W. Ayer & Son's Directory of Newspapers and Periodicals. Philadelphia: N. W. Ayer & Son, 1880– . Annually. Covers the United States and its possessions, Canada, Bermuda, Panama, and the Philippines.

Besterman, Theodore. *A World Bibliography of Bibliographies*. 4 vols. 3rd and final ed. New York: Scarecrow Press, 1955–56. International in scope.

Books in Print. 3 vols.: Author, Title, Subject. New York: R. R. Bowker, 1957– . Annual.

The Bibliographic Index. New York: H. W. Wilson, 1938– . Semiannual. Includes foreign-language works.

Hoffman, Hester R., ed. *The Reader's Adviser and Bookman's Manual*. 9th ed., rev. and enl. New York: R. R. Bowker, 1960. Subtitled "a guide to the best in print in literature, biographies, dictionaries, encyclopedias, Bibles, classics, drama, poetry, fiction, science, philosophy, travel, history."

Publishers' Weekly. New York: Publishers' Weekly, 1872– . Includes both books published and those announced for publication.

Ulrich's Periodicals Directory. 9th ed. New York: R. R. Bowker, 1959. Includes foreign periodicals.

Winchell, Constance M. *Guide to Reference Books*. 7th ed. Chicago: American Library Assn., 1951. Supplements, 1950–52, 1953–55, 1956–58. Evaluates as well as lists reference works.

Government Publications

Boyd, Anne Morris, and Rae E. Rips. *United States Government Publications*. 3rd ed., rev. New York: H. W. Wilson, 1950.
"Explains the nature, distribution, catalogs, and indexes of U.S. Government publications; lists and describes important publications of the departments of the U.S. Government: the executive, legislative, and judicial branches, Con-

gress, the Courts, etc.'' [Jean Key Gates, *Guide to the Use of Books and Libraries,* p. 132.]

Schmeckebier, Laurence F. and Roy B. Eastin. *Government Publications and Their Use.* rev. ed. Washington, D.C.: The Brookings Institution, 1961.

U.S. Library of Congress, Division of Documents. Monthly Checklist of State Publications. Washington, D.C.: U.S. Government Printing Office, 1910– .

U.S. Superintendent of Documents. *United States Government Publications, Monthly Catalog.* Washington, D.C.: U.S. Government Printing Office, 1895– .

——. Price Lists of Government Publications. Washington, D.C.: U.S. Government Printing Office, 1898– .

Wilcox, Jerome Kear. *Bibliography of New Guides and Aids to Public Documents Use, 1953–1956.* New York: Special Libraries Association, 1957. Includes international as well as domestic guides.

SUBJECT FIELDS

Fine Arts—Dance and Drama

Baker, Blanch M. *Theatre and Allied Arts: A Guide to Books Dealing with the History, Criticism, and Technic of the Drama and Theatre and Allied Arts and Crafts.* New York: H. W. Wilson, 1952.

Dictionary of Modern Ballet. New York: Tudor Publishing, 1959. A complete record from Diaghilev and Isadora Duncan to the present day.

Dramatic Index. Boston: Boston Book, 1910–49. Now published as Part II of the Annual Magazine Subject Index.

Ewen, David, ed. *Complete Book of American Musical Theater.* New York: Holt, 1958. Pertinent information concerning more than three hundred productions since 1886.

Hartnoll, Phyllis. *The Oxford Companion to the Theatre.* 2nd ed. New York: Oxford Univ. Press, 1957.

Logasa, Hannah. *Index to One-Act Plays, 1900–1924.* Boston: F. W. Faxon, 1924. Four supplements cover the period from 1924 to 1957.

Nicoll, Allardyce. *A History of English Drama, 1660–1900.* 6 vols. rev. ed. Cambridge, Eng.: Cambridge Univ. Press, 1952–59.

Shipley, Joseph T. *Guide to Great Plays.* Washington, D.C.: Public Affairs Press, 1956. Covers all periods, giving history, production, themes, casts.

Fine Arts—Music

Apel, Willi. *Harvard Dictionary of Music.* Cambridge, Mass.: Harvard Univ. Press, 1956.

Baker, Theodore. *Biographical Dictionary of Musicians.* 5th ed., completely rev. by Nicholas Slonimsky. New York: G. Schirmer, 1958.

Bronson, Bertrand H. *The Traditional Tunes of the Child Ballads with Their Texts According to the Extant Records of Great Britain and America.* 4 vols. et al. Princeton, N.J.: Princeton Univ. Press, 1959– .

Duckles, Vincent, et al. *Guide to Reference Materials on Music.* 3rd ed. Berkeley, Calif.: Univ. of California Press, 1955.

Ewen, David. *Living Musicians.* New York: H. W. Wilson, 1940. First supplement, 1957. Lists the most important works of each composer, with biographical information.

——. *Ewen's Musical Masterworks.* 2nd ed. New York: Arco, 1954. Includes every field of music; summarizes plots of operas and evaluates composers and their works.

——, ed. *Complete Book of American Musical Theater.* New York: Holt, 1958.

Feather, Leonard G. *Encyclopedia of Jazz.* New York: Horizon Press, 1955.

Grove's Dictionary of Music and Musicians. 9 vols. 5th ed., ed. Eric Blom. New York: Macmillan, 1954. Supplementary Volume to fifth edition. Ed. Eric Blom. New York: St. Martin's Press, 1961.

Music Index. Detroit: Information Service, 1949– . Monthly, with annual cumulations.

Scholes, Percy A. *The Oxford Companion to Music.* 9th ed., completely rev. New York: Oxford Univ. Press, 1955. Covers all phases of music, with long encyclopedic articles, including some 1,500 biographies.

Song Index: An Index to More than 12,000 Songs in 177 Song Collections Comprising 262 Volumes. Comp. Minnie E. Sears and Phyllis Crawford. New York: H. W. Wilson, 1926. Supplement. New York: H. W. Wilson, 1934.

Thompson, Oscar. *Intrernational Cyclopedia of Music and Musicians.* 5th ed., rev. and enl. by Nicholas Slonimsky. New York: Dodd, Mead, 1949.

Fine Arts—Painting, Sculpture, and Architecture

American Art Annual. Washington, D.C.: American Federation of Arts, 1898– .

Art Index. New York: H. W. Wilson, 1933– . Quarterly with annual and two-year cumulations. Includes both fine and applied arts.

Chamberlin, Mary W. *Guide to Art Reference Books.* Chicago: American Library Assn., 1959.

Encyclopedia of Painting. Ed. Bernard S. Myers. New York: Crown, 1955.

Encyclopedia of World Art. New York: McGraw-Hill, 1959– . Fifteen volumes are planned, of which three have now appeared. A comprehensive work, covering all phases of art.

Gardner, Helen. *Art Through the Ages.* 5th ed. Revised by Horst de la Croix and Richard G. Tansey. New York: Harcourt Brace Jovanovich, 1970.

Hammond, William A. *A Bibliography of Aesthetics and of the Philosophy of the Fine Arts from 1900 to 1932.* rev. and enl. ed. New York: Longmans, Green, 1934.

Monro, Isabel S., and Kate M. Monro. *Index to Reproductions of American Paintings.* New York: H. W. Wilson, 1948.

——. *Index to Reproductions of European Paintings.* New York: H. W. Wilson, 1956.

Reinach, S(alomon). *Apollo: An Illustrated History of Art throughout the Ages.* Completely rev., with a new chapter by the author. New York: Scribner's, 1935.

Upjohn, Everard M., Paul S. Wingert, and Jane G. Mahler. *History of World Art.* 2nd ed., rev. and enl. New York: Oxford Univ. Press, 1958.

Who's Who in American Art. New York: R. R. Bowker, 1937– . Includes bibliographies of both American and Canadian artists, with a geographical index and a list of open exhibitions.

Poetry

Arms, George, and Joseph M. Kuntz. *Poetry Explication: A Checklist of Interpretations since 1925 of British and American Poems Past and Present.* New York: Swallow Press and Morrow, 1950.

Courthope, William J. *A History of English Poetry.* 6 vols. New York: Macmillan, 1895–1910.

Granger's Index to Poetry. Ed. Raymond J. Dixon. 4th ed., rev. and enl. New York: Columbia Univ. Press, 1953. Supplement to the fourth edition, indexing anthologies published from January 1, 1951, to December 31, 1955. Ed. Raymond J. Dixon. New York: Columbia Univ. Press, 1957.

Granger's Index to Poetry and Recitations. 3rd ed., rev. and enl. Chicago: A. C. McClurg, 1940. Indexes both standard and popular collections.

Sell, Violet, et al., comps. *Subject Index to Poetry for Children and Young People.* Chicago: American Library Assn., 1957.

Tate, Allen. *Sixty American Poets, 1896–1944.* rev. ed. Washington, D.C.: Library of Congress, General Reference and Bibliographic Division, 1954. Includes bibliographies of their writings.

Literature

Baker, Ernest A. *The History of the English Novel.* 10 vols. London: H. F. and G. Witherly, 1924–39.

Baker, Ernest A., and James Packman, eds. *A Guide to the Best Fiction, English and American, including Translations from Foreign Languages.* new and enl. ed. London: G. Routledge, 1932. Includes an index of authors, titles, subjects, historical names and allusions, places, characters, and so forth.

Barnhart, Clarence L., and William D. Halsey, eds. *The New Century Handbook of English Literature.* New York: Appleton-Century-Crofts, 1956. Emphasis is on English writers and their works.

Baugh, Albert C., ed. *A Literary History of England.* New York: Appleton-Century-Crofts, 1948.

Bell, Inglis F., and Donald Baird. *The English Novel, 1578–1956: A Checklist of Twentieth-Century Criticisms.* Denver: A. Swallow, 1959.

Benét, William Rose, ed. *The Reader's Encyclopedia.* 2nd ed. New York: Thomas Y. Crowell Company, 1965. Deals with world literature and the arts and includes mythology and legend.

Blanck, Jacob. *Bibliography of American Literature.* New Haven, Conn.: Yale Univ. Press, 1955– . Work in progress. Three volumes have appeared.

Bond, Donald F. *A Reference Guide to English Studies.* A revision of the *Bibliographical Guide to English Studies,* by Tom Peete Cross. Chicago: Univ. of Chicago Press, 1962.

The Cambridge Bibliography of English Literature. Ed. F. W. Bateson. 4 vols. Cambridge, Eng.: Cambridge Univ. Press; New York: Macmillan, 1941. Supplement, Vol. V. Ed. George Watson. Cambridge, Eng.: Cambridge Univ. Press, 1957. Provides a complete bibliography in chronological order, of "the authors, titles, and editions, with relevant critical matter, of all the writings in book-form (whether in English or Latin) that can still be said to possess some literary interest, by natives of what is now the British Empire, up to the year 1900." (Donald F. Bond, *A Reference Guide to English Studies*)

Cassell's Encyclopedia of Literature. Ed. S. H. Steinberg. 2 vols. London: Cassell, 1953.

Cattell, Jacques, ed. *Directory of American Scholars.* 3rd ed. New York: R. R. Bowker, 1957.

Coan, Otis W., and Richard G. Lillard. *America in Fiction: An Annotated List of Novels that Interpret Aspects of Life in the United States.* Stanford, Calif.: Stanford Univ. Press, 1956.

Columbia Dictionary of Modern European Literature. Ed. Horatio Smith. New York: Columbia Univ. Press, 1947. Treats only the literature of continental Europe of the twentieth century and immediately before.

The Concise Cambridge Bibliography of English Literature, 600–1950. Ed. George Watson. Cambridge, Eng.: Cambridge Univ. Press, 1958.

Dickinson, Asa D. *The World's Best Books.* New York: H. W. Wilson, 1953.

Fiction Catalog: Seventh Edition, 1960: A List of 4,097 Works of Fiction in the English Language, with Annotations. Ed. Estelle A. Fidell and Esther V. Flory. New York: H. W. Wilson, 1961. First published in 1908. Annual supplements, cumulated periodically.

Hackett, Alice Payne. *Sixty Years of Best Sellers, 1895–1955.* New York: R. R. Bowker, 1956.

Hart, James D. *The Oxford Companion to American Literature.* 3rd ed., rev. and enl. New York: Oxford Univ. Press, 1956.

Harvey, Sir Paul. *The Oxford Companion to Classical Literature.* Oxford, Eng.: The Clarendon Press, 1940.

——. *The Oxford Companion to English Literature.* 3rd ed. Oxford, Eng.: The Clarendon Press, 1946.

Hoehn, Matthew. *Catholic Authors.* Newark, N.J.: St. Mary's Abbey, 1948. Covers the period from 1930 to 1947.

Kunitz, Stanley J., ed. *Twentieth Century Authors: First Supplement.* New York: H. W. Wilson, 1955.

Kunitz, Stanley J., and Howard Haycraft, eds. *American Authors, 1600–1900.* New York: H. W. Wilson, 1938.

——. *British Authors before 1800.* New York: H. W. Wilson, 1952.

——. *British Authors of the Nineteenth Century.* New York: H. W. Wilson, 1936.

——. *The Junior Book of Authors.* New York: H. W. Wilson, 1934.

——. *Twentieth Century Authors.* New York: H. W. Wilson, 1942.

Literary History of the United States. Ed. Robert E. Spiller et al. rev. ed. in 1 vol. (2nd ed.) New York: Macmillan, 1959.

Magill, Frank N., ed. *Masterplots.* 3 vols. New York: Salem Press, 1955.

Modern Language Association of America. *MLA International Bibliography of Books and Articles on the Modern Languages and Literature.* New York: Modern Language Association, 1921– .

Nygren, Dorothy, ed. *A Library of Literary Criticism.* New York: Frederick Ungar, 1960. Treats American authors who came into prominence after 1900.

The Oxford History of English Literature. Ed. Frank P. Wilson and Bonamy Dobree. New York: Oxford Univ. Press, 1945– . Twelve volumes are planned, of which three have appeared.

Reader's Companion to World Literture. Ed. Lillian H. Hornstein. New York: The Dryden Press, 1956.

Richards, Robert F., ed. *Concise Dictionary of American Literature.* New York: Philosophical Library, 1955.

Shipley, Joseph T., ed. *Dictionary of World Literature*. New York: Philosophical Library, 1943.

——. *Encyclopedia of Literature,* 2 vols. New York: Philosophical Library, 1946.

Short Story Index: An Index to 60,000 Stories in 4,320 Collections. Comp. Dorothy E. Cook and Isabel S. Monro. New York: H. W. Wilson, 1953. Supplement, 1950–54. New York: H. W. Wilson, 1956. Supplement, 1955–58. New York: H. W. Wilson, 1960.

Thrall, William F., and Addison Hibbard, eds. *A Handbook to Literature*. rev. and enl. by C. Hugh Holman. New York: The Odyssey Press, 1960. Explains terminology of literary study and includes an outline of the literary history of England and America.

U.S. Library of Congress. *A Guide to the Study of the United States of America: Representative Books Reflecting the Development of American Life and Thought.* Prepared under the direction of Roy P. Basler by David H. Mugridge and Blanche P. McCrum. Washington, D.C.: U.S. Government Printing Office, 1960.

Van Doren, Carl C. *The American Novel, 1789–1939.* 2nd ed. New York: Macmillan, 1940.

Myth and Folklore

Benét, William Rose, ed. *The Reader's Encyclopedia*. 2nd ed. New York: Thomas Y. Crowell Company, 1965.

Diehl, Katharine S. *Religions, Mythologies, Folklores: An Annotated Bibliography.* 2nd ed. New York: Scarecrow Press, 1962.

Frazer, Sir James G. *The Golden Bough: A Study in Magic and Religion.* 12 vols. 3rd ed. New York: Macmillan, 1907–15. See also: *Aftermath: A Supplement to "The Golden Bough."* New York: Macmillan, 1936. And an abridgment, *The New Golden Bough.* Ed. Theodore H. Gaster, New York: Criterion Books, 1959.

Harvey, Sir Paul. *The Oxford Companion to Classical Literature.* Oxford, Eng.: The Clarendon Press, 1940. Includes Greek and Roman mythology.

Hastings, James, ed. *Encyclopaedia of Religion and Ethics* . . . 13 vols. in 7. New York: Scribner's, 1928. Includes mythology and folklore.

Larousse Encyclopedia of Mythology. New York: Prometheus Press, 1959. Worldwide in coverage.

Mythology of All Races. Ed. Louis H. Gray and John A. MacCulloch. 13 vols. Boston: Marshall Jones, 1916–32.

Thompson, Stith. *Motif-Index of Folk Literature: A Classification of Narrative Elements in Folktales, Ballads, Myths, Fables, Mediaeval Romances* . . . 6 vols. rev. and enl. ed. Blomington, Ind.: Indiana Univ. Press, 1955–58.

Philosophy and Psychology

Cattell, Jacques, ed. *American Men of Science*. 9th ed. New York: R. R. Bowker, 1956. Volume III: *The Social and Behavioral Sciences*.

Contributions to Modern Psychology: Selected Readings in General Psychology. Ed. Don E. Dulany et al. New York: Oxford Univ. Press, 1958.

Dictionary of Philosophy and Psychology. Ed. James M. Baldwin et al. 3 vols. new ed. New York: Macmillan, 1925–33. A work that is still useful, although it does not include modern developments.

Encyclopaedia of the Social Sciences. Ed. Edwin R. A. Seligman and Alvin Johnson. 15 vols. New York: Macmillan, 1930–35. A comprehensive work that brings out the relationships among the sciences.

English, Horace B., and Ava C. English. *A Comprehensive Dictionary of Psychological and Psychoanalytical Terms*. New York: Longmans, Green, 1958.

Good, Carter V., and Douglas E. Scates. *Methods of Research: Educational, Psychological, Sociological*. New York: Appleton-Century-Crofts, 1954.

Harriman, Philip L., ed. *Encyclopedia of Psychology*. New York: Philosophical Library, 1956.

Harvard List of Books in Psychology. Ed. Edward G. Boring. Cambridge, Mass.: Harvard Univ. Press, 1955. Supplement. Cambridge, Mass.: Harvard Univ. Press, 1958.

Louttit, Chauncey M. *Handbook of Psychological Literature*. Bloomington, Ind.: The Principia Press, 1932.

Miller, Hugh. *An Historical Introduction to Modern Philosophy*. New York: Macmillan, 1947.

Runes, Dagobert D., ed. *The Dictionary of Philosophy*. New York: Philosophical Library, 1942.

——. *Who's Who in Philosophy*. Vol. I. New York: Philosophical Library, 1942.

Russell, Bertrand. *A History of Western Philosophy*. New York: Simon and Schuster, 1945.

Schneider, Herbert W. *A History of American Philosophy*. New York: Columbia Univ. Press, 1946.

Urmson, J. O., ed. *The Concise Encyclopedia of Western Philosophy and Philosophers*. New York: Hawthorn Books, 1960. Treats philosophy from Abelard to the present time; includes up-to-date bibliographies.

U.S. Library of Congress, Reference Department. *Philosophical Periodicals: An Annotated World List*. Washington, D.C.: U.S. Government Printing Office, 1952.

Religion

Attwater, Donald, ed. *The Catholic Encyclopaedic Dictionary.* New York: Macmillan, 1958.

Barrow, John G. *A Bibliography of Bibliographies in Religion.* Austin, Tex.: By the Author, 716 Brown Bldg., 1955.

The Catholic Encyclopedia: An International Work of Reference on the Constitution, Doctrine, Discipline, and History of the Catholic Church. 16 vols. New York: Catholic Encyclopedia Press, 1907–14. Supplement, 1922. Supplement II. Ed. Vincent C. Hopkins. New York: Gilmary Society, 1954. Not limited to subjects of interest only to Roman Catholics.

Coulson, John, ed. *The Saints: A Concise Biographical Dictionary.* London: Burns and Oates, 1958.

Ferm, Vergilius, ed. *An Encyclopedia of Religion.* New York: Philosophical Library, 1945.

Hastings, James, et al., eds. *Dictionary of the Bible.* 5 vols. New York: Scribner's, 1905–09.

Joy, Charles R., comp. *Harper's Topical Concordance.* New York: Harper & Brothers, 1940. Topical index of the King James version of the Bible.

Miller, Madeleine S., and J. Lane Miller. *Harper's Bible Dictionary.* 6th ed. New York: Harper & Brothers, 1959. Addresses all levels of readers.

The Oxford Dictionary of the Christian Church. Ed. F. L. Cross. New York: Oxford Univ. Press, 1957. Second corrected impression, 1958.

Schaff, Philip. *The New Schaff-Herzog Encyclopedia of Religious Knowledge . . .* Ed. Samuel Jackson et al. 12 vols. New York: Funk & Wagnalls, 1908–12. Supplementary volumes: *Twentieth Century Encyclopedia of Religious Knowledge.* Ed. Lefferts A. Loetscher. 2 vols. Grand Rapids, Mich.: Baker Book House, 1955.

Zaehner, Robert C., ed. *The Concise Encyclopedia of Living Faiths.* New York: Hawthorn Books, 1959.

Biological and Physical Sciences—General

The American Yearbook. Publisher varies, 1929– . Summarizes progress in the sciences.

Hawkins, Reginald R., ed. *Scientific, Medical, and Technical Books Published in the United States of America.* 2nd ed. New York: R. R. Bowker, 1958.

The McGraw-Hill Encyclopedia of Science and Technology. New York: McGraw-Hill, 1960.

Technical Book Review Index. New York: Special Libraries Assn., 1935– . Monthly, except July and August.

Biological Sciences

Agricultural Index. New York: H. W. Wilson, 1916– . Monthly.

Blake, Sidney F. *Geographical Guide to Floras of the World: An Annotated List with Special Reference to Universal Plants and Common Plant Names.* Washington, D.C.: U.S. Government Printing Office, 1942.

Cattell, Jacques, ed. *American Men of Science.* Vol. II: *The Biological Sciences.* 9th ed. New York: R. R. Bowker, 1956. Living persons.

Comstock, Anna B. *Handbook of Nature-Study.* 24th ed. New York: Comstock, 1939.

Henderson, Isabella F., and W. D. Henderson. *Dictionary of Scientific Terms . . . in Biology, Botany, Zoology, Anatomy, Cytology, Embryology, Physiology.* 4th ed., rev. by J. H. Kenneth. Princeton, N.J.: D. Van Nostrand, 1949.

Jordan, E. L. *Hammond's Nature Atlas of America.* New York: C. S. Hammond, 1952. For the layman nature lover.

Palmer, Ephraim L. *Fieldbook of Natural History.* New York: Whittlesey House, 1949.

Stedman's Medical Dictionary. 19th ed. Baltimore: Williams & Wilkins, 1957.

Willis, J. C. *Dictionary of Flowering Plants and Ferns.* 6th ed., rev. Cambridge, Eng.: Cambridge Univ. Press, 1931.

Physical Sciences

American Institute of Physics Handbook. Ed. Dwight E. Gray et al. New York: McGraw-Hill, 1957.

Ballentyne, D. W. G., and L. E. Q. Walker. *A Dictionary of Named Effects and Laws in Chemistry, Physics, and Mathematics.* New York: Macmillan, 1959.

Cattell, Jacques, ed. *American Men of Science,* Vol. I: *The Physical Sciences.* 9th ed. New York: R. R. Bowker, 1956. Living persons.

Condon, Edward U., and Hugh Odishaw. *Handbook of Physics.* New York: McGraw-Hill, 1958.

Gray, H. J., *Dictionary of Physics.* New York: Longmans, Green, 1958.

International Dictionary of Physics and Electronics. Ed. Walter C. Michels et al. 2nd ed. Princeton, N.J.: D. Van Nostrand, 1961.

Lindenberg, George C., et al. *Encyclopedia of Chemistry.* New York: Reinhold, 1957.

Mellon, Melvin Guy. *Chemical Publications.* 3rd ed. New York: McGraw-Hill, 1958. A survey, with explanations of ways to use such publications to advantage.

U.S. Department of Interior, Bureau of Mines. *Minerals Yearbook.* Washington, D.C.: U.S. Government Printing Office, 1933– .

Social Sciences—General

Cattell, Jacques, ed. *American Men of Science.* Vol. III: *The Social and Behavioral Sciences.* 9th ed. New York: R. R. Bowker, 1956. Living persons.

Encyclopaedia of the Social Sciences. Ed. Edwin R. A. Seligman and Alvin Johnson. 15 vols. New York: Macmillan, 1930–35.

International Index. New York: H. W. Wilson, 1913– . Quarterly, with annual and two-year cumulations. First published (1907) as a supplement to the *Readers' Guide* in order to index more scholarly and technical periodicals. Since 1955 it has carried the subtitle, *A Guide to Periodicals in the Social Sciences and the Humanities.*

Zadrozny, John T., ed. *Dictionary of Social Science.* Washington, D.C.: Public Affairs Press, 1959.

Social Sciences—Education

Alexander, Carter, and Arvid J. Burke. *How to Locate Educational Information and Data.* 4th ed., rev. New York: Bureau of Publications, Teachers' College, Columbia Univ., 1958.

Education Index. New York: H. W. Wilson, 1929– . Monthly, except July and August, with annual cumulations. Covers the entire field and includes British publications.

Monroe, Paul, ed. *A Cyclopedia of Education.* 5 vols. New York: Macmillan, 1911–13. Valuable for its presentation of the history and philosophy of education.

Rivlin, Harry N., ed. *Encyclopedia of Modern Education.* New York: Philosophical Library, 1943. Explains some of the problems of present-day education.

Who's Who in American Education. Nashville, Tenn.: Who's Who in American Education, 1928– . Biennial.

Social Sciences—Geography

Bartholomew, John W., ed. *Advanced Atlas of Modern Geography.* 3rd ed. New York: McGraw-Hill, 1956.

Encyclopaedia Britannica World Atlas. Chicago: Encyclopaedia Britannica, 1960.

Hammond's Ambassador World Atlas. Maplewood, N.J.: C. S. Hammond, 1961. Includes the 1960 census figures.

Webster's Geographical Dictionary. rev. ed. Springfield, Mass.: G. & C. Merriam, 1959.

Social Sciences—History

Adams, James Truslow, ed. *Dictionary of American History.* 5 vols. 2nd ed., rev. New York: Scribner's, 1942.

Barzun, Jacques and Henry F. Graff. *The Modern Researcher.* New York: Harcourt Brace Jovanovich, 1957.

The Cambridge Ancient History. Ed. J. B. Bury et al. 12 vols. Cambridge, Eng.: Cambridge Univ. Press, 1923–39.

The Shorter Cambridge Medieval History. Ed. C. W. Previte-Orton. 2 vols. Cambridge, Eng.: Cambridge Univ. Press, 1953.

The Cambridge Modern History. Ed. A. W. Ward et al. 13 vols. and atlas. Cambridge, Eng.: Cambridge Univ. Press, 1902–26.

Current, Richard N., T. H. Williams, and Frank Freidel. *American History: A Survey.* New York: Random House, 1961.

Handlin, Oscar, et al. *Guide to American History.* Cambridge, Mass.: Harvard Univ. Press, 1954.

Keller, Helen Rex. *Dictionary of Dates.* 2 vols. New York: Macmillan, 1934. Historical events through 1930.

Lord, Clifford L., and Elizabeth H. Lord, eds. *Historical Atlas of the United States,* rev. ed. New York: Holt, 1953.

The New American Nation Series. Ed. Henry S. Commager and Richard B. Morris. New York: Harper & Brothers, 1954– . Work in progress. Sixteen volumes have appeared, each by a different author.

Schlesinger, Arthur M., and Dixon R. Fox, eds. *History of American Life: A Social, Cultural, and Economic Analysis.* 13 vols. New York: Macmillan, 1929–44.

U.S. Library of Congress, Reference Division. *A Guide to the Study of the United States of America.* Washington, D.C.: U.S. Government Printing Office, 1960.

Other Social Sciences

Burchfield, LaVerne. *Student's Guide to Materials in Political Science.* New York: Holt, 1935.

Clark, Donald T., and Bert A. Gottfried. *Dictionary of Business and Finance.* New York: Thomas Y. Crowell Company, 1957.

Fairchild, Henry Pratt, ed. *Dictionary of Sociology.* New York: Philosophical Library, 1944.

Lazarus, Harold, ed. *American Business Dictionary.* New York: Philosophical Library, 1957.

Nemmers, Erwin E., and Cornelius C. Janzen, eds. *Dictionary of Economics and Business.* Paterson, N.J.: Littlefield, Adams, 1959.

Patterns of Government: The Major Political Systems of Europe. Ed. Samuel H. Beer and Adam B. Ulam. New York: Random House, 1958.

Schlesinger, Arthur M., and Dixon R. Fox, eds. *History of American Life: A Social, Cultural, and Economic Analysis*. 13 vols. New York: Macmillan, 1929–44.

Smith, Edward C., and Arnold J. Zurcher, eds. *New Dictionary of American Politics*. rev. ed. New York: Barnes & Noble, 1955.

Van Royen, William, ed. *Atlas of the World's Resources*. Vol. I: *The Agricultural Resources of the World*. Vol. II: *The Mineral Resources of the World*, by William Van Royen and Oliver Bowles. Englewood Cliffs, N.J.: Prentice-Hall, for the University of Maryland, 1952–54.

EXERCISES

Library problems

1. Interpret the information presented on the sample library catalog card *A*.

A

```
540    Selwood, Pierce, 1900–
Sel       General Chemistry. 6th
          ed. New York, Holt, c1962.

          220p.   illus.

          1. Chemistry
```

B

```
540         General Chemistry.
Sel    Selwood, Pierce, 1900–
            General Chemistry, 6th
       ed.
```

C

```
540         CHEMISTRY
Sel    Selwood, Pierce, 1900–
            General Chemistry, 6th
       ed.
```

2. Identify cards *A, B,* or *C* as either subject, title, or main entry cards.
3. In which books or other materials would you find the following information:

a. periodical articles in the fields of history, economics, philosophy, and allied subjects

b. critics' evaluations of *Another Country* by James Baldwin [c. 1962]

c. a history of the word *God* in the English language

d. a biographical essay on the Duke of Marlborough

e. a biographical sketch of John Adams

f. current material on civil rights

g. general periodical articles

h. a biographical sketch of former President Nixon

i. a quotation from James Boswell

j. an article on Salvador Dali

k. the population of Yap Island in June 1960

l. the number of people employed in the luggage industry in the United States in 1959

m. a description of reference sources of value to library users

1. *Who's Who in America*
2. *Book Review Digest*
3. Pamphlet file
4. *Statesmen's Yearbook*
5. Bartlett's *Quotations*
6. *Oxford English Dictionary*
7. *Social Sciences Index* and *Humanities Index*
8. *Painting in the Twentieth Century*
9. *Dictionary of National Biography*
10. *Readers' Guide to Periodical Literature*
11. *Statistical Abstract of the U.S.*
12. *Dictionary of American Biography*
13. *Winchell's Guide to Reference Books*

4. Interpret this entry from the *Readers' Guide:*

HAPPINESS
Happiness is within you, by Gaylord Hauser.
Read. Dig. 57:42 Jl'47.

5. How are fiction books arranged in the library?
6. After careful research in a good library, mark the correct answers to the following problems.

a. Consult the *Dictionary of Mythology, Folklore, and Symbols,* Vol. 2, and determine the page number of the citation on Mumbo Jumbo.
1) 965   2) 1136   3) 1483   4) 1689

b. Consult the *International Film Guide* (1971) and find out how many custom-built cinemas existed in the U.S.S.R. in 1969.
1) 3,600   2) 4,800   3) 7,320   4) 11,318

c. See the table of contents in the *Sources of Information in the Social Sciences* and determine how many subject areas are covered.
1) 7   2) 8   3) 9   4) 10

d. See *The Interpreter's Bible,* 12 volumes. In Volume I, the history of the interpretation of the Bible begins on page
1) 74   2) 99   3) 106   4) 135

e. In *The American Novel 1789–1959,* page 120 contains references dealing with Hemingway's *For Whom the Bell Tolls.*
1) True   2) False

f. How many illustrations are to be found accompanying the article *Medicine and the Arts,* page 18, in *Britannia Yearbook of Science and the Future,* 1971?
1) 36   2) 30   3) 25   4) 11

g. The call number for the *International Who's Who* is R920.
1) True   2) False

h. The *Dictionary of American Biography* is an excellent source of biographical information on living Americans. (R926)
1) True   2) False

i. The *New Century Cyclopedia of Names* includes mythological and legendary persons and places.
1) True   2) False

j. See the *Oxford Classical Dictionary,* second edition, page 333. Deucalion is the Greek equivalent to which of the following?
1) Abraham   2) Samson   3) Noah   4) Cain

k. Check the *C.Q. Weekly Reports,* Vol. XXIX, No. 27, 2 July 1971, page 1417. Consult the excerpts of nine opinions of the Supreme Court and determine if Justices Douglas and Harlan concurred in their opinions.
1) True   2) False

l. In the *Dictionary of Names* identify Kashake-Darya as
1) musician   2) Persian poet   3) River in U.S.S.R.   4) none of these

m. Find a brief discussion of the life of the English king Alfred, emphasizing his work as an author and educator, listing his principle works, and giving a brief list of other sources about him.
1) *Who Was Who*   2) *Current Biography*   3) *Webster's Biographical Dictionary*   4) *British Authors before 1800*

n. Which one of the following does *not* contain a listing on Willy Brandt?
1) *International Who's Who*   2) *Who's Who in America*   3) *Who's Who*   4) *Dictionary of National Biography*

o. Where would you find a listing of several famous ichthyologists?
1) *Biography Index*   2) *Who's Who*   3) *Cyclopedia of World Authors*   4) *Leaders in Education*

p. Cite the page in *Webster's Biographical Dictionary,* 1943, that states the date on which Henry Auguste Omont became the curator of manuscripts in the Bibliothèque Nationale.
1) 2711   2) 1215   3) 1302   4) 1121

q. By checking *Who's Who in America,* find Daryl F. Zanuck's military rank in the U.S. Army.
1) corporal   2) lieutenant colonel   3) major   4) private

r. Consult *American Authors 1600–1900.* Cite the page of the article on Jonathan Edwards.
1) 230   2) 243   3) 257   4) 306

s. See the *Oxford English Dictionary.* Find the date on which the word "totemism" was first recorded in English.
1) 1791   2) 1311   3) 1914   4) 1806

t. See *Readers' Guide to Periodical Literature.* Give the number of articles on Alcoholics Anonymous in Volume 25.
1) 12   2) 2   3) 7   4) 1

Documentation problems

1. Convert the following information into the proper bibliography form.

   a. A book by Geoffrey Ashe entitled King Arthur's Avalon, copyrighted in 1957 and published by Collins, whose address is St. James's Place, London.

   b. A book called Limits and Latitudes, copyrighted 1965, written by Kevin G. Burns, Edward H. Jones, and Robert C. Wylder, and published in Philadelphia and New York by the J. B. Lippincott Company.

   c. The fifth edition of a book whose title is Writing with a Purpose, authored by James M. McCrimmon and published by Houghton Mifflin Company of Boston, copyrighted 1972.

   d. A two-volume edition of a work called American Literature: The Makers and the Making, edited by Cleanth Brooks, R. W. B. Lewis, and Robert Penn Warren, published in New York by St. Martin's Press, Inc., copyrighted in 1973.

e. Sculley Bradley, and others' edition of The Scarlet Letter by Nathaniel Hawthorne, published in New York by W. W. Norton & Company, Inc., in the year 1962.

f. A translated version of the novel Crime and Punishment by Fyodor Dostoevsky. The translator is Constance Garnett; the copyright date is 1964, published by Bantam Books in New York.

g. Lionel Trilling's article The Meaning of a Literary Idea, reprinted in a book called Exploring Literature, which is edited by Lynn Altenbernd and published by The Macmillan Company in New York, copyrighted 1970.

h. An article entitled The Historical Roots of our Ecologic Crisis, found in a journal called Science, Volume 155, pages 1203 to 1207. That particular issue of the magazine came out on March 10 of 1967.

i. An unsigned news article in the newspaper Los Angeles Times, headlined Nader Links Candles and Lead Poisoning, found in the December 7, 1973 issue, Part I, page 5, columns one and two.

j. An entry from the Encyclopaedia Britannica entitled Seleucid Dynasty. The author is E. R. Bevan. The encyclopedia edition year is 1963.

2. Using page numbers that you make up, turn the previous bibliography entries into proper footnotes, numbered consecutively 1–10.

Note-taking problems

1. Summarize the following paragraph into no more than twenty-five words.

All the objectively observable characteristics of the goose's behavior on losing its mate are roughly identical with those accompanying human grief. This applies particularly to the phenomena observable in the sympathetic nervous system. John Bowlby, in his study of infant grief, has given an equally convincing and moving description of this primal grieving, and it is almost incredible how detailed are the analogies we find here in human beings and in birds. Just as in the human face, it is the neighborhood of the eyes that in geese bears the permanent marks of deep grief. The lowering of the tonus in the sympathicus causes the eye to sink back deeply in its socket and, at the same time, decreases the tension of the outer facial muscles supporting the eye region from below. Both factors contribute to the formation of a fold of loose skin below the eye which as early as in the ancient Greek mask of tragedy had become the conventionalized expression of grief. My dear old greylag Ada, several times a widow, was particularly easy to recognize because of the grief-marked expression of her eyes. A knowledgeable visitor who knew nothing about Ada's history standing beside me at the lake suddenly pointed her out among many geese, saying, "That goose must have been through a lot!"

—Konrad Lorenz, *On Aggression*

2. Paraphrase the following passage, using approximately the same number of words as the original.

In many ways (though by no means in all), Napoleon was insensitive to the forces that were shaping the future. Except in some scattered remarks made at St. Helena, when he had time to reflect on the age, he was blind to the potentialities of steam power and of other inventions that were changing the world. A conservative by temperament, he distrusted innovations of any sort. He sought to establish a dynasty when monarchy was beginning to go out of fashion—and the dynasty he wished to establish was based on the Carolingian model, at that; he created a nobility after a revolution had been fought to abolish it; and in restoring the Church he gave it a position which, as subsequent history has shown, was out of keeping with modern trends.

—J. Christopher Herold, *The Age of Napoleon*

11

Writing about literature

FALLACIES ABOUT LITERATURE

The "author intended" fallacy
The "I like it" fallacy
The "it can mean anything" fallacy

THE GENERAL AND CRITICAL ANALYSIS

The general analysis
The critical analysis

WHAT TO SAY ABOUT FICTION

Point of view
Plot and theme
Tone
Mood
Character

WHAT TO SAY ABOUT DRAMA

Point of view
Plot and theme
Tone
Mood
Character

WHAT TO SAY ABOUT POETRY

Point of view
Plot and theme
Tone
Mood
Character

In this chapter we shall describe three fallacious approaches to interpreting literature and discuss the two major methods of writing about literature: the general and critical analysis. The chapter ends with separate discussions of fiction, drama, and poetry.

FALLACIES ABOUT LITERATURE

The most common fallacies students fall into when writing about literature are:

1. The "author intended" fallacy
2. The "I like it" fallacy
3. The "it can mean anything" fallacy

The "author intended" fallacy

The "author intended" fallacy is the assumption that a literary work can be judged by the intent of its author. This assumption is usually false. First of all, we have no way of knowing what the author's intent really was. Second, he may have had a sincere intent, but failed to carry it out. Students are sometimes quick to point to author intent as support for an interpretation. At best, this is guesswork, since there is no real way of judging intent. Even if the author dogmatically recorded his intent and believed himself to have carried it out, the final judgment must be based on evidence from the work itself. Author intent is frail evidence to base an interpretation on.

There are slight exceptions. For instance, if you were combining a biographical study of an author with a study of his work, you might want to mention any special intent the author claimed for his writing. Generally, however, you should reserve intent for biography and leave it out of interpretation. You should judge and interpret a literary work for what it seems to be, not for what you think it was intended to be.

The "I like it" fallacy

Liking literature is not necessarily a fallacy; but neither is it an interpretation. When you are asked to comment on a literary work, the assignment is intended to measure more than emotional intensity. It is usually aimed at finding out how well you understand the work, how you discriminate, and how logically you think. So, if your instructor asks you to analyze and interpret a poem, and you rhapsodize for three pages on how much you like it, you have failed to meet the assignment.

Furthermore, saying that you like or dislike a poem says something about your taste, but nothing about the poem. You are saying, in effect, that the poem is good because you like it, which is what actors and football heroes say about aftershave lotion in commercials. In an analysis of a poem, however, you are to focus on the poem, not on your response to it. You therefore need to say why you like it by discussing the poem itself, how it is put together, and how well it works. This applies to anything you write about fiction, drama, or any other literary genre. Similarly, the "I dislike it" response is also fallacious for the same reasons.

> **Do not endorse: Interpret!**

The "it can mean anything" fallacy

The "it can mean anything" fallacy usually comes up when a student and an instructor disagree over the meaning of some literary work. The disagreement usually boils down to the following question: If the work means one thing to me and another thing to you, who is to say which interpretation is right?

There are two parts to the fallacious argument that "it can mean anything." Part one says that a work of literature may validly mean one thing to one reader and something different to another—in short, that there is no absolute meaning to any literary work. That part of the argument is true enough. From this, part two infers that since meaning is not absolute, all interpretations of literature are equally valid; in other words, since nobody can be right, nobody can be wrong. But this conclusion does not follow. There are two components of any interpretation: the reader and the work. The formula is:

> reader + work = interpretation

The reader is always different; but the text is always the same, even though each reader may interpret it differently. Some students justify the belief that all interpretations are acceptable on the ground that all readers are different. But they ignore the fact that the text remains the same. To interpret responsibly, you must be able to:

1. Specify the point of view you used in interpreting the literary work
2. Cite evidence from the text to support your interpretation of it
3. Show the logical links leading from the evidence in the text to your interpretation

These are the minimal requirements for a responsible interpretation.

It follows that an interpretation can be wrong in at least these three ways:

1. The point of view used in approaching the literary work may be inappropriate.
2. The interpretation may not be supported by evidence in the text.
3. The interpretation may be illogically derived from the evidence.

Do:
Focus your analysis on the work itself

State reasons for your response to the work

Know and be prepared to defend the assumptions, evidence, and logic behind your interpretation

Do not:
Judge a work by intent
Emote in place of analyzing
Assume that any interpretation is valid

THE GENERAL AND CRITICAL ANALYSIS

Most of the writing you will have to do on literature will involve either a general analysis or a critical analysis.

The general analysis

The general analysis requires you to sum up and trace a theme in a literary work and briefly discuss some elements of technique. This kind of analysis is usually done as an in-class assignment where you are asked to make an impromptu interpretation of a piece of literature. The cardinal rule for the general analysis is this: you should analyze the literary work on the basis of its most significant feature. If you are writing about a poem that uses elaborate imagery but says nothing about the personality of its speaker, you should focus your analysis on its imagery and ignore its speaker. If the story has a threadbare plot but a well-developed character, then you should analyze its character. First, you determine by common sense what is most significant about the literary work to be analyzed; then you analyze that.

For a general analysis of any literary form, use the SQIF format: Summarize, Quote, Interpret, and discuss Form.

Begin your analysis with a *summary* of the work's theme. Extracting theme from literature is the most error-prone phase of any general analysis. You should try to sum up the work in terms of its single dominant idea; the statement of this idea is your version of the work's theme. Naturally, if you are wrong about the theme, your entire analysis is wrong. However, if you use the SQIF format, your instructor will have a chance to reconstruct your thinking and examine the evidence that led you to your mistaken conclusion. Most instructors are gentle with erroneous themes so long as they can trace the thinking process behind them.

If you feel a preamble to your essay is necessary, at least make sure the theme is stated in your opening paragraph. Your summary of theme will serve as a thesis for your analysis and lend structure and direction to it.

Quotations from the literary work serve as evidence for your version of its theme. They anchor your analysis to the text of the work and keep you from going adrift on the sea of speculation. But do not simply string one quotation after another as padding for a skimpy analysis. Use the sandwich principle—bread, then meat, then bread; interpret, then quote, then interpret again. Here is an example:

> The speaker, however, is not so optimistic. He sees that there are "no more clowns . . . no more children . . . no more old ladies" left to inspire the poet/artist. If we take the clowns to mean the ability to laugh in the middle of tragedy, the children to mean innocence in the midst of guilt, and the old ladies to mean gentleness in the middle of cruelty, we can then anticipate the ending of the poem, which is the speaker's conclusion that artists have lost their magic—that is, their illusive talents—and "soon shall be dead." In short, the savagery of war annihilates hope and along with it the artist's inspiration.

Notice that the writer imbeds her quotations between interpretation. Sandwich quotations interfere less with the flow of writing than blob quotations. Here is an example of a blob quotation:

> The speaker seems to be very depressed, as when he says:
>
>   i said
>   no denying
>   essentially, this fact—
>   no denying in places like bergen-belsen

> the world's hope died there—
>   which is narrow, but
>   maybe true—
> the world's hope died
> when auschwitz opened its gates—

A frail point backed up by a massive quotation is a clear signal of padding, to which most instructors respond negatively. Quote to prove your theme, not to elongate your analysis.

In a general analysis, *interpretation* consists of applying the extracted theme to the body of the work and demonstrating that it fits. In short, you trace the way the theme is developed throughout the work. Summarizing the theme puts your interpretation in thesis form: the rest of the analysis consists of expanding on the theme and proving it with evidence from the text. If your summary of theme is concise and accurate, the follow-through interpretation should be easy.

Form refers to the mechanics of a literary work—to its physical characteristics. The form of a poem is its meter, rhyme scheme, imagery, stanza structure, and shape; the form of a play is its division into acts and scenes, its plot, dialog, and setting. Form refers to what a literary work is made up of; content refers to what the work means. This conceptual difference between form and content is frequently used in the analysis of literature. It is possible to analyze a work for its form or its content. When you write about theme you are analyzing content; when you scan a poem for its meter, you are analyzing form.

Most general analyses do not call for long, ponderous commentary on form. The idea is simply to mention and underscore those elements of form that are prominently used to convey theme. If the poem uses a distinctive rhyme to reinforce its theme, you should mention it in your analysis. If a play makes use of the flashback technique (where a character relives a memory for the benefit of the audience) to advance its plot, that, too, should probably be mentioned in your analysis. Only the major elements of form need to be discussed in a general analysis.

Do:
  Focus on the most significant feature of the work

  Use SQIF: Summarize, Quote, Interpret, and discuss Form

  **Tie in all your analysis with your summation of theme
    in the same way that you would hold a paper to its thesis**

Do not:

Wander off into an analysis of some minor feature of the work

Pad your analysis with long, blob quotations

Quote without interpreting

Shift your focus from the work itself

The poem below is followed by an example of a general analysis of it.

EVERY JEW IS A POET

every jew is a poet
steiner said
and i told him yes
i said
  no denying
essentially, this fact—
  no denying in places like bergen-belsen
the world's hope died there—
  which is narrow, but
  maybe true—
the world's hope died
when auschwitz opened its gates—
  and steiner said
every jew a poet
  and i said essentially
  and steiner and i
sat there
in the marketplace
and he said the world lost itself
in the barracks at treblinka
  and i said yes
most definitely—
  and steiner boasted
  every jew a poet
and i told him is magic in that—
  is magic in our people—
and steiner said
  every jew a poet, an artist—
  a creator—
  i said yes steiner yes
    and i said
no more clowns in lublin, steiner,
  no more children in kiev,
  no more old ladies in cracow—

i said steiner i said steiner
  we have lost our magic
and soon shall be dead.

—Neeli Cherry

Title of work to be
analyzed.

AN ANALYSIS OF "EVERY JEW IS A POET"

By Diana Haring

Summary of theme: first
sentence sums up theme
in thesis form; second
sentence expands on it.

In his poem, "Every Jew Is a Poet," Neeli
Cherry tells us that a brutalized society destroys artistic creativity. The poet uses the extermination of the Jews during the Second
World War as a symbol for the kind of excessive brutality that inevitably leads to an extinc-
tion of artistic creativity. Since much of the
world's great art has come from Jews, the
choice is an appropriate one.

Specific focus on the
poem. Answers who,
where, what, as a lead-in
to the interpretation,
which will apply the
theme to the body of the
poem and prove it with
specifics.

The speaker is a Jew sitting in the marketplace of a city, discussing the effects of the
Second World War with another Jew by the
name of Steiner. Their conversation approaches despair as they face the fact that the
Nazi concentration camps and prisoner of war
barracks in such places as Bergen-Belsen, Auschwitz, and Treblinka have suffocated, perhaps
for all time, the hope that turns into magic and
then into poetry. In the process of their conversation, the speaker and Steiner tell us something important about the total creative
process: it can survive only as long as hope
survives; when hope dies, the urge toward artistic creativity dies with it.

Beginning of proof.
Notice the sandwich
effect: quotation, then
comment. The
interpretation part of the
analysis shows how the
poem develops the
theme.

The poem begins with Steiner's comment
that "every jew is a poet," which could mean
that poetry (or in a larger sense, all art)
flourishes during persecution and personal suf-
fering, of which the Jews have had a greater
share than most people. The speaker then re-
torts that this is so only as long as there is
hope, but that in places like Bergen-Belsen and
Auschwitz "the world's hope died." At first,
Steiner cannot accept this tragic view and in-
sists that "the world lost itself," implying that it
can again find its way because, after all, "every
jew a poet, an artist—a creator." This is

Steiner's way of asserting that the human spirit will prevail.

The speaker, however, is not so optimistic. He sees that there are "no more clowns . . . no more children . . . no more old ladies" left to inspire the poet/artist. If we take the clowns to mean the ability to laugh in the midst of tragedy, the children to mean innocence in the midst of guilt, and the old ladies to mean gentleness in the midst of cruelty, we can then anticipate the ending of the poem, which is the speaker's conclusion that artists have lost their magic—that is, their illusive talents—and soon "shall be dead." In short, the savagery of war annihilates hope and along with it the artist's inspiration.

The poem is written in free verse with numerous enjambed lines that create a loose, hesitating dialog, as if the two speakers were experiencing some difficulty concentrating among the many distractions of the marketplace. There are no quotation marks to inform the reader when one speech ends and another begins. This lack of grammatical precision increases the general spontaneity of the dialog by allowing the comments of both speakers to blend. Each speaker says what he feels at that moment, and the effect is that of a casual conversation. The entire poem is concentrated into a single stanza, making it a self-contained unit of thought.

In summary: a growing sense of futility fills the poem as the speaker and Steiner progress in their conversation. In the beginning Steiner maintains his sense of identity by repeating three times, "every jew is a poet," but as the realism about the brutalizing effects of war crowd in on him and on the speaker, the poem ends on a note of despair and resignation: "we have lost our magic/and soon shall be dead."

Continuation of interpretation: notice the use of specifics. Focus does not wander; evidence for the theme compiled in quotes.

Discussion of form begins, which is limited to form as it underscores statement of theme in poem: the use of line and verse devices to create conversational effect.

Ends by summing up theme, providing closure to the analysis.

The critical analysis

The critical analysis is usually the subject of a paper written out of class. It involves selecting a single frame of reference and analyzing the literary work from that point of view. The major frames of reference for approaching literature are: *moral, psychological, sociological,* and *formalist.* In their application to literature, these frames of reference differ only slightly from the way you would apply them to account for any human behavior. If, for example, you knew someone who committed a felony, and you had to explain his behavior to someone else, you could do it in one of several ways:

1. You could describe him as an immoral person who got what he deserved. In this case, your frame of reference is essentially a moral one.
2. You could explain him as the victim of a domineering mother and weak father and subject to compulsions picked up from a traumatic childhood. Your frame of reference is now psychological.
3. You could explain him as the victim of his social environment, bringing in such factors as his race and the income level of his parents. Your frame of reference is now sociological.

Notice that the explanation of why your friend committed the felony shifts with each frame of reference. Each of these frames of reference is available as an approach to interpreting literature, and each brings with it a slightly different emphasis that will eventually affect the outcome of your analysis.

In the *moral* approach to literature, the emphasis is on evaluating and discussing the literary work in terms of contemporary morality. Say, for instance, that you are analyzing a novel whose central character commits a murder and is executed for it after a long trial. Taking the moral approach to this novel does not necessarily mean that you should use the novel as an opportunity to deliver a sermon against murder. However, you could analyze the revenge ethic underlying capital punishment and use the novel to draw conclusions about the moral value the culture places on life.

In other words, the moral approach does more than moralize about simple good versus simple evil. The moral approach assumes that the morality of any culture consists of a ranked set of values that are always changing. Since literature largely deals with people in the state of making choices, it will reflect the prevailing hierarchy of values in the culture. By studying literature we therefore gain insight into the value system we live by.

The following are summaries of possible critical analyses using the moral frame of reference.

A study of the image of man in Beckett's *Endgame:* The writer analyzes the image of man presented through the characters in Beckett's play *Endgame.* He concludes that the characters are drawn after the model of the existentialist's "absurd man" whose life is futile and pointless. The writer focuses on the notion of "life as a game," which he concludes is pivotal to Beckett's philosophy in the play. He ends with a summation of the "absurd man's" values as they are presented in the play.

The morality of war in Stephen Crane's *Red Badge of Courage:* The writer examines the moral change that takes place in Henry Fleming's values as part of his initiation as a soldier. She shows how Fleming's values are altered by war and examines his early cowardice and his subsequent emergence as a leader in battles. She concludes that Fleming had come to value demonstrations of his manliness in battle over his civilian respect for human life. She ends with a discussion of the cultural value and definition of manliness as it is reflected in the novel.

Notice that both of these critical analyses were focused on some aspect of our value system. The first analysis investigates the values of Beckett's "absurd man," which in turn is a reflection of man's image of himself as seen through the eyes of a major playwright. In the second analysis the writer examines our definition and value of manliness and how it changes during a time of war as reflected by the changes in Fleming. This is the focus of the moral frame of reference: on literature as it reflects our value system.

As the name implies, the *psychological* approach to literature focuses either on the behavior and psychological makeup of characters in literature, or on the psychological makeup of an author as it is revealed through his or her work. Using the psychological approach to a novel about a person who commits a murder, you could try to construct a psychological explanation accounting for motives based on the evidence given in the novel.

The psychological approach to literature assumes that literary characters behave according to the same psychological consistencies and probabilities as real people, and that the motives for their behavior can be discovered and a psychological explanation inferred from a study of the text itself. If the characters behave in a way that is not explainable by the psychological cues in the text, they are considered to be faultily drawn.

The psychological approach can also be used in a biographical study of an author. The author's work can be analyzed in conjunction with his or her life and used to explain stages in his or her development. A single work may also be taken to reflect the psychological self of the author and analyzed for what it tells about him or her. This use of the psychological approach assumes that an author symbolically projects his or her private self into the artistic work.

Here are some examples of critical analyses using the psychological approach:

An analysis of Raskolnikov's dreams as they reflect his motive for murder in Dostoevsky's *Crime and Punishment:* Using the technique of Freudian dream analysis, the writer analyzes two dreams of Raskolnikov's and shows how they symbolically depict his true motive for the murder.

A psychological analysis of "Every Jew Is a Poet": The writer analyzes the poem "Every Jew Is a Poet" for what it reveals about the poet and his creativity. (This analysis is included at the end of this section, pp. 307–9.)

Both of these analyses typify the focus of the psychological approach to literature. This frame of reference is concerned primarily with behavior, either of a character or of the author, as it is symbolically reflected in the literary work.

The *sociological* approach to literature is used in two ways. First, it is used to analyze and explain characters from a sociological frame of reference. The emphasis in such an analysis is on the sociological background of the character—social class, income level, religious training, race, and so on. The character is analyzed in a sociological context and with reference to the mores, norms, and role expectations of the society he or she lives in.

Second, the sociological approach is used to understand and explain an earlier society through its literature. The literary work is treated as sociological evidence of how an earlier society was stratified, what its norms and mores were, and how its various classes related to each other. This kind of analysis assumes that a literary work, especially novels and plays, faithfully reflects the social environment of its time.

The following are examples of sociological analyses:

Social class in the nineteenth century as reflected in Thomas Hardy's novel *Jude the Obscure:* The writer focuses on class conflict and layering in nineteenth-century England as it is seen in the novel *Jude the Obscure.* She concludes that most of Jude's problems were caused by the lack of vertical mobility, that is, upward movement from one class to another, in nineteenth-century England.

The role of the salesman in our society: a study of Willy Loman in Arthur Miller's *Death of a Salesman:* The writer uses Willy Loman as the typical salesman and analyzes role expectations exerted on him by the society. He concludes that Willy Loman undergoes an identity crisis caused by his internalization of the salesman's role and his inability to regain contact with himself when faced with retirement. The writer describes the salesman's role as requiring self-image manipulation in a variety of sales situations where the salesman is trying to please the customer.

305

Like the psychological approach, the sociological approach to literature is concerned with the way people behave. However, it focuses not on the inner person, but on the external and social causes of behavior. That is essentially the difference between these two frames of reference.

Finally, we come to the only frame of reference you could not use in explaining the behavior of your felon friend. The *formalist* approach is peculiar to literature. Its focus is on form, not on content (see p. 299). It deals primarily with the physical characteristics of a literary work. Typical formalist studies of literary works examine structure, language, symbolism, imagery, meter (in poetry), and other physical features. The formalist approach is less interested in *what* a literary work means, and more in *how* it means. How does imagery function in the work to convey meaning? What part in a poem's meaning does its meter play? The focus is on the mechanics that generate the meaning of a literary work. Here are two examples:

The use of color imagery in Stephen Crane's *Blue Hotel:* The writer analyzes *The Blue Hotel* for its use of color imagery. He concludes that part of Crane's technique is to identify each character with a single color and to then repetitiously use that color in images that describe him.

An analysis of style in Hemingway's *In Our Time:* The writer analyzes Hemingway's style in the novel *In Our Time*. She concludes that Hemingway's style is based on short sentences, sparing use of adjectives, and heavy use of adverbial phrasing.

Neither of the above analyses has anything to do with content; they are studies directed at form. That is the overwhelming aim of the formalist approach, as its name implies.

Before you write your critical analysis, you must select a frame of reference for approaching the literary work. The decision to select one frame over another is a matter of common sense. You must first decide whether or not the work is approachable from that frame of reference. A small poem about a bumblebee will probably contain little psychological or sociological evidence, and will not lend itself well to analysis by these approaches. Neither is it likely to yield anything under moral analysis. But by using the formalist approach you could ignore the bee and its meaning and analyze the poem for imagery, meter, stanza, structure, and rhyme scheme. Before you begin your analysis, be sure that the approach you intend to use is appropriate.

A frame of reference in approaching a literary work is valuable because it pinpoints your focus on a specific aspect of the work. If you use a sociological frame, you would consider the sociological evidence in the work; if you use the moral frame, you would zoom in on what the work implies about humans and human values. In each case, you are examining a different aspect of the literary work and analyzing that. It might occur to you that such selectivity leads to a version of literature similar to the blind men's description of the elephant. In a critical analysis you do end up with an interpretation of a single strand of the work's meaning, but you do not claim that this interpretation is definitive of the whole work. All the strands woven together will reveal the work's richness and complexity. Some works of literature are analyzable from all frames of reference; they will yield up something different to each and still store vast and unexplored meanings.

SQIF is also the recommended format for the critical analysis (see pp. 298–99), but the F part is optional. You should summarize the findings of your analysis in a thesis statement, back it up with specific quotations from the text itself, and demonstrate its applicability to the literary work. With a critical analysis your thesis will be narrower than a simple statement of the work's theme, and will focus instead on some aspect in the work that is related to the frame of reference you are using. In the following analysis of "Every Jew Is a Poet" (see pp. 300–301) the writer uses a psychological frame of reference. She begins with the major assumption that the poem reflects a psychological crisis in the poet, and that both Steiner and the speaker represent different sides of the poet's personality:

A PSYCHOLOGICAL CRITIQUE OF "EVERY JEW IS A POET"

by Virginia Parra

From a psychological point of view, this poem appears to depict a spiritual struggle between the positive and negative forces of the poet's nature. Perhaps the word *struggle* is a little too strong, for, while there is movement in the poem, or a constant shifting of positions, it is always amicable. It is possible that the poet is really just tossing these two opposing views out into the open for the purpose of analyzing them more objectively and thus arriving at some sort of solution. In any event the conflict seems to end badly, as the poem closes with the negative forces having the last word and a deep depression setting in.

First, let us look at the title, "Every Jew Is a Poet." It is interesting to note that the poet elected to use the adjective "every," which makes no exception or omission. Had he merely said "Jews are poets," we could have assumed that he was making a general statement and, conceivably, some Jews are not poets, including himself. However, while the poet's creativity is not under scrutiny in the poem, it does appear to be in jeopardy at the end of the poem. The main question here is whether the poet should go in the direction of love or in the direction of hate, or, as Shakespeare said through Hamlet, "To be or not to be." For to love is to live, or to be, and to hate is to die, or not to be.

Two of several definitions given by the Random House unabridged dictionary for the word *Jew* are: 1) a person whose religion is Judaism, and 2) one of a scattered group of people that traces its descent from Biblical Hebrews. Both of these definitions give substance to the poem. As an adherent of Judaism—the monotheistic religion from which some of our present religions, including Christianity, are off-shoots—the poet displays a definite pride in his people, the original defenders of belief in one God, Yahweh. However, as a member of "a scattered group of people" who have been ostracized and expelled from one country after another, he feels depression tinged with bitterness.

It is more difficult to find a symbolic meaning for the word *poet*. For, even among themselves, poets seem to be unable to agree in this regard. However, in order to perceive the world around them with the depth and perception demanded by their art, they must possess acute sensitivity to both interior and exterior stimuli, or, in other words, have a very high degree of "aliveness." The impressions they receive with icy clarity are recorded for their benefit and enjoyment, as well as for the benefit and enjoyment of their less creative brothers, with the hope of sparking them to life. As Alexander Pope said in his "Imitation of Horace," "Vain was the chief's, the sage's pride! They had no poet, and they died."

Now let us discuss the poem itself. The poem consists of a dialog between Steiner, the optimist, and I, the pessimist. Steiner struggles to buoy up the pessimist by reciting no less than four times that "every jew is a poet," and actually succeeds in mustering up the pessimist's enthusiasm just before he plunges into a final depression.

At the beginning, after Steiner has first stated that "every jew is a poet," the pessimist is somewhat noncommittal. He agrees with Steiner, but with reservations—note the word *essentially*. Then the pessimist goes on to mention two of the six Second World War extermination areas mentioned in the poem, stating that the world's hope died there. This could be looked at from two angles. First, since the poet, so to speak, gives life to the world, as stated above, exterminating the Jew, who is also a poet, will, figuratively speaking, cause the world to die as well. Second, since hatred is a two-edged sword, which while killing the hated also destroys the hater, the world so consumed with hatred for the poet's people, to the point of exterminating them, will ultimately succeed in destroying itself. However, the poet qualifies his comment by conceding that this is perhaps a "narrow" way of thinking. Perhaps somewhere in his subconscious he feels for a moment that there is still a spark of love left to ignite and save the world.

All of this takes place in the marketplace, a place long associated with the Jew. Additionally, it seems fitting that this discourse should occur in a place where people customarily exchange one thing for another, which is precisely what happens. In a surprise move, Steiner momentarily allows himself to cross over to the pessimist's corner by stating that "the world lost itself/in the barracks at treblinka." Perhaps this was his way of letting the reader know that although optimistic, he was not out of touch with reality and felt the plight of the Jew with deep intensity. However, he does not dwell there very long, returning to his litany of optimism with even greater force. Steiner's enthusiasm is contagious, and the pessimist is caught up in it for a while. But the poet's pessimism is too engrained in his soul, and he soon reverts to his role of gloom and destructive thinking, stating that there are "no more clowns in lublin, steiner, no more children in kiev, no more old ladies in cracow." I do not know whether the poet mentioned "clowns," "children," and "old ladies" for a special reason. If he did, the clown probably depicts the "schlemiel," or hapless victim, who, as Robert Kirsch said in a recent book review, "survived not only because of his ability to make a harassed and persecuted people laugh, but because beneath that laughter was the last laugh: the reality of survival." The reference to children was probably because they have always been an important part of the Jewish family. "Old ladies" perhaps embodies the famous "Jewish mother." The thought of their demise at Lublin, Kiev, and Cracow is too much for the poet to bear, and the poem ends with his finally giving in to his destructive thoughts and dragging Steiner along with him—note the use of the word *we* in "we have lost our magic." With this forfeiture of hope, the poet has put his creativity in jeopardy and, consequently, will soon be spiritually dead.

Compare this critical analysis with the general analysis of the same poem given on pages 301–2. Notice that the focus here is specifically related to the psychological frame of reference. Once the initial assumption is granted—that the poem tells something about the psyche of the poet—the rest of the analysis logically follows. Notice also that the writer does no analysis of form. With the more specific critical analysis, a discussion of form is optional. Do it if it adds something to your thesis; otherwise, ignore it.

To sum up, the critical analysis is usually given as an outside writing assignment like the term paper, and it involves selecting a frame of reference for approaching the literary work and then formulating an interpretation of it based on the emphasis of that frame. Although one of the frames of reference we have described will usually be selected, an analysis could be formulated that would straddle two or more frames of reference. Some blurring is bound to occur here, as with everything else.

All the previous cautions given for the general analysis also apply to the critical analysis. In addition,

> **Do:**
>> **Be sure the work is approachable from your chosen frame of reference**
>>
>> **Clearly identify your frame of reference**
>
> **Do not:**
>> **Force an inappropriate frame on the work**
>>
>> **Switch frames in mid-analysis**

WHAT TO SAY ABOUT FICTION

Whichever genre of literature you choose to write about, the central principle remains the same: you should focus on the most significant feature of the work and analyze that. Some stories emphasize character; others emphasize mood, and others plot. With still others, tone may be more significant than either character, mood, or plot. In each case, you should concentrate on the emphasis in the work and focus your analysis on it.

One or more of the following features is generally touched on in any analysis of fiction: point of view, plot and theme, tone, mood, and character. We will discuss these features as they apply to both the short story and the novel.

Point of view

Point of view refers to the perspective from which a story is told. The main points of view are: omniscient, first-person, and stream of consciousness.

With the *omniscient* point of view, the story is narrated from the perspective of an invisible author who refers to the characters as ''he'' or ''she.'' Here is an example:

> The old gentleman at the tea-table, who had come from America thirty years before, had brought with him, at the top of his baggage, his American physiognomy; and he had not only brought it with him, but he had kept it in the best order, so that, if necessary, he might have taken it back to his own country with perfect confidence. At present, obviously, nevertheless, his journeys were over and he was taking the rest that precedes the great rest.
>
> —Henry James, *The Portrait of a Lady*

The omniscient point of view allows an author to centralize a view of his characters and their behavior through his implied observer's presence. He can describe a character's appearance, tell what he or she is thinking, then move to another character and do the same. The effect is one of shifting intimacy which carries the reader from one character to another through the invisible presence of the author.

Where the omniscient point of view is used, the author's attitude toward his story or his characters is sometimes revealed through tone. We will discuss this point later when we deal with tone.

The *first-person* point of view tells the story through the mind of a single character who refers to himself or herself as "I." Here is an example:

> I'm a sick man . . . a mean man. There's nothing attractive about me. I think there's something wrong with my liver. But, actually, I'm not even sure what it is about my sickness; I'm not even sure what it is that's ailing me.
> —Feodor Dostoevsky, *Notes from the Underground*

A first-person narrative is colored by the personality of the character who tells it. We see everything through his eyes, and everything he says or describes tells us something about him. A chief difficulty with this point of view is judging the reliability of the narrator and evaluating what she says. Other implications for characterization also follow from the use of this point of view. We will discuss these when we deal with character.

The *stream of consciousness* point of view is an extension of the first-person point of view, but it involves an unusual technique. Stream of consciousness is an attempt to reconstruct the mental processes of a character on a page, to show how his or her mind actually sounds inside. The idea is not simply to capture the conscious or rational side of a character's mind, but to plumb the unconscious and irrational side of it as well. Here is an example:

> Through the fence, between the curling flower spaces, I could see them hitting. They were coming toward where the flag was and I went along the fence. Luster was hunting in the grass by the flower tree. They took the flag out, and they were hitting. Then they put the flag back and they went to the table, and he hit and the other hit. Then they went on, and I went along the fence. Luster came away from the flower tree and we stopped and I looked through the fence while Luster was hunting in the grass.
> —William Faulkner, *The Sound and the Fury*

This is the description of a golf game as seen through the mind of an idiot. Notice the simplicity of his language and his descriptions. He perceives everything as occurring in rigid sequence.

Here, in contrast, is a recollection in the mind of a suicidally depressed character:

I didnt look back the tree frogs didnt pay me any mind the grey light like moss in the trees drizzling but still it wouldnt rain after a while I turned went back to the edge of the woods as soon as I got there I began to smell honeysuckle again I could see the lights on the courthouse clock and the glare of the town square on the sky and the dark willows the light still on in Benjys room and I stooped through the fence and went across the pasture running I ran in the grey grass among the crickets the honeysuckle getting stronger and stronger and the smell of water then I could see the water the colour of grey honeysuckle I lay down on the bank with my face close to the ground. . . .
—William Faulkner, *The Sound and the Fury*

Stream of consciousness writing typically abandons traditional grammar and sentence structure on the assumption that these are superficial devices not observed by the mind in the thought process. In the above passage, the character is reliving a traumatic and painful memory; his thoughts are jumbled with vivid impressions that run through his mind almost incoherently. The passage recreates the experience as the character lived it in his mind.

A story written from a stream of consciousness point of view cannot be read literally. Such a point of view does not attempt to be factual or rational since it is based partly on the Freudian notion that the mind is subjected to irrational and absurd forces. You therefore have to infer about the character, rather than simply accept what he or she says literally.

To sum up, point of view in fiction is analogous to camera angle in a movie. Each of the different points of view allows an author to process and construct information about a character and his or her world in a slightly different way. It is important, therefore, that you begin your analysis of fiction with a clear idea about who is telling the story, what his or her attitude toward the narrative is, and whether or not his or her version of the story can be taken as factual and honest.

Plot and theme

Plot refers to the sequence of events or actions in a story. Plots are as numerous as the imagination of writers allows and vary in importance from one story to another. At the heart of plot is conflict—a character in opposition either to himself or herself, to something or someone else, or to the environment. The formula is:

PLOT + CONFLICT = THEME

For instance, if the plot recounts a "second honeymoon" trip taken on a fiftieth wedding anniversary, and the conflict exists in the husband between the demands of his wife and his personal need for privacy, the overall theme can probably be expressed as a criticism of marriage, depending on how the story turns out. If it turns out badly—the husband feels cramped, the wife is unhappy, yet they decide to spend the rest of their lives together in spite of their personal misery—then the theme may be the brutalization of romantic feeling by marriage. The idea is not to be glib, but to sum up plot and conflict into a major idea that becomes the theme.

A caution: do not ramble on for pages about plot. Many instructors regard this as a padding device. Here is an example from a student paper on Melville's *Bartleby the Scrivner:*

> The story is about a man who is hired as a Scrivner or clerk by the narrator. At first, he seems a little sluggish, but does what he's told. Then, after a while, he begins to object to doing little things that are part of his job. For instance, on the third day when the narrator asks Bartleby to help him examine a paper, he refuses and says, "I would prefer not to," which is what he always says when he refuses to do as he's asked. At first, his boss could hardly believe his ears, but he was so busy that he decided to forget the incident and asked Nippers to help him examine the papers instead.

The paper goes on in this vein for a couple of pages, unnecessarily so, because the instructor has obviously read the story and does not need to have it retold. What the assignment calls for is a statement of the major idea in the story and a tracing of this idea throughout the narrative using the SQIF format. Here is the opening sentence of a better analysis:

> The theme of *Bartleby the Scrivner* is society's inability to deal with a nonfunctioning human who withdraws and becomes cut off from its materialistic values.

This opening touches on plot, conflict, and theme. The plot is Bartleby's gradual withdrawal; the conflict is between him and his society; the theme is the sum of the two—how a function-conscious society that evaluates its members for their work is at a loss to deal with an individual on a solely human basis.

Combine plot and conflict and formulate a statement of theme that will become your thesis. After that, follow the SQIF format as you document your thesis by referring directly to passages in the story.

Tone

Tone is an abbreviation for *tone of voice*. A writer tells a story and does it in a voice. Because we must read rather than hear the story, the tone of

voice of its teller may be hard to detect. However, it is vital that you understand the author's tone, since it affects the way a story can be validly interpreted.

Tone is used both to project the personality of a character on the page
and to reveal the attitude of the author toward the narrative. An author's
tone of voice will signal whether he or she is taking the story seriously,
comically, bitterly, ironically, or otherwise. Compare these openings from
two different novels:

> Studs Lonigan, on the verge of fifteen, and wearing his first suit of
> long trousers, stood in the bathroom with a Sweet Caporal pasted in
> his mug. His hands were jammed in his trousers' pockets, and he
> sneered. He puffed, drew the fag out of his mouth, inhaled and said
> to himself: "Well, I'm kissin' the old dump goodbye tonight."
>
> —James T. Farrell, *Studs Lonigan*

> In the last years of the seventeenth century there was to be found
> among the fops and fools of the London coffee-houses one rangy,
> gangling flitch called Ebenezer Cooke, more ambitious than talented,
> and yet more talented than prudent, who, like his friends-in-folly, all
> of whom were supposed to be educating at Oxford or Cambridge, had
> found the sound of Mother English more fun to game with than her
> sense to labor over, and so rather than applying himself to the pains
> of scholarship, had learned the knack of versifying, and ground out
> quires of couplets after the fashion of the day, afroth with "Joves" and
> "Jupiters," aclang with jarring rhymes, and string-taut with similes
> stretched to the snapping point.
>
> —John Barth, *The Sotweed Factor*

Both openings draw introductory portraits of the main characters. In the
first example, the writer uses slang to describe Studs Lonigan; for example,
"his mug" for "his face," and "the fag" for "the cigarette." Notice that
when Studs Lonigan speaks, his language follows the same city slang the
author used to describe him. The tone of the description adds to the portrait
by giving us the flavor of Studs's personality—his tough-guy mask. That is
the function of the slang words in the description, to inflect the language
with a tough-guy tone that implies something about Studs's personality.

In the second example, the language is archaic and burlesque, the sentence long and cumbersome. The major character is referred to as "one
rangy, gangling flitch . . . more ambitious than talented, and yet more
talented than prudent." He is a poet pretender who "grinds out quires of
couplets." The comic, burlesque tone of the passage obviously reflects the
author's attitude toward Ebenezer, not Ebenezer's attitude toward himself.
Once the stage is set, the satire operates because of the chasm between the

way Ebenezer regards himself and the way he is regarded by his author. Ebenezer considers himself a serious poet and writes passionately after the fashion of the day. His author takes him for a mock poet and delights in poking fun at his versification. And the signal to the reader that the author is treating Ebenezer as a comic figure is given through the tone of the passage.

Both of these examples are taken from contemporary novels. In the first, the tone is used to project and imply the personality of the major character; in the second, tone is used to set comic distance between the author and the major character.

The point is this: you must be sensitive and alert to tone, or you will miss the undercurrents of fiction. There are no hard and fast rules when it comes to recognizing tone. Most native speakers of English have an intuitive sense for the appropriate language on any occasion. The subtleties of tone are ordinarily achieved by an author twisting language in such a way that it deviates from what is appropriate and causes slight reverberations that we call tone. Consider this example:

> Braggioni loves himself with such tenderness and amplitude and eternal charity that his followers—for he is a leader of men, a skilled revolutionist, and his skin has been punctured in honorable warfare—warm themselves in the reflected glow, and say to each other: "He has a real nobility, a love of humanity raised above mere personal affections." The excess of this self-love has flowed out, inconveniently for her, over Laura, who, with so many others, owes her comfortable situation and her salary to him.
> —Katherine Anne Porter, *"Flowering Judas"*

In the story, the description of Braggioni is given from Laura's point of view, and the tone of the language is inflected with irony, to convey her dislike for him. It is ironic overkill to say that someone loves himself with "tenderness and amplitude and eternal charity." The same applies to phrasing like, "his skin has been punctured in honorable warfare." If we rewrite the passage in more appropriate language, much of the ironic tone will disappear:

> Braggioni loves himself. He is a leader of men, a revolutionist. He has been injured in the war. His followers warm themselves in his glow and say to each other, "He has a real nobility, a love of humanity raised above personal affection." He likes Laura who, like so many others, owes her comfortable situation and her salary to him.

But, as it stands in the short story, the description of Braggioni is ironic; that is, it says one thing but means another. The ironic tone sums him up as

315

a cynical and egotistic opportunist, implies that his followers are duped by his humanitarian pretensions, and conveys Laura's dislike for him.

Good dialog will also convey a separate tone of voice for each character. Sometimes, tone in dialog is inflected to reveal conflict, as in this example from a Hemingway story, "Hills Like White Elephants" (1927):

> "And we could have all this," she said, "And we could have every-thing and every day we make it more impossible."
> "What did you say?"
> "I said we could have everything."
> "We can have everything."
> "No, we can't."
> "We can go everywhere."
> "No, we can't. It isn't ours any more."
> "It's ours."
> "No, it isn't. And once they take it away, you never get it back."
> "But they haven't taken it away."
> "We'll wait and see."
> "Come back in the shade," he said, "You mustn't feel that way."
> "I don't feel any way," the girl said, "I just know things."
> "I don't want you to do anything that you don't want to do . . ."
> "Nor that isn't good for me," she said. "I know. Could we have another beer?"

The couple are somewhere in Mexico where the woman is about to undergo an abortion. The man tries to humor and reassure her and seems on the surface as if he would give in to her wish not to have the abortion. But he really wants her to go through with it, and in spite of his assertions to the contrary, she knows it. The conflict between them is subtly conveyed through tone. At the end, she even anticipates one of his pat lines:

> "I don't want you to do anything that you don't want to do . . ."
> "Nor that isn't good for me," she said. "I know. Could we have another beer?"

A tone-sensitive reader will hear the resigned sarcasm in her final line.

In writing about tone in fiction, several common tacks are:

1. To analyze and write about the tone in the work as it indicates the attitude of the author
2. To analyze tone as it reveals personality and conflict
3. To analyze tone as it is used to depict characters

Whether or not you analyze the literary work strictly for its tone, you should be alert to its use in fiction in these ways.

Mood

Mood is the dominant impression to come out of scenery descriptions in the work. It usually functions in fiction about the same way as setting does in a play, to provide a backdrop for the action and an external equivalent for the conflict taking place in the story. Here, for instance, is how Joseph Conrad's *Heart of Darkness* (1902) begins:

> *The Nellie,* a cruising yawl, swung to her anchor without a flutter of the sails, and was at rest. The flood had made, the wind was nearly calm, and being bound down the river, the only thing for it was to come to and wait for the turn of the tide.
>
> The sun-reach of the Thames stretched before us like the beginning of an interminable waterway. In the offing the sea and the sky were welded together without a joint, and in the luminous space the tanned sails of the barges drifting up with the tide seemed to stand still in red clusters of canvas sharply peaked, with gleams of vanishing flatness. The air was dark above Gravesend, and farther back still seemed condensed into a mournful gloom, brooding motionless over the biggest, and the greatest, town on earth.
>
> The Director of Companies was our captain and our host. We four affectionately watched his back as he stood in the bows looking to seaward. On the whole river there was nothing that looked half so nautical. He resembled a pilot, which to a seaman is trustworthiness personified. It is difficult to realize his work was not out there in the luminous estuary but behind him, within the brooding gloom.

Heart of Darkness tells the story of a man who goes to Africa and while there succumbs to the darkness inside himself and becomes the leader of a cannibal tribe. Notice how the opening descriptions emphasize a mood of becalmed gloom. The air is described as "condensed into a mournful gloom, brooding motionless over the biggest, and the greatest, town on earth." Later on in the novel, the words *gloom* and *brooding* occur again and again in the descriptive passages.

Mood is usually consonant with the conflict in the story. If the story is about a man who succumbs to an internal darkness, we expect that the author will set up an external equivalent in the description of the landscape to prepare us for the character's downfall. Obviously, it would seem incongruous to tell a story about a man who falls victim to an inner dark force and have the whole affair take place in clear sunlight at the foot of a pink mountain. The mood must be modulated to be consistent with the line of conflict. The same is true of mood manipulation in movies. Vampires come out on dark overcast nights when black clouds hang over a sinister moon. But when the sun comes out and flowers are blooming, Mary Poppins flies down on the end of her umbrella. The mood is manipulated through the use of appropriate background scenery. Some stories are known as mood stories because they emphasize mood to the exclusion of everything else. A mood story generally turns on a minimal plot, has little action, and projects its characters' state of mind and conflict into the imagery used to describe scenery.

The key principle in writing about mood is to locate and identify the correspondences between the mood in the descriptive passages and the theme of the story.

Character

Most writing about character involves an analysis of action and motive. The writer must expand on evidence in the text that implies something about the character. We have already talked about how tone can be inflected to depict character and how mood can provide an external equivalent to the conflict. All parts of fiction—point of view, plot, theme, tone, and mood—generally have some bearing on, or meet in, the central character. A story written from the first-person point of view has the mind of the character who tells it as a common denominator to all its parts. A story written from an omniscient point of view will orchestrate all its parts to be consistent with the conflict experienced by its main character. It follows that analysis of character must take account of the context in which the character operates and will most likely have to touch on one or more of the other features of fiction. The use of the SQIF format will force you to observe the context of the story as you discuss its main character.

A caution: beware of identifying with a character. This is a common student error. Here is an example excerpted from a student paper on Hemingway's "Hills Like White Elephants":

> The woman was such a beautiful person, I really liked her. I personally thought that her lover, at least I think that that was what he was or he would not have wanted her to have the abortion, was very patronizing to her. He didn't understand her point of view, and all he could do was try to agree with her. I hated his attitude. But she had more pride than he did, because even though she knew that he was lying to her all the time, she didn't try to force him to accept the baby. He reminds me of a lot of callous men I know.

In addition to its other flaws, the excerpt suffers from an overidentification by its writer with the woman in the story. There is no point in moralistically condemning one character while adulating another. The idea is to analyze the character in such a way that your analysis of him or her sheds light on the story.

There are a finite number of methods available to an author in drawing a character. Characterization comes about by:

1. What a character does, says, or thinks
2. What an author says about a character
3. What a character says about himself or herself
4. What another character says about him or her

In most novels written from the omniscient point of view, all four combine to produce a single picture of a character. In James's *Portrait of a Lady*, for instance, Isabel Archer is partly drawn by what she does, thinks, and says. This dialog occurs on her first meeting with her aunt:

> . . . And then, since the girl [Isabel] stood there hesitating and wondering, this unexpected critic said to her abruptly: "I suppose you're one of the daughters?"
> Isabel thought she had very strange manners. "It depends upon whose daughters you mean."
> "The late Mr. Archer's—and my poor sister's."
> "Ah," said Isabel slowly, "you must be our crazy Aunt Lydia!"

We are therefore led to infer that Isabel can be blunt and outspoken.
She is also characterized by what the author tells us about her:

> It may be affirmed without delay that Isabel was probably very liable to the sin of self-esteem; she often surveyed with complacency the field of her own nature; she was in the habit of taking for granted, on scanty evidence, that she was right; she treated herself to occasions of homage. Meanwhile her errors and delusions were frequently such as a biographer interested in preserving the dignity of his subject must shrink from specifying.

What she says about herself also characterizes her:

> "I don't like everything settled beforehand," said the girl, "I like more unexpectedness."
> Her uncle seemed amused at her distinctness of preference.
> "Well, it's settled beforehand that you'll have great success," he rejoined, "I suppose you'll like that."
> "I shall not have success if they're too stupidly conventional. I'm not in the least stupidly conventional. I'm just the contrary. That's what they won't like."

Other characters add to her characterization. For example, the aunt comments:

> I don't know whether she's a gifted being, but she's a clever girl—with a strong will and a high temper. She has no idea of being bored.

And a friend notes:

> I call people rich when they're able to meet the requirements of their imagination. Isabel has a great deal of imagination.

All combine to give a multiangled camera shot of Isabel's personality and her struggle to become unconventional.

In contrast, in a story written from the first-person point of view, characterization must come from a single source: what the character says and what can be inferred about his or her personality from the way he or she tells the story. Here, for instance, is an excerpt from Ring Lardner's short story "The Golden Honeymoon" (1926) that suggests something about the personality of the narrator:

> We went to Trenton the night before and stayed at my daughter and son-in-law and we left Trenton the next afternoon at 3:23 PM.
> This was the twelfth day of January. Mother set facing the front of the train, as it makes her giddy to ride backwards. I set facing her, which does not affect me. We reached North Philadelphia at 4:03 PM and West Philadelphia at 4:14, but did not go into Broad Street. We reached Baltimore at 6:30 and Washington, D.C. at 7:25. Our train laid over in Washington two hours till another train come along to pick us up and I got out and strolled up the platform and into Union Station.

He is trite, orderly, and bored; his life is taken up with pointless trivia such as the arrival and departure times of the train he is riding on. Notice that what conclusions we come to about him have to be inferred from the way he sees and reports on his world, and not from anything an outside narrator directly tells us. Plot, theme, mood, conflict, tone, and point of view all cluster into a single source: the personality of the ''I'' who tells the story.

In summary, bear in mind that you should analyze the work of fiction for its most significant feature. If a story turns on an intricate plot to the exclusion of everything else, then its plot should be the focus of your analysis. The most significant and highly developed feature of a story, whether its point of view, plot, tone, mood, or character, is frequently the source of its main idea or theme, and that is what your analysis should develop.

320

WHAT TO SAY ABOUT DRAMA

Much of what we said about fiction also applies to drama. Both make use of plot, tone, mood, and character, although in slightly different ways.

Point of view

Generally, a play is not mounted from a single point of view. A play may tell a story about a character, and it may focus on the character's interrelationships with people and the world. But the author customarily does not intervene with comments on behalf of the character or to tell all his or her intimate thoughts, nor does a narrator tell all or most of the story to the audience.

The essence of drama is interaction of characters with each other, played out through action and dialog on a stage. Some modern plays distort characterization and action for effect and have an implied point of view that is linked with the playwright's theme. Ionesco's *The Bald Soprano* (1948), for instance, opens with the following:

> Mrs. Smith: There, it's nine o'clock. We've drunk the soup, and eaten the fish and chips, and the English salad. The children have drunk English water. We've eaten well this evening. That's because we live in the suburbs of London and because our name is Smith.
>
> Mr. Smith: (*Continues to read, clicks his tongue.*)
>
> Mrs. Smith: Potatoes are very good fried in fat; the salad oil was not rancid. The oil from the grocer at the corner is better quality than the oil from the grocer across the street. It is even better than the oil from the grocer at the bottom of the street. However, I prefer not to tell them that their oil is bad.

This version of reality is uniquely the playwright's, and implies the equivalent of a first-person point of view. Ionesco is parodying the smug and shallow life in the English suburbs, which accounts for the peculiar and banal dialog. As a rule, however, serious drama operates on the "slice of life" that is arranged to accord with all the probabilities of conventional reality. Satirical and absurd plays are exceptions in which the playwright frequently distorts the drama until it symbolically reflects the version of reality seen from his or her point of view.

Plot and theme

Early dramatists conceived of a play as having unity. Whatever occurred at the end of a play must be caused by something that existed in its beginning. This concept of plot gave rise to the technique of foreshadowing—a means by which dramatists hint the presence of something that will later play a significant part in the outcome of the plot. For instance, in Odets's *Awake and Sing!* (1935), Jacob suddenly introduces the fact that he has an insurance policy on his life:

> Jacob: (*Taking a large envelope from pocket.*) Please, you'll keep this for me. Put it away.
> Morty: What is it?
> Jacob: My insurance policy. I don't like it should lay around where something could happen.
> Morty: What could happen?
> Jacob: Who knows, robbers, fire . . . they took next door. Fifty dollars from O'Reilly.
> Morty: Say, lucky a Berger didn't lose it.
> Jacob: Put it downtown in the safe. Bessie don't have to know.
> Morty: It's made out to Bessie?
> Jacob: No, to Ralph.
> Morty: To Ralph?
> Jacob: He don't know. Some day he'll get three thousand.

Later in the play, Jacob will commit suicide in his attempt to bequeath Ralph the three thousand and a new beginning. By introducing the insurance policy before it was needed to resolve the complications of the plot, the playwright foreshadowed the significant part it would later have. When the suicide eventually takes place and the policy comes up, we are not surprised. It seems a natural turn of events.

Foreshadowing is part of standard plotting technique in almost all drama, both on stage, in film, and on television. If, at the opening of a segment in a television series, a character makes mention of an umbrella for no apparent reason, it means that the umbrella is destined to play a part in the outcome of events before the half hour or hour is up. The failure to foreshadow causes a *deus ex machina* effect. This Latin term means "god by machine," and comes from the Greek playwrights' occasional use of a machine to lower a god onto the stage to resolve difficult and sticky plots.

To this day, melodrama continues to call on *deus ex machina* devices to solve its peculiar problems. After showing the misery and poverty of a family—the wolf and bill collector at the door and the starving children—the play is then resolved by the entrance of a long-lost and wealthy cousin, thereby resorting to a *deus ex machina*. The cousin would be the equivalent of the god by machine whose presence was unaccounted for at the beginning of the play and whose abrupt entrance into the play signals that the playwright is imposing a moralistic and improbable solution on its plot.

The formula we gave earlier under fiction, plot + conflict = theme, is generally equally applicable to drama. The plots of many three-act plays have the following arrangement: Act I introduces the conflict; Act II complicates it; Act III resolves it. In addition, there may be a subplot branching off the main plot. Some plays do not observe this simple three-act arrangement; others have no subplots, only a main plot. Most plays, however, will have at least one speech somewhere, usually toward the end, in which a character sums up its theme. At the end of *Awake and Sing!* for instance, Ralph's final speech sums up the exhortation to live that is both the play's theme and title:

> Ralph: Right here in the house. My days won't be for nothing. Let Mom have the dough. I'm twenty two and kickin'! I'll get along. Did Jake die for us to fight about nickels? No! "Awake and Sing," he said. Right here he stood and said it. The night he died, I saw it like a thunderbolt! I saw he was dead and I was born! I swear to God, I'm one week old! I want the whole city to hear it—fresh blood, arms. We got 'em. We're glad we're living.

A play may also state its theme symbolically, as in Ionesco's *Rhinoceros* (1959) where the grotesqueness of conformity is expressed through the gradual metamorphosis of its characters into rhinoceroses.

Tone

As in fiction, tone of voice in drama is inflected in dialog to reveal the character's personality. Here, for example, is what George Bernard Shaw's version of a poet sounds like:

> Octavius: Jack; we men are all coarse: we never understand how exquisite a woman's sensibilities are. How could I have done such a thing!
> Tanner: Done what, you maudlin idiot?
> Octavius: Yes, I am an idiot, Jack: If you had heard her voice! If you had seen her tears! I have lain awake all night thinking of them. If she had reproached me, I could have borne it better.
>
> —George Bernard Shaw, *Man and Superman*

Notice the shrill and prissy tone Octavius, the poet, uses.

The burden of tonal characterization in drama rests entirely with dialog since the characters are on stage and must talk for themselves.

Mood

Mood is partly a function of physical setting and partly of descriptive language. If you are reading a play rather than seeing it performed, you must take into account the descriptions of setting as given by the playwright. These, in part, imply the mood the scene is written to be played in. If you are seeing a play, the stage setting, lighting, and pace of dialog will all operate to evoke the desired mood. Early playwrights who wrote for stages lacking in setting and lighting facilities often built descriptions of scenery into the character's dialog to create an appropriate mood. Here, for instance, from Shakespeare's *Macbeth*, Lennox describes the night of the king's murder:

> Lennox: The night has been unruly. Where we lay,
> Our chimneys were blown down, and as they say,
> Lamentings heard i' th' air, strange screams of death,
> And prophesying, with accents terrible,
> New hatched to th' woeful time. The obscure bird
> Clamoured the livelong night. Some say, the earth
> Was feverous, and did shake.

Again, the principle is the same as in fiction: to create a mood equivalent to the conflict through the use of description. To the Elizabethan, the storm would mirror the unnaturalness of the king's murder and imply a breach of the cosmic order; it is also a good mood equivalent to the turbulence in Macbeth's mind.

The playwright also manipulates dialog and action on stage to create and evoke mood. Here, for example, from Chekhov's *The Cherry Orchard* (1904), is part of a scene dominated by a dreamy, wistful mood:

> Mme. Ranevskaya: Now you want giants! They're only good in fairy tales; otherwise they're frightening.
> (*Yepihodov crosses the stage at the rear, playing the guitar.*)
> Mme. Ranevskaya: (Pensively.) There goes Yepihodov.
> Anya: (Pensively.) There goes Yepihodov.
> Gayev: Ladies and gentlemen, the sun has set.
> Trofimov: Yes.

When you read a play, you should be alert to the fluctuations of mood indicated by the content and pace of its dialog.

Character

Characterization in drama is achieved by what a character does or says and by what other characters say about him. Dramatic characters vary widely in individuality. Some are used symbolically to stand for an idea and have no unique identity outside of the concepts they represent. Others are sharply drawn and uniquely constituted as separate personalities. Extreme examples of these two are to be found in Mrs. Smith from Ionesco's *The Bald Soprano,* who is a stereotype of the English suburbanite, and in Shakespeare's Hamlet, who plays his own agonized self. Mrs. Smith's speech is stuffed with banalities, which suit her representational nature:

> Mrs. Smith: Mrs. Parker knows a Rumanian grocer by the name of Popesco Rosenfeld, who has just come from Constantinople. He is a great specialist in yogurt. He has a diploma from the school of yogurt-making in Adrianople. Tomorrow I shall buy a large pot of native Rumanian yogurt from him. One doesn't often find such things here in the suburbs of London.

Hamlet's dialog, in contrast, is edged with his personal torments:

> Hamlet: O that this too too solid flesh would melt,
> Thaw, and resolve itself into a dew,
> Or that the Everlasting had not fixed
> His canon 'gainst self-slaughter. O God, God,
> How weary, stale, flat, and unprofitable
> Seem to me all the uses of this world!
> Fie on't, ah, fie, 'tis an unweeded garden
> That grows to seed. Things rank and gross in nature
> Possess it merely.

The use of characters to stand for ideas is a technique both of serious and satiric drama, although it is more widely found in the second. Early morality plays of the Middle Ages used characters in serious drama to symbolically personify the war between the forces of good and evil in biblical stories. The technique has survived even today in serious drama. In Arthur Miller's *Death of a Salesman,* for example, Uncle Ben represents to Willy Loman both the lure of success and missed opportunity. A typical line is the following:

> Ben: William, when I walked into the jungle, I was 17. When I walked out I was twenty-one. And, by God, I was rich!

A play's theme may also be wholly embodied in its characters as in *The Bald Soprano* where the characters both act out and stand for the thematic ideas. You need to decide early in your analysis of a play whether its characters are more representational than real.

Writing about drama is not significantly different from writing about fiction. The difference is primarily one of approach and emphasis. As with any literary work, you have a choice in writing about a play between a general analysis and a critical analysis, depending on which is more appropriate to the purpose of your assignment.

WHAT TO SAY ABOUT POETRY

When analyzing poetry, the primary purpose remains the same: analyze the poem for its most significant feature. Poetry is more compressed than either fiction or drama, and makes use of rhythm and rhyme as a means of conveying tone. Poetry has also evolved some further conventions of its own. In general, however, poetry is as analyzable through the use of the five features of literature—point of view, plot and theme, tone, mood, and character—as is either fiction or drama.

Point of view

The convention in poetry assumes that behind each poem is a speaker who speaks the poem. Occasionally, the speaker may be identified with the poet, especially when the subject of the poem seems obviously related to the poet's life as deduced from its title. Theodore Roethke's poem "Elegy for Jane My Student, Thrown by a Horse" falls into this category, as its title implies. An elegy is a poem lamenting the death of someone, and since the poet tells us in the title of the poem that the lamented someone was once his student, we can assume that the grief is his own, and not a speaker's. But even this cannot be assumed to be true of all elegies. In the past, it was customary for a bereaved family to pay a poet to write an elegy for its deceased member. The resulting poem would also have a speaker called "I," who would lament the passing of the family member in a most personal way.

More often than not the speaker's attitude does not necessarily coincide with the poet's. It is more usual to assume that the speaker, who almost always refers to himself as "I," is simply a point of view constructed for the sake of the poem. There are at least two good reasons for assuming that the speaker's point of view is not the poet's. First, many poems are too brief and contain too little evidence on either the speaker or the poet for it to matter. Second, even if the contrary is assumed—that the speaker and the poet are the same—the assumption usually adds nothing to understanding either the speaker, the poet, or the poem. Take for instance, this poem by William Carlos Williams:

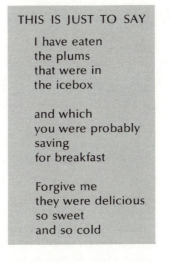

THIS IS JUST TO SAY

I have eaten
the plums
that were in
the icebox

and which
you were probably
saving
for breakfast

Forgive me
they were delicious
so sweet
and so cold

If the speaker is assumed to be the poet, all we know is that he has raided an icebox at one time or another. Nothing else comes out of the assumption that the speaker is the poet. Moreover, who ate the plums is insignificant, whether it was the poet or the speaker.

Point of view in poetry is conventionally assigned to a speaker who is assumed to be an undifferentiated "I," a point of view constructed for the sake of the poem. This is the assumption you would make in a general analysis and in most critical analyses. In a psychological critique, however, your approach would be quite different: the speaker would be assumed to be the same as the poet, or, at least, to be some reflection of the poet.

Plot and theme

Most poems do not have a plot, but every poem has a context that is related to its theme. A poem's context is the frame of reference it begins with. It must begin somewhere, with some idea, act, event, or discovery as its initial frame. From then on, it proceeds within this assumed context. Consider this poem:

DESIGN

I found a dimpled spider, fat and white,
On a white heal-all, holding up a moth
Like a white piece of rigid satin cloth—
Assorted characters of death and blight
Mixed ready to begin the morning right,
Like the ingredients of a witches' broth—
A snow-drop spider, a flower like a froth,
And dead wings carried like a paper kite.

What had that flower to do with being white,
The wayside blue and innocent heal-all?
What brought the kindred spider to that height,
Then steered the white moth thither in the night?
What but design of darkness to appall?—
If design govern in a thing so small.

—Robert Frost

The context of this poem is provided in its first two lines: "I found a dimpled spider, fat and white,/On a white heal-all, holding up a moth." These lines mean exactly what they say: that the speaker found a spider and a dead moth. The rest of the poem is made up of the speaker's elaboration on his discovery and his speculation on what it means. We cannot call this a plot: plot refers to a sequential series of events, one thing happening as the result of another. But this discovery, though it is too static to be a plot, is the initial context of the poem; from then on, we expect the poem to stay within the context of that discovery, and it does.

But even if a poem has no plot, it will have a theme—a dominant idea that all its parts add up to. Frequently, the theme of a poem will be stated in its imagery. The theme of Frost's poem is partly hinted at by its title, "Design," and is expressed through the images it uses to describe the spider and the moth. The spider is described as "fat and white"; the moth is also "white"; the flower, normally blue, as the speaker tells us, is also "white." White is the color we associate with innocence, which leads the poet to ask:

What had that flower to do with being white,
The wayside blue and innocent heal-all?
What brought the kindred spider to that height,
Then steered the white moth thither in the night?

The entire cosmos seems implicated, by coincidence, in the murder of a mere moth. Having raised the question, the poet then answers it with another question: "What but design of darkness to appall?" and then questions his own answer: "If design govern in a thing so small." The imagery assembles a scene of fantastic coincidence: a dead white moth in the clutches of a white spider on top of a white flower. And all three came together in a dark night. We are left speculating about innocence versus destiny—and that is the dominant idea or theme of the poem.

The initial context in which a poem opens will often be implied by its title. Below are the titles of various poems together with a paraphrase of the context of each poem:

"Snake," by D. H. Lawrence: The speaker describes his encounter with and reaction to a snake.
"To His Coy Mistress," by Andrew Marvell: The speaker is berating his mistress for being coy.
"On Looking at Stubb's Anatomy Of The Horse," by Edward Lucie-Smith: The speaker has a daydream as he examines a book titled *Anatomy Of The Horse* by Stubb.

Many poems will use their titles in this way—to establish an initial context or frame that the first line of the poem will then abruptly plunge the reader into. Frequently, a reader who misses the implications of a poem's title will miss its starting point and be unable to follow it. This use of title partly accounts for the conciseness of poetry. While a short story will often expend the first few paragraphs or pages establishing the context for the narrative to follow, a poem will simply flash a title, take its context for granted, and begin.

We began by saying that most poems do not have a plot, but all poems have a context. A few poems, however, do have a plot. The ballad is a poem that tells a story, and therefore generally has a plot, much like a short story does. "Ringo" and "Frankie and Johnny" are two well-known ballads that have been set to music. Plot poems, or ballads, while being more terse than fiction, will often use their plots similarly. Much of what we said about plots in the fiction section therefore applies to ballad poetry.

Some poems are skimpy in length, and consequently contain very skimpy themes. While the size of a poem does not necessarily reflect the complexity of its theme or main idea, it is generally a factor. Students, however, are seldom content to accept the shallowness of a poem's theme at its face value. Generally, they cling to the belief that there must be more, and it must be probed for in the poem's symbolism. Every poem is believed to have some vast "hidden meaning." This is not so: some poems mean exactly what they seem to. There is a surface meaning, and nothing underneath. Here, for example, is one such poem:

THE EAGLE

He clasps the crag with crooked hands;
Close to the sun in lonely lands,
Ringed with the azure world, he stands.

The wrinkled sea beneath him crawls;
He watches from his mountain walls,
And like a thunderbolt he falls.
—Alfred, Lord Tennyson

The poem is a vivid, poetic rendering of an eagle, almost like a word painting. It is nothing more than that. If you hunt for symbols in it, you will produce nothing but a forced and artificial interpretation.

In writing about a poem's theme, you should:

1. Identify the poem's initial context
2. Trace the development of the poem from its context to its conclusion
3. Study the imagery the poem uses

Tone

As in fiction or drama, tone in poetry is inflected to vary with the seriousness of the subject and to project the personality of the speaker. Poetry, however, uses rhythm and rhyme to convey tone. Compare this stanza:

Break, break, break,
On thy cold gray stones, O Sea!
And I would that my tongue could utter
The thoughts that arise in me.
—Alfred, Lord Tennyson

with this one:

A sweet, a delicate white mouse,
A little blossom of a beast,
Is waltzing in the house
Among the crackers and the yeast.
—Stanley Kunitz, from "The Waltzer in the House"

The difference in tone between these two stanzas is partly a result of what their words mean, and partly a result of the way they sound. There is a complex interplay between the rhythm of the words and their meanings. Poetic rhythm is this manipulation of words in a line to produce a sound that underscores the subject of the poem. If the poem deals with a gloomy and weighty topic, as in the first example above, we expect its lines to sound heavy and laborious; if its subject is light and frothy, as in the second example, we expect its lines to sound likewise. As the poet Alexander Pope once put it, "The sound must seem an echo to the sense." This principle of modulating the sound of a poem to produce a tone appropriate to its subject, is basic to the use of rhythm in poetry.

Frequently, the rhyme of a poem will similarly underscore its meaning. Here is an example:

DADDY

You do not do, you do not do
Any more, black shoe
In which I have lived like a foot
For thirty years, poor and white,
Barely daring to breathe or Achoo.

Daddy, I have had to kill you.
You died before I had time—
Marble-heavy, a bag full of God,
Ghastly statue with one grey toe
Big as a Frisco seal

And a head in the freakish Atlantic
Where it pours bean green over blue
In the waters off beautiful Nauset.
I used to pray to recover you.
Ach, du.
                    —Sylvia Plath, from "Daddy"

The poem goes on in this vein for sixteen stanzas. Notice, however, that in the three stanzas reprinted above the primary rhyme is on the "do, shoe, Achoo, you," sound. The title of the poem is "Daddy" and the speaker in it addresses her father in rhymes that capture the gurgle of baby talk. The rhyme underscores the psychological conflict of the speaker, who seems caught between a simultaneous impulse to hate and love her father.

In addition to its use of rhythm and rhyme, poetry also uses other devices common to both fiction and drama, such as appropriate diction and phrasing, to convey its speaker's tone. Most poems are written from the vantage point of a speaker who refers to himself or herself as "I"; the tone of voice in the poem is therefore his or hers, and is partly the means by which we are convinced of the credibility of the speaker, and therefore of the poem. If the speaker's tone and statements are at odds with one another, the poem will seem artificial and false, as if the speaker were contriving to be poetic for our benefit. For the poem to convince us, we must be convinced of the sincerity of its speaker, and that sincerity is partly a function of an appropriate tone. Consider this poem:

> ### UNLUCKY BOAT
>
> That boat has killed three people. Building her
> Sib drove a nail through his thumb, and died up by
> Bunged to the eyes with rust and penicillin.
> One evening when the Bring was a bar of silver
> Under the moon, and Mansie and Tom with wands
> Were putting a spell on cuithes, she dipped a bow
> And invited Mansie, his pipe still in his teeth,
> To meet the cold green angels. They hauled her up
> Among the rocks, right in the path of Angus,
> Whose neck, rigid with pints from the Doundy market,
> Snapped like a barley stalk . . . There she lies,
> A leprous unlucky bitch, in the quarry of Moan.
>
> Tinkers, going past, make the sign of the cross.
> —George MacKay Brown

We have no way of knowing who the speaker is, but the tone of the poem implies that he is a simple person, probably a fisherman, who lives somewhere in the British Isles. We infer this first, from the names of the people associated with the boat: "Sib, Mansie, Angus"; second, from the place names used in the poem: "Doundy market, quarry of Moan"; and finally, from his diction and phrasing, "when the Bring was a bar of silver"—*Bring* apparently meaning *sea*—and from his neck "rigid with pints," which is an Anglicized way of saying that he was drunk either on beer or ale. The last line, "Tinkers, going past, make the sign of the cross," adds to the impression that the speaker probably lives somewhere in the British Isles where Roman Catholicism is the dominant religion and where people are typically superstitious. His story of the unlucky boat is believable because it is exactly what we would expect from the point of view of a simple and superstitious fisherman. We would probably not believe the poem if it were inflected with the tone of a sophisticated New Yorker. But as it stands, the tone of the poem adds to the speaker's credibility and convinces us of his sincerity.

In summary, tone in poetry is commonly achieved by the use of rhyme and rhythm appropriate to the subject of the poem, and the use of diction and phrasing appropriate to the speaker of the poem.

Mood

The function of mood in some narrative poetry remains the same as in fiction and drama—to provide an external equivalent for the conflict taking place in the mind of the speaker. Here, for example, is a poem by John Keats:

LA BELLE DAME SANS MERCI

O what can ail thee, knight-at-arms,
Alone and palely loitering?
The sedge has withered from the Lake,
And no birds sing!

O what can ail thee, knight-at-arms,
So haggard, and so woe begone?
The Squirrel's granary is full
And the harvest's done.

I see a lily on thy brow
With anguish moist and fever dew,
And on thy cheeks a fading rose
Fast withereth too—

I met a Lady in the Meads,
Full beautiful, a faery's child
Her hair was long, her foot was light
And her eyes were wild—

I made a Garland for her head,
And bracelets too, and fragrant Zone
She look'd at me as she did love
And made sweet moan—

I set her on my pacing steed
And nothing else saw all day long
For sidelong would she bend and sing
A faery's song—

She found me roots of relish sweet
And honey wild and manna dew
And sure in language strange she said
I love thee true—

She took me to her elfin grot
And there she wept and sigh'd full sore,
And there I shut her wild wild eyes
With kisses four.

And there she lulled me asleep
And there I dream'd, Ah Woe betide!
The latest dream I ever dreamt
On the cold hill side.

I saw pale Kings, and Princes too
Pale warriors, death pale were they all;
They cried, La belle dame sans merci
Thee hath in thrall.

I saw their starv'd lips in the gloam
With horrid warning gaped wide,
And I awoke, and found me here
On the cold hill's side.

And this is why I sojourn here
Alone and palely loitering;
Though the sedge is withered from the Lake
And no birds sing.

The title translates, "The beautiful woman without mercy," and the poem tells of a knight's seduction by an illusive woman who abandons him on a hillside. Notice the description of his surroundings: "the sedge has withered from the Lake/And no birds sing"; and, "the Squirrel's granary is full/And the harvest's done." The knight's story is told against a backdrop of autumn, the season that poetically corresponds to old age and is therefore a suitable equivalent for his disillusionment. His loss of the beautiful lady is complexly echoed throughout the poem in its descriptions. As he says, he awoke and found himself on "the cold hill's side," which invites a comparison in the reader's mind between the desolation the knight feels and the desolation he describes. The one is mirrored in and intensified by the other. The same principle of mood manipulation is at work that we talked about in fiction, where the descriptions of landscape reflect the conflict and feelings in the mind of the speaker.

Mood is an important feature in narrative or ballad poetry, but less so in other shorter poems. For instance, the poem "This Is Just to Say" (page 327) does not use description to reflect conflict, which is a primary technique for evoking mood. When this technique is used in poetry, as in "La Belle Dame Sans Merci," it differs very little from the way it is used in fiction or drama. The principle is the same in all three genres, to use description to provide an external equivalent for the conflict and feelings of the speaker or character.

Character

Some poems are not simply told from the point of view of an undifferentiated speaker, but are full-blown characterizations. It is, however, difficult to distinguish between when a poem is characterizing and when it is simply using a speaker to make comments about the external world. Poetry, as we said earlier, generally is written from the first-person point of view. The convention assumes that this first person who calls himself "I" is simply a point of view constructed for the sake of the poem. This convention evolved partly because most poems are too brief for us to conclude anything about their speaker's personality or character traits. In the poem "This Is Just to Say" (p. 327), we said that nothing could be concluded about the speaker except that he likes to eat plums. Or in the poem "Unlucky Boat" (p. 332), we concluded from its tone only that the speaker is probably a fisherman somewhere in the British Isles. What else can we know about him from the poem? Very little. The focus in the poem is on the boat and its history, and not on the speaker.

There are other poems, however, where the vision the speaker has is so peculiarly his own that we come away thinking that what we have read is more symptomatic of his mind than of an external reality. Such poems are generally long, and have a chance to articulate the speaker's point of view more completely. Frequently, the character study poem takes the form of a long speech delivered by the speaker, called a *dramatic monolog,* during which a full range of his or her foibles and quirks is revealed. In such cases, the person behind the poem is called a *persona,* from the Latin word meaning "mask." The assumption is that the poet has, for the duration of the poem, put on the mask of this person, for the sake of laying bare his or her character in the poem.

The burden of characterizing the persona in a dramatic monolog falls partly on what the speaker says and does, and partly on the imagery he or she uses. The techniques for characterizing are essentially the same in poetry as in fiction, with this exception: poetry is more likely to draw more heavily on the use of imagery. In T. S. Eliot's "Love Song of J. Alfred Prufrock," for instance, Prufrock's frame of mind is objectified in his imagery. To him, the evening is "like a patient etherized upon a table." And we get an idea of how desolate and lonely Prufrock feels when he says, "I should have been a pair of ragged claws/Scuttling across the floors of silent seas." Throughout the poem, the case for the way Prufrock thinks and feels is made partly by his response to people, partly by his paralysis and indecision in love matters, and partly by the imagery he uses that tells us how he views the world. Otherwise, the techniques of characterization in fiction, especially in a story written from the first-person point of view, are essentially the same in poetry. In both cases we have to infer about the character from what he tells us about himself and the language he uses to do it.

12
Writing for the sciences

THE SCIENTIFIC POSTURE

Science assumes a special posture and therefore requires a special kind of writing. The scientific posture is based on objectivity, neutrality, and observation; consequently scientific writing is primarily denotative and factual. Understanding the nature of this assumed posture is of primary importance to anyone attempting to write a scientific paper.

Objectivity

Objectivity as an absolute quality is arguable. We might even grant that it is impossible for anyone to be totally objective. But objectivity in the scientific framework simply means that anyone using the same methodology and the same data should have a reasonable expectation of coming to the same conclusions. The method of reaching conclusions must be openly displayed; inferences drawn from the data must be clearly shown along with data; interpretation must be labeled as interpretation. These precautions in the presentation of scientific studies guard against human frailty and guarantee some objectivity. See Chapter 8 for a more complete discussion of these precautions.

Neutrality

Neutrality requires a scientist to consider all relevant data and to be willing to modify or reject his or her thesis if it proves insupportable. This posture is more one of dispassionateness than neutrality and accounts for the impersonal tone of scientific papers. Science is a system whose ground rules are independent of any one person. If an idea is scientifically true for one person, it is therefore scientifically true for all people. Consequently, the convention in scientific papers is to avoid the use of "I" to refer to the writer. However, avoiding the use of "I" does not guarantee neutrality any more than does the use of "I" corrupt neutrality. Your posture toward a thesis or project is neutral so long as you consider all the relevant data and are prepared to modify or reject your thesis as new data becomes available.

Observation

The third characteristic of science is that it is based on observation. Nothing is preconceived or taken for granted: data are gathered through observation and used to construct a thesis. Or, alternatively, a thesis is constructed and data gathered to either verify, modify, or reject it. Most scientific writing is therefore denotative, factual, and descriptive.

WRITING THE SCIENTIFIC PAPER

In many ways, a paper written on a scientific subject will have much in common with a paper written on a subject in the humanities. Both papers observe the conventions of grammar, paragraphing, and in some ways, of organization. However, because of objectivity and neutrality on the observer's part, scientific papers tend to be more dependent on data. Judgments are sparingly made, and always with a great deal of caution.

In the humanities, in contrast, the situation is just the reverse. Writers frequently make cosmic generalizations without an ounce of substance or proof behind them. Reasoned and intuitive generalizing is commonly accepted. Literary critics who have spent their lives cocooned in the study of the literature and culture of a certain century will emerge with definitive but metaphorical pronouncements about that century's literary output. Here, for instance, is such an off-the-cuff pronouncement made about the eighteenth century:

> To read normal eighteenth-century verse and prose is to have a cleansing and refreshing bath—not a Carlylean "Baphometic Fire-baptism"—in cool and masculine rationality, to be persuaded that man is a civilized and cosmopolitan being in an orderly, uniform, and rather comfortable world, and the writers who have such qualities and induce such moods deserve better praise than Arnold's damaging "our excellent and indispensable eighteenth century."
> —Douglas Bush, *Mythology and the Romantic Tradition in English Poetry*

This value judgment, and that is what it is, would probably be readily accepted by most students of literature. The writer's method of arriving at his conclusion would not be questioned, because writers in the humanities are licensed by the discipline to both write and think in this way.

In science, however, the rules are different; the formula for writing scientific papers consequently reflects this difference in approach and methodology. The following format has evolved for papers that report experiments or research projects, and is generally accepted both in the social and physical sciences. A paper reporting on an experiment or research project is divisible into five parts:

1. An introductory paragraph that describes the hypothesis to be tested and sometimes also sums up concisely any other research relevant to the hypothesis.
2. A section that describes the method and procedure used in the experiment
3. A section that reports the data
4. A section that discusses and interprets the data
5. A section that sums up the experiment and its findings

In addition to the above, the paper should have a title that encapsulates the aim and purpose of the experiment. The following hypothetical report on an experiment demonstrates this format:

THE EFFECT OF AN AUTHORITY'S PRESENCE ON THE BEHAVIOR OF MOTORISTS AT A STOP SIGN

Only the relevant research that provides a background context to the experiment is summarized.

This paper reports on an experiment to determine whether the visible presence of an authority at a stop sign affects how long drivers pause at that sign. Various research has reported on the effects of authority on behavior. Stempel, in her study of college coeds, reported that the visible presence of the dorm mother in a room altered the length and substance of conversations between the coeds. Similarly, Bancroft and Goldstein have reported on the changes in the behavior of college seniors when a professor is present. In line with their findings, it was hypothesized that the visible presence of an authority at a stop sign would affect how long drivers stopped at the sign before proceeding in the flow of traffic.

You should be as concise as you can in this paragraph. Lead immediately to the thesis. The final sentence here is the thesis.

Procedure

The procedure used in the experiment should be carefully and concisely detailed here.

A uniformed highway patrolman on his motorcycle was used as the authority. The experiment was conducted at the intersection of Fifth Street and El Molino during peak traffic hours between 8 and 10 A.M. on January 16th and January 17th. Between 8 and 9 A.M. on January 16th with no policeman present, the pause of fifty random drivers at the stop sign was timed with a stop watch and recorded. Between 9 and

10, the policeman stationed himself at the stop sign in view of approaching traffic, and the pause of another fifty drivers at the stop sign was timed and recorded. On January 17th, the times were reversed. The policeman was present between 8 and 9, and absent between 9 and 10, and the pause of fifty random drivers was again timed and recorded in each one-hour period. Each driver had to come to a complete stop before the length of his pause was timed. If a driver did not completely stop, he or she was indicated by an S, and not timed.

Findings

This section lists all the raw data obtained in the experiment.

On the first day, while the authority was present, drivers paused an average of 10.5 seconds. Without the authority's presence, the pause dropped to an average of 7.5 seconds. Moreover, on the first day, there were 6 S's, drivers who did not come to a complete halt when the authority was absent, but none when he was present.

The results on the second day were similar. While the authority was present, the average pause at the stop sign was 10.7 seconds. During his absence, the pause dropped to an average of 6.2 seconds. With the authority present, there were no S's: in his absence there were 5 S's. The data are reproduced in Table 1.

Discussion

Your interpretation of the data belongs here.

The findings confirm the hypothesis that the presence of an authority affects how long drivers pause at a stop sign before proceeding into traffic. On the first day, with the authority present, the average pause at the stop sign increased by 3 seconds. On the second day, with the authority present, the average pause increased by 4.5 seconds. Moreover, with the authority present, all drivers came to a complete stop at the sign. During his absence on the first day, 6 drivers did not completely stop; and on the second day, 5 drivers did not completely stop while the authority was absent.

Conclusion

In short papers this section may be combined with the one immediately before it.

These findings are consistent with the results obtained by Stempel, and by Bancroft and Goldstein. The results of this experiment suggest that the presence of a policeman at an accident-prone intersection will at least slow down traffic at the stop signs and possibly improve the accident rate.

The study reported above is hypothetical, as are the figures and characters. The format, however, is real and should be followed in writing up the results of experiments. Notice that the table in which the findings would be reproduced is not included. The study was fictitious, and so there were no data to reproduce. However, in a real study, the raw data as they were recorded would be reproduced in a separate table.

Most of your writing in science will probably involve reporting on experiments such as this one. However, some of your writing will be merely commentary on some topic in an essay and will require no special format. All of our previous suggestions on writing an essay will apply when writing this type of scientific essay. You should, however, bear the following points particularly in mind.

Begin with a manageable thesis

Science has grown fantastically in the past years, especially in the quantity of research done on various miniscule topics. A broad thesis may commit you to reading and reporting on vast quantities of research that you might not be able to assemble coherently in a single paper. Bear in mind, as you formulate your thesis, that science is characterized by its microscopic focus. We suggest that you consult with your instructor before selecting a thesis to research, or a topic to write on. He or she can advise you if you are being too ambitious.

State your thesis concisely

Everything we have said in the past about the need for precision and conciseness is especially true of scientific writing. A paper in science is likely to be technical and crammed with data, which intensifies the need for structure and organization. The thesis gives a paper its framework and direction. If the thesis is incoherent or otherwise poorly worded, the paper is likely to suffer from flawed organization, and the data will appear jumbled. Reread Chapter 3 if you have doubts about the thesis of your own paper.

Frequently, the thesis and the title are worded similarly. Notice the parallel between the title of the hypothetical study above and the wording of its thesis. The parallel wording of thesis and title helps to hold both in focus and contributes to their mutual conciseness.

Define ambiguous words and terms

If your thesis contains any word or term that is essential to its meaning but ambiguous, it should be defined as early as possible. Here is an example from a paper entitled "Behavior Modification and the Brat Syndrome."

> The purpose of this paper is to describe a behavior modification program designed for one "brat." A brat will be defined as a child who engages in tantrums, assaultiveness, threats, and so forth, which are highly aversive and serve to render others helpless in controlling him or her.

The word *brat* is crucial to the paper's thesis, but ambiguous. The writer therefore defines it in his second sentence. If you have trouble defining a term, turn to Chapter 6 and review the section on definition there.

Science relies on its use of technical language to avoid multiple and frequent definitions. A technical word will usually have one specific meaning and require no definition. Unfortunately, while a technical vocabulary allows for more precision, its use can also blur and confuse. Remember to choose words in an earnest effort to communicate rather than to impress your reader with your use of a technical vocabulary.

Word statements cautiously

Science and its writing are steeped in caution. Few assertions are ever made dogmatically; few ideas are ever regarded as "facts." This is entirely as it should be for any discipline whose ideas are dictated by data rather than by faith. Here is an example of an assertion worded to allow a cautious edge:

> A number of geophysical and biological processes *are known* in which CO is produced. The processes include volcanic action, natural gas emission, electrical discharge during storms, seed germination and seedling growth, and marsh gas production. The contribution of CO to urban atmospheres by these sources *is thought* to be relatively small.

The statements are straightforward but cautious. The use of "are known" and "is thought" qualifies the assertion as provisionally true with the present state of knowledge, implying that it may later prove to be untrue when more is known. The wording makes the assertion specific, yet cautious.

Choose words carefully

Since the aim of most scientific writing is to communicate theories and data, it follows that the use of denotative language will probably serve this aim best with a minimum of misunderstanding and ambiguity. Reread Chapter 7 for a more complete discussion of the differences between connotative and denotative words.

Do not attempt to practice whimsical diction in a paper on a scientific subject. Avoid the use of neologisms (newly coined words) and, emphatically, of slang. These words will merely draw attention to themselves and away from your paper's content.

Words should be chosen primarily for their precision. Somewhere you may have picked up the idea that it is improper to use the same word twice in the same sentence. This is not true: the use of different words to refer to the same concept or object in a sentence may cause much confusion. Here is an example.

> In a *set* of *dishes*, the *plates* are the elements or members of the *collection*; similarly, George Washington is a member of the *set* of Presidents of the United States.

The writer uses *set* and *collection* to refer to the same concept, and *dishes* and *plates* to refer to the same objects. The meaning is clearer when only *set* and *dishes* are used:

> *Rewrite:* In a set of dishes, the dishes are the elements or members of the set; similarly, George Washington is a member of the set of Presidents of the United States.

SOME SUGGESTIONS ON STYLE

Many of the stylistic problems found in nonscientific writing will also roost in scientific writing. However, the following stylistic errors are especially common in scientific prose.

Overuse of the passive voice

The passive voice is legitimately and widely used in scientific writing for a variety of reasons. First, it eliminates "I" constructions and is therefore suited to the scientific posture. Second, it emphasizes the action rather than the agent; the approach and method of science have a similar emphasis. Data, method, and results are more important than the researcher, and this focus is ideally reflected in passive constructions. Here is an example:

> In some cases the incompatibility of the statuses *is* sufficiently *recognized* that their occupancy by the same person *is* socially *discouraged*.

Recognized by whom? Presumably by society. The passive sentence and its verb implicate no one directly in any action, and therefore seem open to implicate everyone. Used in this way, passive constructions add an air of universality to an assertion. To the extent that language should reflect the assumed posture of a writer, use of the passive voice by a scientific writer is justifiable.

But it is easy to overuse passive constructions and to do so unnecessarily. The passive voice tends to encourage an overuse of nouns and is generally more difficult to read. Here is an example:

> Two statuses with conflicting roles come to be infrequently *occupied* simultaneously for three reasons. In some cases the incompatibility of the statuses *is* sufficiently *recognized* that their occupancy by the same person *is* socially *discouraged*. An example of this *is* the treatment *accorded* females who aspire to be airline pilots.

These three sentences are unnecessarily burdened with passive verb constructions. It is easy to rewrite them in the active voice and still retain a proper tone of objective and neutral detachment.

> *Rewrite:* A person may simultaneously occupy two statuses with conflicting roles for three reasons. In some cases society may recognize that the two statuses are incompatible and discourage a person from occupying both at the same time. An example of this is the way women who want to be airline pilots are treated.

The sentences are now clearer and easier to read because the verbs are assigned subjects and put into the active voice.

Use the passive voice when you want to emphasize an action over its agent, or when you want to eliminate a subject. For example:

> Between 8 and 9 A.M. on January 16th with no policeman present, the pause of fifty random drivers at the stop sign was timed with a stop watch and recorded.

Here, what is important is not who did the timing (the agent), but what was timed (the pause) and how it was timed. The passive voice therefore serves its purpose well.
Again:

> A uniformed highway patrolman on his motorcycle was used as the authority.

Here, the passive construction eliminates the "I" subject. Otherwise the sentence would have read:

> I used a uniformed highway patrolman on his motorcycle as the authority.

This second version is no less neutral nor less objective than the first. However, the convention in scientific writing seems to favor as few "I's" as possible, and in deference to this the passive construction is used.

Use of jargon

Jargon refers to the overuse of technical language. All disciplines necessarily have their own concepts and ideas that are labeled by a specialized vocabulary. Jargon, however, is something other than the legitimate use of technical language. It is the use of technical language where plain language will work just as well. Here is an example:

> One cannot assume from this example, however, that *universalistic principles of recruitment in the occupancy of a status* means that anyone and everyone can occupy the status without facing role conflict.

"Universalistic principles of recruitment in the occupancy of a status" simply means that the status is open to everyone without regard to differences. The phrasing here is unnecessarily burdened with jargon. A rewrite should strip the sentence clean of jargon and use plain words instead:

> *Rewrite:* One cannot, however, assume from the example that a status open to everyone will involve no role conflict for anyone.

Science legitimately relies on technical language for the sake of precision. Jargon, however, is neither precise nor communicative. It is simply another barrier between the reader and your content.

Overuse of nouns

Verbs are the action elements of a sentence. Sentences with a higher ratio of verbs to nouns are generally easier to read than sentences whose verb-to-noun ratio is low. The tendency in scientific writing is to overuse nouns and underuse verbs, and especially to use noun combinations in long phrases that function as a subject. Here is an example:

> In still other cases *the inability to conform to the roles of one or both of the statuses* leads to the person's being deprived of one or both statuses.

The italicized words make up the subject for the verb *leads;* the proof is that the entire phrase can be replaced by a single pronoun, *it,* and the sentence remains intact.

> In still other cases *it* leads to the person's being deprived of one or both statuses.

Where a frail verb is responsible for such a massive subject, arteriosclerosis of the prose is inevitable. The following rewrite involves dismantling the noun phrase and replacing it with a verb.

> *Rewrite:* In still other cases, a person *may be unable to conform* to the role of one or both statuses and may consequently be deprived of either or both.

Noun phrases frequently occur in sentences written in the passive voice. Rewriting these involves converting the sentence into the active voice, and converting one of the nouns to its verb form. Here is another example:

> *The failure of the participant's performance* was regarded by the experimenters as the crucial factor.
>
> *Rewrite:* The experimenters regarded the participant's failure *to perform* as the crucial factor.

Frequently, with a minimum of effort, noun phrases in a sentence in the passive voice can be converted this way, by changing to the active voice and using a verb form in place of the noun. Since science relies on the passive voice to convey its implied posture, a high degree of noun phrasing is inevitable. You will relieve your reader's burden if you bear this in mind and convert, wherever possible, to the active voice.

In summary, when you write on a scientific subject, your prose should convey the posture of objectivity, neutrality, and precision of observation that you are expected to assume toward your subject. In addition, all other conventions of grammar and paragraphing apply as much to scientific prose as to prose on any other subject.

13
Writing reports

DETERMINING THE PURPOSE OF YOUR REPORT
THE EVALUATIVE REPORT
THE PROBLEM-SOLVING REPORT
THE ANALYTICAL REPORT
THE DESCRIPTIVE REPORT

Reports are the workhorses of all organizations, and well-written reports are much sought after these days. Executives everywhere loudly lament the fact that few of their subordinates can write readable reports. In this chapter we attempt to give you some general guidelines for writing short, narrative, operational reports of the kind most commonly required by business firms or civil service organizations. Because of their highly specialized nature, the following reports are not included in this chapter:

1. Printed form reports built to a predetermined plan
2. Professional reports, such as legal briefs, medical case histories, or engineering proposals
3. Reports based on tables, graphs, or illustrations
4. Long, formal, analytical reports

The information in this chapter *will* prove particularly useful in writing the following:

1. Advertising reports
2. Aeronautics reports
3. Attitude surveys
4. Committee reports
5. Employee appraisals
6. Employee bulletins
7. Improvement reports
8. Interview reports
9. Market surveys
10. Police reports
11. Problem-solving reports
12. Procedure statements
13. Product analyses
14. Progress reports
15. Sales reports

While we cannot provide examples of each specific report, we have divided the field of short narrative reports into four general types which include most of the above. The four types are:

1. Evaluative reports
2. Problem-solving reports
3. Analytical reports
4. Descriptive reports

Each of these reports follows a general format that is flexible enough to fit various situations. Once you understand the basic framework, you can adapt it to suit a specific circumstance.

Needless to say, all the writing skills you have learned so far can be applied to reports. Principles such as developing an idea coherently, using concrete words, and being yourself are as important in writing a report as they are in writing a creative essay. A good report does not have to be a literary masterpiece, but most busy executives do have certain similar expectations from written reports. These can be summarized in four points:

1. A visible method of organization; that is, a pattern the reader can see
2. A purposeful direction in which the report moves
3. Sparse language to fit the reader's limited time
4. Accurate evidence to support assertions

DETERMINING THE PURPOSE OF YOUR REPORT

All the writing talent in the world cannot disguise a report that leads nowhere. Unless your reader can tell at first glance what you intend to report, you have not communicated. Therefore, begin your report with a statement of purpose that encapsulates the core of your report. This statement then becomes a peg on which you can hang the rest of your report. Make this statement of purpose clear and concise. Do not waste words building suspense or stating the obvious.

> *Wrong:* Here in the Philadelphia plant of NICON Corporation we have had a problem for a long time that has to do with the rapid expansion of the number of employees and their time computations. We believe we can solve this problem.
>
> *Better:* This report proposes the installation of time clocks for the Philadelphia NICON Corporation because it will result in greater efficiency in the accounting office, in improved accuracy of time computations, and in less tardiness among employees.
>
> *Wrong:* Heritage Gardens Convalescent Hospital has a dreadfully high turnover in nurses' aids, the reasons for which are not agreed on by everybody involved.
>
> *Better:* The turnover in nurses' aids at Heritage Gardens Convalescent Hospital is due to three factors analyzed in this report: 1. the competitive wages paid by the nearby Veterans Hospital, 2. poor personnel relations on the part of the head nurse, 3. lack of variety in patient care.
>
> *Wrong:* The introduction of a line of Anne Klein belts would maybe give prestige to our store, but we would lose our shirts because the stock would not move.

> *Better:* The analysis that follows will indicate that introducing a line of Anne Klein belts is not economically feasible at the present because, although the markup on the Anne Klein line is high, the decrease in stock turnover would more than offset the profit margin.
>
> *Wrong:* Financial statements presented by corporate enterprises to shareholders are often a broken and winding path.
>
> *Better:* The objective of this report is threefold: 1. to point up specific areas where there was lack of communication in this year's stockholders report, 2. to analyze the causes for this failure in communication, 3. to suggest some changes that will remedy the problem.

The first step in writing a report is to summarize your findings in a concise statement of purpose.

THE EVALUATIVE REPORT

The evaluative report passes critical judgment on a subject. The most common is the report evaluating a person (also called a personal reference). It is often requested of people in supervisory positions. Evaluative reports must be kept confidential, to be discussed only with those individuals directly involved in the hiring, firing, or promoting of the person evaluated. In writing an evaluation, you have every right to assume complete confidentiality. You also have the responsibility to be honest and objective. An evaluation is no place for undeserved praise nor for disparagement based on personal grudges. Tell the truth the way you actually see it. The person asking for an evaluation is depending on your judgment as a basis for his or her decision. If you provide overblown compliments or sarcastic criticisms, you are of no help.

Your evaluation of a person should include the following information:

1. Statement of purpose summarizing your attitude toward the person being evaluated
2. Name and position of person being evaluated
3. Length of person's association with you, and your relationship
4. Job description
5. Most valuable assets
6. Least valuable assets
7. Personal traits, including the person's public relations, interoffice relations, character integrity, and presentability
8. Final summary statement

Be sure to back up general statements with specific evidence, particularly if the statement is a negative criticism. Avoid hackneyed phrases, such as:

> In the line of duty . . .
> With a character beyond reproach . . .
> My considered opinion of her is . . .
> Above and beyond the normal average . . .

Unless you are filling out a particular personnel form, the following questions will help you in evaluating a person:

1. Does he/she have adequate skills?
2. Does he/she make sound decisions?
3. Does he/she plan ahead?
4. Does he/she work well with others?
5. Does he/she consider the welfare of the organization?
6. Does he/she interfere with the performance of duties by others?
7. Does he/she communicate?
8. Does he/she get jobs done?
9. Does he/she have personal integrity?
10. Does he/she look presentable?

SAMPLE EVALUATIVE REPORT

Statement of purpose

It is my pleasure to recommend Karl L. Folger. He worked for me as part of a three-person clerical pool from January 1, 1972, to November 19, 1973. During this time, he was expected to answer my correspondence, handle my appointments and phone calls, and organize the office files. His job was complicated by the fact that he was responsible to two

Job description

other sales managers besides me. Keeping three employers happy during hectic periods was no small task.

Most valuable assets

Mr. Folger's most valuable asset is his total commitment. During the two years that he worked for me, he rarely allowed work to pile up, but would prefer working at the office on weekends rather than getting noticeably behind. I could usually count on beginning the week with a clean slate.

Most of Mr. Folger's work involved typing, which he did accurately and efficiently as long as he could copy or transcribe from dictation.

Least valuable assets

He was, however, reticent about composing memos or other material on his own. Such original work always had to be checked for precision in form and content. For instance, I could not rely on him to take committee minutes or to write a letter based on a few kernel ideas. In this area Mr. Folger needs further training.

Public relations

An important function of our office is serving the public. Nervous, disgruntled clients come in expecting immediate attention. Some of them are occasionally rude. In this area of our business Mr. Folger showed poise and maturity. He was friendly, unflustered, and dignified. During the two years he worked for me, I did not receive any complaints about him from clients, which in itself is a remarkable recommendation.

Interoffice relations

Mr. Folger worked well with the other clerks in our firm, but he did not waste time talking with them or taking excessively long coffee breaks. He avoided getting entangled with "gripe" factions as well as courting special favors. He was perhaps somewhat of a "loner," but I believe he saw his job as a job and not as a place where he satisfied his social needs.

Personal appearance

In his personal appearance Mr. Folger was adequate. He was well groomed and dressed appropriately.

Integrity

I do not hesitate to praise Mr. Folger's honesty and discretion. Our transactions involve dossiers that must be handled discreetly. Never have I known Mr. Folger to give out private information or twist the truth. I respect his integrity fully.

Final summary

In brief, except for his inability to write original material, Mr. Folger is a capable, loyal, and efficient secretary.

Signed: _____

Title: _____

Date: _____

Make your evaluation report objective, specific, and fair.

THE PROBLEM-SOLVING REPORT

The problem-solving report provides a workable plan to get an organization out of trouble. Companies such as the Chase Manhattan Bank or Standard Oil rely for their solution to problems on highly sophisticated methods of investigation and prediction. The executives of these huge corporations have at their disposal professional analysts with computers that can process in minutes what ordinarily would take years of painstaking information gathering and classifying. Business problems are translated into symbols, numbers, or mathematical formulas that the computer then processes and reads back.

Most small organizations, however, still have to rely on human investigation unaided by computers. But the steps involved in solving an organizational problem are basically the same, regardless of whether you use a computer or your own resources. No matter how simple or complicated, a problem-solving report proceeds in four steps:

1. Pinpointing the problem
2. Establishing a goal
3. Finding methods to achieve the goal
4. Applying the methods

Your first step is to *pinpoint the problem* for your reader. More than likely your employer will have done this for you when assigning the report. However, if finding the problem is part of your report, then you must locate it by the best means available. Check the company files; interview reliable workers who might know something about the problem; talk to authorities in the problem area. If you need information requiring public reaction, you may want to initiate your own survey by phone, interview, or questionnaire. As a hypothetical case, let us look at the Edwards Brothers Roofing Tile Company, a small manufacturing concern with assets of approximately $200,000. One of the owners is ill, and you have been hired as assistant manager to help solve the company's problem of operating at a $500 per month deficit. When writing the report, first state the problem: The company is losing $500 per month.

Your second step is to *establish the goal* that ultimately must be achieved in order to solve the problem. In the case of the Edwards Brothers Roofing Tile Company, the goal is to convert the malfunctioning company into a profitable business.

The third step, *finding the methods to achieve the goal,* usually involves the most creative part of your report. You must answer the question, What will it take in order to turn the Edwards Brothers Roofing Tile Company into a profit-making business? After careful investigative research, you come up with the following answers:

1. The Company must update their equipment in order to reduce the number of faulty tiles coming off the production line.
2. The company must create a greater demand for the tile by a stepped up sales force and increased advertising.
3. The company must wrest a share of the market from existing competitors by stressing the unique qualities of its tile.

Your report will point out that if the three above-mentioned conditions are met, the goal will be achieved, and the problem will be solved.

Step four, *applying the methods,* is the core of your report because it sets up the mechanism by which the problem will be solved. At this point it is difficult to separate skillful investigation from skillful reporting. In order for your report to be helpful, the suggestions it contains must be helpful. Bad ideas cannot be masked by elegant language. Likewise, good ideas cannot be recognized if they are reported in fuzzy language. The ideal is to match up good ideas with good reporting. Providing you with good ideas is beyond the scope of this book; however, we can give you some help with the reporting aspect.

Suppose that these are your specific proposals for the Edwards Brothers Roofing Tile Company:

1. To borrow $25,000 from the bank, to be used as follows:
   a. $10,000 to convert the present equipment
   b. $ 5,000 for advertising and promotion
   c. $ 5,000 to pay off accumulated debts
   d. $ 5,000 in ready reserves
2. To replace the present sales manager with a new one who knows the market and knows how to train other salespersons.

You might also want to include in your report an alternative solution, which in this case might be to liquidate the company at the going rate and invest the money in some suitable way. Your alternative solution will probably be discounted by the information you supply in support of the solution you are proposing. But your inclusion of an alternative solution indicates that you have studied the problem carefully and considered all possible solutions before advising the company on what course to take.

Your final report should read something like the following.

SAMPLE PROBLEM-SOLVING REPORT

To: Edwards Brothers Roofing Tile Company

From:_____

Statement of purpose

The purpose of this report is to propose a bank loan of $25,000 in order to make the company's product competitive, or, as an alternate plan, to liquidate the company at the going rate and invest the money in a suitable way.

The Edwards Brothers Roofing Tile Company is a family business, which in the last year has experienced a steady slump in profits. The land, building, and equipment are currently appraised at $200,000, although it is doubtful that the company could be liquidated at that figure.

Pinpointing the problem

Establishing a goal

If the Edwards Brothers Roofing Tile Company is to survive, it must be converted from its present debt-ridden state into a profitable business.

Finding the methods to achieve the goal

Research into the company's books and files, conversations with competitors, and interviews with steady customers have convinced me that the main problem lies with the tile itself: too many tiles leak. Everyone I talked with agrees that the tile is beautiful and strong, but that it is not consistently leak-proof. Apparently the problem of leakage has developed recently as the result of obsolete equipment. This problem can be solved by updating the equipment. Numerous builders in the Napa Valley wish to use the tile, but they want a guarantee that it will not leak.

Lack of promotion is another problem, especially since Mr. Daniel Edwards has been ill. Edwards Brothers tile has no significant competitors since the tile is a unique blend of the modern bar tile and the old-fashioned Spanish tile. Many designers are pleased with the striking looks of the tile, but rumors of leakage have reached their ears, and they hesitate to commit themselves. The company needs a salesperson who will allay these fears and push the product. At the same time, the company must put out some effective ads in the form of flyers, newspaper inserts, and write-ups in trade magazines.

The promotion just suggested must stress that Edwards Brothers tile is different from any other tile. It must be pointed out that Edwards Brothers tile is the nearest thing to handmade pottery.

The competition in this location consists

only of two building emporiums that stock bar tile imported from Oregon and regular red Spanish tile. No other company in the area offers a product that approaches the individuality and beauty of Edwards Brothers tile. This lack of competition is the key factor in my suggestion that the company should not close down. I am convinced that if it can present a leak-proof tile, it can regain a big share of the tile market.

Applying the methods

Now I come to two specific proposals on how to solve the Edwards Brothers Roofing Tile Company's financial problems. My first suggestion is to borrow $25,000 from the bank, to be appropriated as follows:

1. $10,000 to update the present equipment in order to decrease the number of faulty tiles
2. $5,000 for immediate advertising and promotion
3. $5,000 to pay off accumulated debts
4. $5,000 in ready reserves

My second suggestion is to replace the present sales manager with one who is successful in persuasive strategy and who knows how to train and inspire other salespeople. According to my findings, this is something the Edwards Brothers Roofing Tile Company has never had, but has an urgent need for.

Conclusion

The only other option available is to liquidate the company at the going rate and invest the money in some suitable way. However, I do not see this second option as financially nearly so feasible as the first, which is to keep the company, improve the product, and step up promotion.

Signed:_____

Title:_____

See to it that your problem-solving report presents a step-by-step plan to clear up the difficulties that are holding up progress.

THE ANALYTICAL REPORT

Any analytical report answers the question, What is the nature of the subject? It investigates by noting how a thing functions or what its characteristics are. It differs from a descriptive report in that its emphasis is on breaking the subject into parts in order to see how these parts function in relation to the whole. In other words, an analytical report can break up a process to scrutinize each stage in it, or it can break up a subject in order to get a better look at the components involved. Analytical reports are of particular value in the area of salesmanship, consumer reaction, and market surveying.

The most important requirement of a good analytical report is logical organization. If, for instance, you are assigned the job of analyzing a certain city to see if direct-mail solicitation of the teenage market would be profitable to your company, your investigation must result in an organized analysis. The following breakdown is a possibility:

1. Actual number of teenagers in the designated market
2. Number of teenagers forecasted for the next ten years
3. A comparison of the size of this market with other market targets in other age brackets
4. The potential spending force the teenage market represents
5. The kinds of merchandise teenagers in the designated area are most likely to buy

But if you were asked to analyze for your firm the advantages of a tax deferred annuities program, your breakdown would be entirely different. You might settle on the following:

1. Advantages as a savings fund
    a. You invest a regular portion of your monthly income in a stable mutual fund at a guaranteed interest
    b. Your annuities can be cashed in at any time
    c. You receive a monthly statement that informs you of the separate unit purchase price and of the accumulated value of your investment

2. Advantages as a tax deferment
    a. You pay no tax on the money you invest until you cash in some shares
    b. The assumption is that you will hold on to the investment, letting it accumulate until you have retired and are in a lower tax bracket than you are in now.

Regardless of the organization chosen, you must comment appropriately on each entry in your outline in order to give your reader a clear view of the total subject. The kind of assignment will dictate the breakdown you will choose.

Below is a sample analysis of the market for a political science and comparative government college textbook. The publishing company involved has written a letter to one of their field representatives requesting that she survey the market and report her findings in a memorandum. Notice how all the findings are summarized for quick assessment by the reader.

SAMPLE ANALYTICAL REPORT

To: Ken Bancroft
From: Judith King
Subject: Possible market for McFarland manuscript

This is in reply to your memo requesting information on the size of the introduction to political science and comparative government markets at the college level in my territory. An analysis follows. Included are also my recommendations for possible reviewers of the McFarland manuscript.

1. *Market*
   a. *Junior Colleges*
      The market at this level is good, but not especially large. I estimate the California junior college market in any given spring semester to be about 3,000 students. This includes both the comparative government and introduction to political science courses, as these course titles tend to be used interchangeably in many college catalogs. The fact is that most, if not all, introduction to political science courses are essentially courses in comparative government. They deal with political science methodology as it exists in theory and as it applies to the study of various governments. The countries selected for study are usually: Great Britain, France, Germany, and Russia.
      My estimate of the Arizona junior college market is 1,000 students in any given spring semester. The total junior college market in my area is therefore about 4,000 students.
   b. *Four-year colleges*
      The four-year college market is difficult to estimate. In California I estimate the enrollment to be about 1,000 in any given spring semester, in Arizona about 300. In my territory junior colleges outnumber four-year colleges about ten to one, which accounts for the difference in enrollment. I am also assuming that the book is pitched strictly for the undergraduate course and will not be used on the graduate level.
   c. *To sum up the market:*
      1) My estimate of the total market in my area, including both four-year colleges and junior colleges, is 5,300 students in

---

363

any given spring semester. I emphasize "any given spring semester" because the junior colleges tend to offer this course only in the spring. Some of the larger colleges will offer it in both fall and spring semesters, but these are few when compared to the entire junior college market.

2) At the junior college level comparative government and introduction to political science tend to be the same course. If the junior college offers a course in introduction to political science, it will not offer a course in comparative government; if it has a course in comparative government, it will offer no course in introduction to political science.

3) The course is usually taken by political science majors or by social science majors.

4) I estimate the national market to be about 250,000 students in any given spring semester.

2. *Recommended reviewers for the McFarland book*

The following persons will do a competent review for us:

Rita Specht
Political Science Department
Sierra College

Jeb Janicki
Political Science Department
Sierra College

Prof. Specht has done reviews for Harper & Row and is familiar with what is involved.

3. *To sum up*

There is a good market that is worth publishing for. The only reservation I have is that the McFarland manuscript does not deal with all the countries usually studied in this course. I think we should pursue this point carefully with the reviewers.

Signed _____

In an analytical report, decide on the main points to be developed and organize them so that they will unify and clarify your analysis.

THE DESCRIPTIVE REPORT

The descriptive report aims at verbally recreating an object, a person, or an incident so that the reader can portray in his mind's eye what is being described. It is not the aim of such a report to create fictitious or fanciful impressions such as we find in poetry or stories. The aim here is to reproduce faithfully what is being described, without personal coloring or emotive suggestion. Police reports, real estate notices, weather reports, or accident reports are descriptions of this kind. The following three paragraphs are examples of uncolored, objective reporting:

FOR SALE

Regency-type house in College Hills, overlooking the Interstate Freeway. 3 bedrooms, living room 15' × 25', family room with sunken conversational area near marble fireplace. Modern kitchen with microwave oven and General Electric built-ins. 3 baths and a 2-car garage. Corner lot 150' × 200' surrounded by cyprus hedge. Little yard upkeep due to ivy. Radiant heat and central air conditioning. Excellent residence for professional or businessperson. Price:$60,000

WANTED BY THE UNITED STATES MARSHAL

Harry Foster, alias "Stan Porter." Escaped after committing armed robbery of a house in the Chevy Chase Estates. White, male, aged 26, black hair, brown eyes, 5' 11", weighs 165 lbs. Occasionally wears a beard and mustache. Missing thumb on right hand. Walks with hitching gait due to knee injury. $1,000 reward for information leading to his arrest.

THE WEATHER

Bay Area: Mostly cloudy today with chance of rain in the afternoon. Rain likely at times tonight with snow on the hills. Clearing Wednesday, then fair. Not so cold at night. High today and Wednesday in the 40's. Winds becoming westerly 10 to 20 m.p.h. today. Chance of rain 40 percent today and 60 percent tonight.

These descriptions are literal, factual, and photographic. They do not go beyond the simple enumeration of parts and characteristics.

Another kind of objective description is found in reports that recreate an incident the way it happened. Police and insurance agents are often required to submit such descriptions. Success in writing them depends on the use of clear, factual language and on careful observation of the event to be reported. The reporter must arrange all the details systematically either according to how they took place chronologically or where they happened geographically. He should not shift from a chronological sequence to a geographic sequence or vice versa. In other words, he must maintain a single organizational scheme. The following paragraph stresses chronology:

The victim stated that at approximately 11:40 P.M., as he was unlocking his vehicle parked behind the Crest Theater on Vachel Avenue, Suspect No. 1 grabbed him from behind, put his right hand over his mouth while keeping him in a wrestling hold with his left arm, and then forced him to the ground. Next, Suspect No. 2 grabbed his briefcase from his hand and rammed his fist in his face. Leaving the victim stunned and bleeding from his nose, both suspects fled down a dark alley next to the theater.

The following paragraph stresses geography:

My client stated that she was driving her 1970 Camaro south on Barton Road in Springfield. She stopped for the stop sign at the intersection of Barton and Benton, looked to the left and right, then proceeded slowly across the intersection. The next thing she remembers is seeing a two-ton Ford truck bearing down on her from the west. My client says she tried to speed up to avoid a collision, but she was too late. Before she could escape, the truck had rammed into her broadside, crushing the entire right side of her car.

Whether the stress is on chronology or geography, a description is coherent only when the order of events is arranged in a manner that the reader can follow and interpret. Descriptions must never range erratically forward and backward in time, or willy-nilly left, right, up and down in place. Such descriptions confuse.

Below is the description of an arrest as reported by the police. Only the narrative portion of the report is provided here. The person arrested is charged with wife-beating.

SAMPLE DESCRIPTIVE REPORT

While working as Desk Man at the Hillhurst Station on the above date, Officer Thomas Bolen observed the defendant standing in front of the station and asked him what business he had in the neighborhood. The defendant stated that his wife was in the station filling out a crime report for wife-beating and that he was waiting to talk with her. He stated: "I don't want to do anything. I just want to talk to her for about five minutes or so. Then I'll leave town. When I broke through the window Friday, I did it because I wanted to talk to her, and she didn't want to open the door for me. Yes, I had a knife that I took from the kitchen, but I wasn't going to kill her. I was just going to scare her. I don't want a divorce. I want to go back to her. I don't want to break up the marriage."

The victim's crime report alleges that on February 24, 1972, between 10:00 and 10:15 P.M. the above defendant, who is the victim's husband, broke into the victim's apartment and attacked her. The victim has been separated from the defendant since January 3, 1972. After breaking into the apartment, the defendant took a butcher knife from the kitchen sink and lunged toward the victim, threatening, "I'm going to kill you." The defendant then attacked the victim, who struggled to protect herself and in the process sustained a slight laceration on the left side of her neck and a deep cut on her left ring finger. The defendant then knocked the victim to the floor and stepped on her face with his shoe. The defendant then fled on foot.

Because of the circumstances involving the crime report, Officer Bolen took both the defendant and the victim to the Hillhurst Station detectives for interrogation. Upon the detectives' orders, Officer Bolen booked the defendant on charges of wife-beating.

Photographs have been taken of the left side of the neck, left cheek, and left ring finger of the victim.

The knife used by the defendant to threaten the victim has been booked as evidence and marked "MJG" for identification.

While checking the defendant's record through the City Police Department and Sheriff's record through the City Police Department and Sheriff's Record, the defendant was found to have a traffic warrant (#T95505) from Oakville J.C. for $46.

A descriptive report must be accurate and objective and must reflect a systematic organizational scheme.

INDEX

A	8
B	9
C	0
D	1
E	2
F	3
G	4
H	5
I	6
J	7